SCHOOLING CHRISTIANS

Schooling Christians

"HOLY EXPERIMENTS"
IN AMERICAN EDUCATION

edited by

Stanley Hauerwas *and* John H. Westerhoff

William B. Eerdmans Publishing Company
Grand Rapids, Michigan

Copyright © 1992 by Wm. B. Eerdmans Publishing Co.
255 Jefferson Ave. S.E., Grand Rapids, Mich. 49503

Printed in the United States of America

Library of Congress Cataloging-in-Publication Data

Schooling Christians / edited by Stanley Hauerwas and John H. Westerhoff.
p.   cm.
ISBN 0-8028-0404-7 (pbk.)
1. Christian education — United States. 2. Education — United States.
I. Hauerwas, Stanley, 1940-   . II. Westerhoff, John H.
BV1467.S36   1992
268'.0973 — dc20   92-17171
CIP

Contents

v

CONTENTS

HIGHER EDUCATION

THE SCHOOL OF THE CHURCH

Introduction

This book is an attempt to begin an argument, or at least to stimulate a conversation. It may be thought that there is little difficulty in beginning a debate about almost anything in this society, but it is part of the argument of this book that conversations about the schooling of Christians are hard to initiate and/or to sustain.

For a variety of reasons Christians in modern liberal societies desire to avoid conflict. In particular they fear coming into conflict with their societies' dominant liberal presuppositions. Yet it is one of the major presumptions of this book that our failure to engage in such conflict has resulted in our inability as Christians to sustain the "schooling of Christians." By "schooling" we understand the manifold ways, in schools and out, in which Christians are made.

In order to start to think about how to begin this argument, we thought it useful to bring together people who we knew had thought hard about what it means to school Christians in a liberal society. With the generous aid of the Lilly Foundation we were able to invite those represented in this book to a consultation to discuss what Christian education might look like if it were willing to challenge some of the mythologies of liberalism. The invitation to the consultation stated:

> There is a growing conviction that we have reached the moral limits of liberalism, with its understanding of community founded upon the virtue of tolerance and its understanding of education founded upon a common school as the crucible for national identity. Liberal-

ism's advocacy of respect as non-interference and of commonness as neutrality, along with its conviction that harmony in the social order can be achieved by minimizing or obliterating differences, has resulted in moral relativism and indifference, as well as social disease.

Similarly, there is a growing conviction that we require a new understanding of society, one that rejects both a social order founded upon a co-existence devoid of conflictual interaction and a "melting pot" devoid of distinctiveness and uniqueness. One alternative understanding of society assumes distinctive, unique, identity-conscious communities interacting with each other in ways that do not compromise their integrity, but make possible various and diverse contributions to our common life.

For Christians, the integrity of the church assumes an alternative community alongside and within a society where intolerance and interference are accepted. Christian families need to be able to shape the convictions by which they are to live and by which they hope their children will live. Christian schools and other agencies of Christian education need to be able to do the same. Christian churches need to be able to stand outside the social order exposing whatever is false, dehumanizing, and contrary to gospel practices so as to engage in selective participation and to provide a sign of an alternative way of life.

This consultation intends to explore these convictions and thereby provide the foundations for an alternative way of envisioning life in the United States and the ways by which Christian churches, families, and agencies of education (mass media, schools, etc.) might live faithfully in relationship to the social order.

This book is the result of that consultation. We thought the papers of such quality that we ought to try to make them available to as wide a readership as possible. We do not pretend that any of the papers individually "solves" the issues confronting the formation of Christians in a liberal society. What we would claim is that, taken together, these papers offer a challenge to the conventionalities concerning how Christians are schooled that at least initiates the argument that we should be having, but unfortunately are not.

It will be obvious to anyone reading through these essays that there is no single position or "story line." The authors of the various essays represent quite diverse and sometimes antagonistic views. These differences often involve different theological perspectives and/or understandings of our social history. For example, Skillen's attempt to provide a theory for the differentiated society is obviously based upon different presumptions from those of Hauerwas. Moreover, the authors have quite different interpretations of the nature of liberalism and the challenge it presents. Yet we believe the differences among the authors of these essays help to frame a challenge for the schooling of Christians in a society such as ours, and to focus our minds on a conflictual situation typically avoided.

Alasdair MacIntyre makes the point in his *Three Rival Versions of Moral Enquiry: Encyclopedia, Genealogy and Tradition* that one of the primary functions of the contemporary university has been to dissolve antagonism and to emasculate hostility in the interest of making the university culturally irrelevant.[1] Such emasculation is crucial if the university is to exist in liberal society, for it becomes the task of the university in such a cultural context to domesticate conflict by educating everyone to view his or her commitments as opinions and/or interests. As a result we fail to see how the university continues to serve as an ideological agent for hegemonic power within liberal social orders.

MacIntyre notes that the pre-liberal modern university depended upon enforced and constrained agreements. The liberal university in contrast aspired to be an institution of unconstrained agreement, so it was necessary to abolish all religious and moral tests. Of course the very presumption that the liberal university was constituted by unconstrained agreements was an illusion, since clearly it excluded and excludes alternatives that would challenge the myth that the liberal university is "open." That, of course, is how Christian theology became a problematic subject matter in the contemporary liberal university.

This can be nicely illustrated by the recent report of the American Academy of Religion's task force on the development of religious studies as a discipline, entitled "The Religion Major: A Report." This report celebrates the loss of any "confessional" approach to the study of religion. Rather, the "academic study of religion" now requires "that the student have more than a superficial acquaintance with at least one other tradition, in the context of its attendant culture. It requires the knowledge of at least two traditions to study religion in depth. It does not, in principle, matter which two traditions are studied. That would

---

1. Alasdair MacIntyre, *Three Rival Versions of Moral Enquiry: Encyclopedia, Genealogy and Tradition* (Notre Dame: University of Notre Dame Press, 1990), p. 219.

depend largely on the local conditions such as the training and resources of the faculty. But religion cannot be studied academically without comparative insight."[2] It is clear that the very constitution of the academic study of religion so conceived is meant to emasculate the possibility that Christians, Jews, and Muslims in a religious studies department might actually think they could locate a disagreement among themselves.

In contrast, MacIntyre argues that the goal of the contemporary university ought to be that place where constrained disagreements are possible. That is, the university should initiate students into substantive traditions, one of which is liberalism, so that they might understand how they conflict and why there are no ready resolutions for those conflicts. MacIntyre acknowledges that such a goal is utopian, but refuses to privilege the bureaucratic-minded who gets to define what constitutes utopian alternatives. We should like to think that the essays in this book are exactly that kind of utopian challenge to liberalism's attempt to domesticate the kind of conflict Christians ought to be initiating about schooling in such cultures.

Our primary principle for organizing the essays in this book has been to group those essays together according to emphasis. Obviously each essay deals, for example, with the current cultural context in which our efforts to school Christians occur. The first three essays by Wolterstorff, Schwehn, and Elshtain are meant to set the issues before us. The next section is grouped primarily to include those who are dealing more directly with the issue of public education in America and its moral presuppositions. The next three essays are grouped because they each address questions of Christian higher education. The final section is in many ways the most challenging of the book. The essays by Michael Warren and John Westerhoff make clear that the issue of schooling Christians in our society cannot be limited to explicit questions of educational institutions.

We should note that the essays by Elshtain, Skillen, and Cartwright have been added to the book after our colloquium. We thought each of them made a significant contribution and fit so well the general issues

---

2. "The Religion Major: A Report," p. 10. Reprints of this report are available through the AAR Executive Office, 501 HL, Syracuse University, Syracuse, New York 13244-1170. The members of the AAR Task Force that produced the report were Stephen Crites, Frederick Denney, Carole Myscopski, Albert Rabil, and James Wiggins.

raised by the book that it was important to have them included. We are indebted to each of them for their willingness to let us use their essays in this manner.

Of course, the essays could have been arranged in a different manner, and the reader may choose to read them in another order. For example, the essays by Schwehn, Skillen, and Hauerwas deal with the epistemological issues that shape the current debate about educational policy. In like manner, the essays by Elshtain, Jung, and Warren would have made a natural grouping since each in its own way makes the process of teaching and learning central. We hope the reader will find it a strength that the issues in one section also come up in another, since the issues surrounding the question of schooling Christians are inseparable from each other. For example, the question of where Christian schooling occurs cannot be distinguished from who is to do the teaching and what is to be taught. Often discussions about Christian education are limited to the "where" issue. That is quite understandable given the importance of institutions in determining our habits and expectations. But as the essays in this book make clear, it does Christians little good to have universities sponsored by the church if that makes no difference concerning who is teaching there and what they are teaching. Of course, equally important are questions of *how* our education is done. As Warren and Westerhoff remind us, the most important schooling often takes place outside explicit educational institutions, and what is taught in these situations is all the more powerful precisely because people do not notice that they are being "schooled."

That the hidden curriculum is so powerful in our culture makes it all the more important that Christian educational institutions exist. We confess that we remain agnostic about the continued viability of so-called public education in America for Christians. Certainly the essays by Skillen, the Glenns, and Patti Jung provide rich resources for considering those questions. Equally challenging are the essays by Burtchaell and Cartwright concerning the Christian commitment to support higher education. As they make clear, unless that commitment is reinvigorated by a substantive vision, Christians will not be able to sustain any significant challenge to the reigning ideologies of liberalism — and in particular that of capitalism, depicted so powerfully by Wolterstorff.

In this respect we hope this book provides a significant alternative to the many discussions we hear about religion in the public schools, the importance of teaching values, and/or moral education. Those ways of describing the issues before us continue to reflect the very problems we confront. For as Wolterstorff makes clear, discussions of moral education cannot succeed in our so-called public schools in an amoral society. The very claims to "respect" pluralism are producing people who believe in nothing other than that everyone's opinion ought to be respected. In contrast, Mark Schwehn's argument is that education, at least the education of Christians, requires the enculturation of virtues such as humility, faith, and self-denial.

We hope, however, that this book will not be seen as a diatribe against liberalism as such. Indeed, it will be clear in reading through these essays that many of the authors have a positive attitude toward liberalism. For example, Patti Jung makes it quite clear that liberalism is not based upon a myth of neutrality but does indeed have a morality and commensurate virtues. We certainly do not mean to foreclose the possibility of positive relationships between the schooling of Christians and the educational practices of this society. Rather, we are trying to challenge the assumption that the schooling of Christians and the schooling that takes place in so many of our educational institutions, whether they are secular or at least allegedly Christian, may well be problematic.

It is our hope that, through the publication of this book, others will take up the issues raised. We are acutely aware that in many ways this is just the beginning, but we think it is a good one.

Stanley Hauerwas and John H. Westerhoff
Duke University Divinity School
The Transfiguration of our Lord 1991

THE ISSUE

The Schools We Deserve

NICHOLAS WOLTERSTORFF

Though the line of argument in the first part of my paper may prove somewhat complex, the main point is simple: It is as true for American society today as it has been for most societies that fundamental ailments in its educational practice not only cause but are caused by fundamental ailments in the society itself and cannot be cured without a cure of those social ailments. We Americans at almost every turn talk and act on the opposite assumption. We typically assume that, in the interaction between society and school, school is culprit and society victim. The consensus of those in political power over the past decade has been that throwing money at the schools solves no problems; their own solution, insofar as they have had one, has been to deliver hortatory speeches. My own view is that throwing money and delivering hortatory speeches are equally futile. But whether it is money that is thrown or exhortations that are delivered, the assumption is that our society is not getting the schools it deserves.

I shall argue in the first part of my paper that we *are* getting the schools we deserve. Our present educational morass is the consequence of ideological convictions, social structures, and social dynamics deep in the American system. I am not a social determinist; American schools and schooling might be different in many of their details while social structures and dynamics and our formative ideologies remain the same. Nonetheless, the extent and mode of deficiency of our educational practice is not simply the consequence of sloth, turpitude, or wrongheadedness on the part of school personnel.

3

Once I have argued this case I will, all too briefly, indicate in the second part of my paper where we could have taken, and where we still can take, some different turns — though I shall also warn, in the light of the preceding discussion, against naive optimism as to the success of such turns.

But first, let us have before us a clear specimen of treating the school as culprit and of thinking, correspondingly, that by a combination of hortatory talk and pressure of one kind or another we can correct what ails our educational practice. So as not to take cheap shots, let us look at one of the better examples of oblivion to the fact that schools are not only *for* society but also *by* society; namely, the thoughtful symposium on educational reform published a few years ago in *Harper's* under the title of "How Not to Fix the Schools."[1] All nine participants agreed that our schools need fixing; and all agreed that the then current rage for fixing the schools by imposing tighter regulations and tougher requirements would prove no cure at all. What ails the schools, they said, is not insufficient money or inadequate regulation but the goal that the schools set for the education they offer. The symposiasts suggested that the dominant goal of American schools today is to induct students into the job market — to teach them the knowledge and skills necessary for entering the economic system as productive workers. The cure for the sickness of the schools is for them to adopt a different and better goal.

Let me halt for a moment here to observe that although the *Harper's* symposiasts regarded themselves as painting a dark picture of the American schools, in one important respect it was not dark enough. Quite clearly our society presently operates on the assumption that the productive side of our economy can proceed quite nicely even if a rather large proportion of the members of our society receive at best minimal education for holding down a job. In particular, we assume that urban blacks are pretty much dispensable and disposable. It's simply not true that our society does its best to educate everyone so that he or she can become a productive worker.

But let's proceed. We need a better goal for the schools, say the symposiasts. What might be that better goal? One of the participants, A. Graham Down, took it as obvious that education's "abiding, all-encompassing purpose must be to equip people with the taste for

1. "How Not to Fix the Schools," *Harper's* 272 (Feb. 1986).

4

lifelong learning." And Ernest L. Boyer insisted that one of the two fundamental purposes of education is "personal empowerment." But neither of these is the purpose that gained emphasis in the discussion. Instead, what Boyer proposed as the other proper aim of education — namely, "civic engagement" — did. Our schools are to aim at equipping students to perform the role of citizen. Here is how Walter Karp put it:

> One simple concept includes *all* those purposes: Americans do not go to school in order to increase the social efficiency or economic prosperity of the country, but to become informed, critical citizens. A citizen is not a worker. The Soviet Union has workers, the American republic has citizens. A citizen is a political being; he has private powers and a public role. As Jefferson wrote, the education of a citizen must "enable every man to judge for himself what will secure or endanger his freedom."
>
> In practice, that goal is persistently betrayed. It is essential that citizens be able to judge for themselves and have the courage and confidence to think for themselves. Yet America's high schools characteristically breed conformity and mental passivity. . . . Our schools do not attempt to make citizens; they attempt to break citizens.[2]

That is the most eloquent and most insistent statement of the point. But others in the symposium expressed the same view, leading the moderator, Mark D. Donner, to summarize the drift of the conversation this way:

> You educators seem to be in a rather embarrassing minority position here. You think of schools as places where people are taught how to think critically and how to become vigilant citizens, whereas most adults and students apparently believe the schools exist to keep kids out of trouble for a few years and help them get jobs.[3]

The fundamental ailment of our schools is that the education they offer is aimed at the wrong goal; adopting a better goal is the cure. The assumption is that schools can pull themselves up by their own bootstraps. The assumption is that while society remains fundamentally unchanged, our schools can adopt this new goal for the education they offer and, that done, can succeed in achieving it. The assumption is that educational reform can succeed without social reform.

2. Ibid., p. 43.
3. Ibid., p. 44.

But let's dig deeper and look at the particular proposal offered by the *Harper's* symposiasts. The symposiasts were suggesting that our schools should aim at producing a certain quality of character and the virtues and skills that go with that type of character. They were proposing that the schools should aim at inculcating a certain *ethic.* They were suggesting that the illness of the schools lies in the fact that they see their task as teaching only how-to-do-it matters when they ought to be inculcating in their students a way of living. Let me say that with this assumption I heartily agree.

But immediately a difficulty faces us. When a society is committed to common schools and its members agree on the sort of character and attendant virtues they wish their children to exhibit, it is then immediately relevant for the society to reflect on how its schools must be organized and their education conducted so as to encourage the formation of that character and those virtues. Correspondingly, when a society is not committed to common schools nor do its members agree on the sort of character and attendant virtues they wish their children to exhibit, it is then relevant for the subcommunities of that society within which there is agreement on the ethic desired for their children to band together and organize schools and education with that ethic in mind. But when a society whose members do not agree on the sort of character and attendant virtues they desire in their children nonetheless commits itself to a common school, then prior to all how-to-do-it questions, that society faces the difficult question, "*Whose* view as to good character and *whose* view as to right virtues are the schools to adopt?" American society is this last kind of society.

The proposal of the *Harper's* symposiasts for the reform of the schools coincides with one of the classic American answers to this question. The public educational institutions of our land are to cultivate in students such qualities of character and such dispositions as are required for playing the role of citizen in our liberal-democratic, republican, polity. They are to cultivate the ethic of citizenship. The *Harper's* symposiasts do little to defend this view. But there is a defense regularly offered for this position which goes as follows: Our society has the right to impress its formative Idea on its citizens; the formative Idea of American society is that of a liberal-democratic, republican polity; and this Idea incorporates the ideal of every adult playing the role of citizen.

Let me make some brief preliminary comments about this line of thought before I probe the issue that will lead us into our main topic.

For one thing, I myself think that to describe the formative Idea of American society as that of a liberal-democratic, republican polity is to give an idealized formulation of that Idea. We Americans not only tolerate but also actively embrace various forms of duress; that too, then, belongs to our formative Idea. Of course American society is not peculiar in this regard; the formative Idea of any society will be, to use scriptural language, a "fallen" Idea. But anyone who suggests that our schooling be guided by the formative Idea of American society is in effect recommending that we perpetuate bias and oppression of certain sorts.

Let it also be noted that the content of the ethic of citizenship is by no means clear and uncontested. The ethic of the physician is the subject of vigorous debate in our society; so too is the ethic of the lawyer. It is no different for the ethic of the citizen. In their fascinating and controversial book, *Habits of the Heart*,[4] Robert N. Bellah and associates argued that an essential component in the character of the republican citizen is concern for the common good over private interests; the *Harper's* symposiasts say nothing about that but insist instead that the citizen needs a critical habit of mind. Both of these may be right; yet there is, if nothing more, a stark difference of emphasis here. And whose voice is to be decisive in determining the content of the common good?

Thirdly, for the schools to shape their education by the ethic of the citizen is by no means for them to be as neutral as might at first appear. For one thing, there are people in our society who consciously and reflectively reject the ethic of the citizen in a liberal-democratic, republican polity. I suppose it might be said, in response, that such people are here only by a kind of sufferance. So let me go on to note that the policy of letting the ethic of the citizen in a liberal-democratic, republican polity shape the education of our common schools is not even neutral among all those who have no particular objection to this ethic. This can be seen by noting that although an ethic of the citizen is perhaps more comprehensive than would at first sight appear, nonetheless for the schools of our land to confine themselves to the inculcation of this ethic is to leave a great many facets of character, disposition, and action untouched.

One of the burning moral issues in our society is abortion on

4. Robert N. Bellah et al., *Habits of the Heart* (Berkeley: University of California Press, 1985).

demand. But the Supreme Court of the United States has declared that one can be a fully entitled member of our society and not only advocate abortion on demand but secure one on demand. Hence if the education conducted by the schools is to have the ethic of citizenship as its sole content, the schools will have to avoid taking a stand on this moral issue. Instead of cultivating sensitivities on one side or the other, they will have to confine themselves to cultivating such qualities of character as are necessary for participating in debates on the matter. The same will be true for a vast number of other moral issues. Now for those who not only agree that the school should inculcate the ethic of citizenship but are also content to have the rest of the ethical education of their children occur in one place or another outside the common day school, there is no problem. But there are some in our society who are persuaded that education into citizenship in our earthly commonwealth will always be distorted if treated outside the context of life before God; and such people will regard a day-school education shaped purely by the ethic of the citizen as not so much falling short of their educational goals for their children but, *in* its falling short, as inimical to those goals. We begin here to spy a dilemma about which I will say more later.

But rather than dwelling on any of these points, important though I think they are, I wish instead to argue that our kind of society is inimical toward any ethic whatsoever shaping the education of our common schools, be it the ethic of the citizen or some other. We get the schools we deserve. I shall begin with some fairly standard socio-logical observations.

A drama is a set of interlocking roles that persons can repeatedly perform. It proves illuminating to think of a society as structured like a drama. Every society creates an interlocking set of roles — that is, coherent and typical ways of acting — that members of the society then learn to perform. Now in most of the world's societies, a high proportion of the social roles that people played or were expected to play were simply ascribed to them, rather than allotted on the basis of their choice. The eldest son of the king was born to be king; it was his nature to be king. The son of a serf was born to be a serf; it was his nature to be a serf. Such ascriptivism has increasingly disappeared in modern Western society. It is true that a person's choice of social role in our society is often made under considerable duress, and that the availability to a given person of certain social roles is conditioned on that person's possession of various indigenous abilities. Nonetheless role assignment in modern society is grounded on *will* to an extent never before known in history. And this, of course, invites us to think of our personal identity as something *behind* all our social roles rather than as in part determined *by* our roles. Our roles are mainly things that we can and do put on or take off as we decide to do so, with our perceived self-identity being that which abides amidst all our actual and contemplated changes of garment.

But not only is the proportion of social roles allotted by ascription much lower in our society than it was in previous ones; the roles themselves are typically both different and understood differently among us. Traditionally, to play a certain social role was not just to act in a certain typical and coherent way, but was to see oneself and be seen as subject to a specific cluster of requirements, the fulfillment of these being enforced and reinforced by social expectations. To have the role of serf was to be required to spend a high proportion of one's time laboring for the lord on the manor; to have the role of lord was to be required to provide protection and security to one's serfs. These requirements were for the most part not legal requirements. Neither were they merely instrumental requirements — that is, causal conditions for achieving one's goals. They were *moral* requirements, matters of duty and right. And in good measure they were not just *general* moral requirements pertaining to all persons in all roles whatsoever; rather, a particular role comprised a specific ethic. To occupy a certain station in life was to be subject to a specific set of duties and to enjoy a specific set of rights. In Christian Europe of the Middle Ages one can see the beginnings of our modern idea of *human* rights and duties — that is, of rights and duties attached to all human beings whatsoever. But these were almost obscured by the whole array of rights and duties pertaining to particular roles: there was an ethic of the knight, an ethic of the goldsmith, an ethic of the physician, etc. Furthermore, the recognition of all these moral requirements, specific and general, was customarily caught up in a picture of the universe according to which all of us not only have duties with respect to human beings and social institutions, but also have duties with respect to the sacred, the divine. Indeed, the duties and rights comprised in one's social roles were understood as grounded, in one way or another, in one's duties to the divine.

It was in the context of societies thus structured and the understanding that accompanied them that the role of citizen of a republic emerged — first in some of the city-states of ancient Greece, then later

9

in some of the cities of Renaissance Italy, in the provinces of seventeenth- and eighteenth-century Netherlands, in the villages of nineteenth-century America, etc. To play the role of citizen was to act in a certain coherent and typical way. But more than that, it was to see oneself and be seen as subject to a specific complex of rights and duties. It was to see oneself and be seen as subject to the ethic of the citizen. Typically, of course, only certain of the adults within the community were allowed and required to play this role, the allotment depending not on one's will but on one's gender, age, race, freedom, inherited religion, property, etc. Speaking of nineteenth-century America, Bellah and his associates remark that

> the basic unit of association, and the practical foundation of both individual dignity and participation, was the local community. There a civic culture of individual initiative was nurtured through custom and personal ties inculcated by a widely shared Protestant Christianity. . . . These autonomous small-scale communities in the mid-nineteenth century were dominated by the classic citizens of a free republic, men of middling condition who shared similar economic and social positions and whose ranks less affluent members of the population aspired to enter, often successfully. . . . Tocqueville's America can be viewed as an interlocking network of specific roles: those of husband, wife, child, farmer, craftsman, clergyman, lawyer, merchant, township officer, and so on. But the distinctive quality of that society, its particular identity as a "world" different from other societies, was summed up in the spirit, the mores, that animated its members, and that spirit was symbolized in the representative character of what we can call the independent citizen.[5]

Of such ascribed and ethically infused social roles there are only traces left in the lives and consciousness of contemporary Americans. Perhaps the clearest trace is to be seen in the role of son and daughter. Not only do we not choose to occupy the role of child of parents, but probably most of us still understand this role as incorporating a specific complex of rights and responsibilities. One has duties to one's parents that one has to no one else, just by virtue of being their child; and they, correspondingly, have duties to their child.

One of the principal causes of the near disappearance in reality

5. Ibid., pp. 38-40.

and consciousness of such ethically infused social roles has been the rise and spread of industrial and post-industrial capitalism — and let me make clear that when I speak of "capitalism" I have in mind not only the capitalism of non-command economies but also the state capitalism known as communism. A prominent feature of the spread of capitalism into new sectors of society is that more and more things are put on the market, with the result that the presence of contractual relations among human beings is increased enormously and the loyalty — and expectations of loyalty — to persons and institutions characteristic of traditional societies is destroyed. Under capitalism a worker puts his labor on the market and makes a contract with some owner of capital whereby for such-and-such quality and quantity of labor he will receive such-and-such pay; in most societies there was no such thing as a labor market. Under capitalism land is put on the market and contracts are signed whereby title is transferred for such-and-such payment; in most societies it was impossible to transfer title to land by contract. Under capitalism, the ethic of contract becomes more and more the pervasive ethic of society. The range of that for which one *must* contract is expanded, and the limits on that for which one *may* contract are removed; the duty to keep the contracts one has made looms larger and larger in the whole body of one's duties. The corollary of this increase of contractual relations under capitalism is of course that one's occupation of social roles is increasingly determined by decision rather than ascription. And a natural if not inevitable consequence is that choosing a social role is understood less and less as taking onto oneself a specific range of duties, and more and more as choosing a way of acting that promises to satisfy one's private goals. Even such a social bond as marriage is increasingly understood not as a complex of rights and duties into which one enters by commitment or ascription but as a contractual arrangement to provide benefits for benefits received.

The pervasive marketing of land and labor in capitalist economies also makes a mobility of population possible, and sometimes necessary, of proportions totally unknown in earlier societies except in times of great social upheaval. This too contributes to the shift of which we have been taking note; for when large and rapid shifts of population occur, then the disciplinary effect of social expectations on the performance of duties is drastically weakened, and loyalties to persons and institutions are diminished.

One more feature of a capitalist economy is worth noting —

11

namely, the increasing differentiation, or sectoring, of social roles. In particular, the occupations of persons, their "work," are increasingly differentiated from their other social roles. And given the other features of the system, persons are invited to choose and practice their occupations not by reference to intrinsic satisfactions or social benefits, but solely by reference to whether or not those occupations serve their private goals of a large paycheck, a conspicuous career, or whatever.

And what then shapes life outside of work? Well, it turns out that the regimented, bureaucratized, differentiated, competitive character of work in an economy of industrial capitalism leaves fundamental sides of a person's nature unsatisfied and unfulfilled. And that, combined with the diminishing presence of ethically infused social roles, yields the phenomenon to which many sociologists have called our attention — namely, that in the core areas of our world-economy persons outside the workplace tend to look for love and intimacy and pleasure and self-expression in family, in sports, in religion, in art, in shopping, in sex. A pervasive privatism, heavily colored with hedonism, begins to characterize the lives of people outside of work. Here is how Bellah and his associates describe the situation:

> The most distinctive aspect of twentieth-century American society is the division of life into a number of separate functional sectors: home and workplace, work and leisure, white collar and blue collar, public and private. . . . Particularly powerful in modeling our contemporary sense of things has been the division between the various "tracks" to achievement laid out in schools, corporation, government, and the professions, on the one hand, and the balancing life-sectors of home, personal ties, and "leisure" on the other. . . . Domesticity, love, and intimacy increasingly become "havens" against the competitive culture of work.[6]

6. Ibid., p. 43. Compare this passage in ibid., p. 45: "Like the entrepreneur, the manager also has another life, divided among spouse, children, friends, community, and religious and other nonoccupational involvements. Here, in contrast to the manipulative, achievement-oriented practices of the workplace, another kind of personality is actualized, often within a social pattern that shows recognizable continuity with earlier American forms of family and community. But it is an outstanding feature of industrial life that these sectors have become radically discontinuous in the kinds of traits emphasized and the moral understanding that guides individuals within them. 'Public' and 'private' roles contrast sharply. . . ."

What sort of educational goals would one expect a capitalist society such as ours to set for its schools? Surely twofold. One would expect it to ask of its schools that they teach students — most of them — the knowledge, skills, and dispositions necessary for participating in the labor force. And one would expect it to ask of its schools that they enable students — many of them — to satisfy their expressive desires: offering athletic programs for those who have a taste for the peculiar bodily and emotional satisfactions which come from competitive sports; offering courses in the world's religions for those who have a taste for religion; etc. This, I said, is what one would expect a society such as ours to ask of its schools. And that is what it does ask. The *Harper's* symposiasts see our schools as oriented toward job preparation. I agree, with the qualification cited earlier; but I would add that they are also oriented toward equipping students to find personal satisfaction in those sectors of their lives outside of job and career.

Now it is for a society such as ours and schools such as these that it is proposed by the *Harper's* symposiasts that the schools inculcate the ethic of the citizen. In addition to the questions posed earlier about this proposal, the question we are led to ask by the reflections we have just followed is this: Is there any likelihood whatsoever that this proposal, or any other proposal concerning the ethic of common day-school education, will be generally adopted? For who are the teachers who staff, and the board members who govern, the public schools of our land? They are members of this very public from which the ethically infused role of citizen has virtually disappeared in reality and consciousness; not even our elected officials put the public good ahead of private careers. Teachers and board members do not constitute, for the most part, some counter-cultural subcommunity within our society; on the average, they think and act like the average.

But suppose that somehow, someway, somewhere, this proposal is embraced by the board and staff of some public educational institution. What that school will then have to do, before anything else, is explain to its students what this ethically infused role of citizen is. Students do not come knowing what that role is. They come to school with an understanding of the role of professional baseball player, for they have seen people playing this role. They have not seen many old-fashioned citizens, nor have they often seen those who do not play the role of citizen suffering under social disapproval. Militating against success in this explanatory project is the fact that the concept of an ethically infused social role in general, no matter of what specific sort, has less and less application in our society, and is less and less recognized as applicable where in fact it is.

But perhaps the necessary explanations can be given, with the aid of history and fiction. Then what the schools would have to try to do is produce in students the disposition to play this role: to perform these actions and embrace this ethic, including the principle that one ought to place considerations of the common good ahead of personal interests. And obviously what militates against success in this project is the fact that students live in a society pervasively structured so as to invite them to give pride of place in their choice and practice of roles to purely private ends. We must, indeed, restrain ourselves from thinking that this is entirely true in our society. Patriotism and its close relative nationalism lead people away from private interests to larger concerns, and it is evident that they have by no means disappeared from the contemporary scene. So too the natural affections present in families and among friends lead us out of our shells. But the ethic of the citizen is not grounded in familiar affection, nor in feelings of patriotism or nationalism. Indeed, these feelings of loyalty and affection all tend to collide at crucial points with what is called for by the ethic of the republican citizen.

I can imagine someone replying to these last points, with their despairing tone, by saying that of course it will be difficult to go against the grain of society and both communicate to students the concept of this ethically infused role of citizen and produce in them the disposition to embrace it. When modelling and discipline are missing, then two of the main dynamics for the cultivation of dispositions are absent. But there remains the possibility of the schools giving students *reasons* for taking up this role — and perhaps supplementing those reasons with inspiring examples culled from history and fiction.

What might those reasons be? Well, given the ethically infused nature of this role, the obvious answer is that playing the role of citizen is one of the *responsibilities* of adults in our society. It is their *duty* to play the role of citizen.

I myself believe that we adults in our society do have a duty to play the role of citizen; I hold it to be one of our responsibilities. Thus I believe that this is a right and correct thing for the schools to say to their students. But I also believe that there are reasons for thinking that, in the climate of our society, the schools will find this reason to be

14

distressingly unpersuasive. Already we have had some indication of why that is so. But let us now expand the picture by adding to the social factor that we have been discussing a certain cultural factor, taking note of one facet of the characteristic ideology of our society. For that complex of practices, laws, and institutions that constitute capitalism do not operate independently of the *ideas* that members of society have as to the nature of reality, humanity, and the good. The ideas influence the practices, laws, and institutions — just as the latter influence the former. Ideas and practices *inter*act. Idealism and materialism are equally mistaken.

I think Bellah and his associates, along with a great many other observers of the contemporary scene, are correct in their suggestion that the ideology most prominent in American society since the latter part of the nineteenth century has been what they — and of course many others — call "individualism." I think they are also right in distinguishing two versions, or two applications, of this ideology: *utilitarian* individualism and *expressive* individualism. Benjamin Franklin, they suggest,

> gave classic expression to what many felt in the eighteenth century — and many have felt ever since — to be the most important thing about America: the chance for the individual to get ahead on his own initiative. Franklin expressed it very clearly in his advice to Europeans considering immigration to America: "If they are poor, they begin first as Servants of Journeymen; and if they are sober, industrious, and frugal, they soon become Masters, establish themselves in Business, marry, raise Families, and become respectable Citizens."[7]

Just as Franklin is the classic spokesman for utilitarian individualism, so Walt Whitman is the classic spokesman for expressive individualism. "For Whitman, success had little to do with material acquisition. A life rich in experience, open to all kinds of people luxuriating in the sensual as well as the intellectual, above all a life of strong feeling, was what he perceived as a successful life."[8]

What has eventually emerged, of course, is that the contemporary American thinks of work in terms of utilitarian individualism and thinks of his or her life after work in terms of expressive individualism

7. Ibid., p. 33.
8. Ibid., p. 34.

— with the former enabling the latter. "The split between public and private life correlates with a split between utilitarian individualism, appropriate in the economic and occupational spheres, and expressive individualism, appropriate in private life."[9]

Bellah and his associates discuss the ideology of individualism purely in the context of American society, inviting in their readers the thought that individualism is an American peculiarity. But to think thus would be profoundly mistaken. Our American ideology of individualism must be seen within the context of a vast change of mentality throughout the West that began around the time of the late Renaissance. Historically, human beings have thought of the world as being inherently meaningful — as being like a text — and of the point of human existence as being found in discerning and responding to that meaning. The people of traditional tribes saw the world and the rhythms of life as the product of the foundational acts of the gods, and saw themselves in their work and rituals as imitating and thereby even renewing those foundational acts. Plato saw the world as mirroring the transcendent structured world of the Forms, and regarded true happiness as consisting in contemplating and imitating that transcendent world. And the ancient Jews saw the structure of the world and the course of history as the result of God's will, and saw the path to shalom as learning and following that same will — walking in the path of the *Torah*.

In the opening chapter of his well-known book *Hegel*, Charles Taylor suggests that the essential difference between that older view of things and the modern view that came to birth in the seventeenth century is that "the modern subject is self-defining, where on previous views the subject is defined in relation to a cosmic order. . . . [T]he view of the subject that came down from the dominant tradition of the ancients, was that man came most fully to himself when he was in touch with a cosmic order. . . . The situation is now reversed: full self-possession requires that we free ourselves from the projection of meaning onto things."[10] Taylor adds that "the modern shift to a self-defining subject was bound up with a sense of control over the world — at first intellectual and then technological. That is, the modern certainty that the world was not to be seen as a text or an embodiment of meaning was not founded on a sense of its

9. Ibid., pp. 45-46.
10. Charles Taylor, *Hegel* (Cambridge: Cambridge University Press, 1975), pp. 6-7.

baffling impenetrability. On the contrary, it grew with the mapping of the regularities in things, by transparent mathematical reasoning, and with the consequent increase of manipulative control."[11] Later, of course, the idea arose that the subject defines itself not only by its control of a world shorn of intrinsic meaning but by one or another form of expressive activity.

In the traditional picture of humanity in the world, moral requirements were seen as something required of us by God, or by the gods, or by the Good. To the question "Who requires this of me?" or "What requires this of me?" there was an answer. But what place can this notion of requirement have in our modern mentality, where the subject is regarded as self-defining through its actions of domination and expression? At best what can be said is that our own nature somehow or other requires of us that we act morally — which is exactly what the later Enlightenment philosophers attempted to show (and perhaps the Romantic philosophers with their ideology of nationalism). But I reveal no secret when I tell you that most philosophers today judge that attempt of their Enlightenment predecessors to be a failure. And in any case, our society in general has scarcely been persuaded that the answer to the question "Who requires this of me?" is "Your own nature requires it."

So to the students who arrive at school or university with little or no disposition to engage in the practices and to embrace the ethic of republican citizenship, a teacher can indeed speak of their duty to do so. But will that answer prove persuasive? Are the social and cultural conditions for the success of such a moral appeal satisfied? The notion of duty is the notion of requirement. But if the student asks, "Who or what requires of me that I take up this role of citizen?" what is the school to say? The traditional answer in the West was "God." The answer that Jefferson and his associates gave when they formulated the ideal of American republican citizenship in the eighteenth century was both "God" and "human nature." But large numbers of our students no longer believe in a god or in anything else transcendent that requires things of them. And in any case, our public schools are not permitted to affirm that God requires of us the duties of citizenship. Now we can each speculate as to the long-range effectiveness of a school's insistence to its students that the role of citizen is required of them, when many or most of those students do not believe that there is anything tran-

11. Ibid., p. 7.

scendent requiring this of them and when the school cannot affirm that there is. My own speculation is that as our modern ideology of the self-defining subject settles ever more firmly into our consciousness, in its characteristic American forms of utilitarian and expressive individualism, moral appeals will prove less and less effective. They will find less and less to attach themselves to.

But perhaps our situation is even worse. Perhaps the demise of the conviction that someone or something requires certain things of us not only threatens the persuasiveness of appeals to moral requirement but also threatens our grasp of the very concept of a moral requirement. So, at least, argues Alasdair MacIntyre in his book *After Virtue*.[12] MacIntyre argues that, given our characteristic modern framework of beliefs, moral precepts have lost their function. It is their function to instruct us on what to do so as to move from how we happen to be, to how transcendent reality and our own true end *(telos)* require us to be. But if the belief in an inherent meaning of the world and an intrinsic end of our existence disappears, then, though we may continue for some time to think in terms of duty and ought and right and responsibility, the whole point of such thinking will have been lost. And if the point of such thinking is lost, then we must expect that eventually, though the words *duty* and *ought* and *right* and *responsibility* may remain in our vocabulary, they will no longer be used to express moral requirement. That, says MacIntyre, is already becoming our situation. More and more these words are used simply to evince attitudes and to influence others.

What may be added to MacIntyre's analysis is that, under the impact of individualism, more and more it is the case that, in reflecting on the choices facing them, members of our society do not even use the vocabulary of morality. They speak instead of what would make them "feel comfortable," of what would make them "feel good," of what would advance "Number One," etc. The concept of a *causal* requirement for the achievement of one's goals is obviously alive and well among us. The concept of a *moral* requirement appears sick unto death. Of course our society does still proffer an "order of life, with character ideals, images of the good life, and methods of attaining it. Yet it is an understanding of life generally hostile to older ideas of moral order. Its center

12. Alasdair MacIntyre, *After Virtue* (Notre Dame: University of Notre Dame Press, 1982).

18

is the autonomous individual, presumed able to choose the roles he will play and the commitments he will make, not on the basis of higher truths but according to the criterion of life-effectiveness as the individual judges it. . . . The expressive culture, now deeply allied with the utilitarian, reveals its difference from earlier patterns in its readiness to treat normative commitments as so many alternative strategies of self-fulfillment. What has dropped out are the old normative expectations of what makes life worth living."[13]

But if the ungroundedness of moral thinking in our society not only eats away at the effectiveness of moral reasons for action but also eats away at our very grasp of moral concepts, then of course the endeavor of the school to produce in students the disposition to play the ethically infused role of citizen by offering them moral reasons for doing so will prove increasingly ineffective. The conditions for success in this enterprise will be missing. Where capitalism alters society so that its basic ethic becomes the ethic of contract, individualism alters our understanding of reality so that honoring the ethic of contract recedes from view in favor of calculating the conditions for personal satisfaction. Moral education cannot succeed in the common public schools of an amoral society.

It must be noticed that it does not follow straightforwardly from this that the schools cannot give their students effective reasons of any sort whatsoever for performing the actions of citizenship. In principle they might offer them persuasive prudential reasons for doing so. Offering such reasons is what Richard Rorty recommends — persuaded as he is that our convictions cannot be grounded in anything transcendent and ahistorical. Identifying himself as a "postmodernist bourgeois liberal," he proposes to suggest "how such liberals might convince our society that loyalty to itself is morality enough, and that such loyalty no longer needs an ahistorical backup." "I think," he says, that "they should try to clear themselves of charges of irresponsibility by convincing our society that it need be responsible only to its own traditions, and not to the moral law as well."[14] But if the school confines itself to offering purely prudential reasons to its students, then, as Rorty would readily

---

13. Bellah et al., pp. 47-48.

14. Richard Rorty, "Postmodernist Bourgeois Liberalism," in R. Hollinger, ed., *Hermeneutics and Praxis* (Notre Dame: University of Notre Dame Press, 1985), pp. 216-17.

acknowledge, the role of citizen will have to be conceived differently from how we have described it: not as an ethically infused way of acting but simply as a way of acting. And if the school offers merely prudential reasons for acting in the manner of the citizen, then it is not moral character that it develops but prudential alertness, not ethical sensitivity but pragmatic shrewdness. It does not teach the student how to appraise actions with moral concepts; neither does it teach her moral principles for action, nor how to discover such principles.

And what, we may also ask, might such persuasive prudential reasons be? One might, as Rorty suggests, display the dignity of our society as compared to others of which we are aware. One might further, as he also suggests, construct a historical scenario as to the sad consequences for this society of ours if its adults cease to engage in the actions of citizenship. But what is the school to say to the student who grants all this but wishes himself to be a freeloader? And what is it to say to the millions who see themselves as deprived of most of the benefits of this society? Rorty speaks of "loyalty" to our society and of "identifying" ourselves with our society. And our century does teach us that there are ways of stirring up the loyalties and the identities of patriotism. The painful truth, however, is that the most effective ways of stirring up such loyalties and identities are at the very same time effectively destructive of the actions of citizenship.

I have suggested that our social-economic system of capitalism and our cultural ideology of individualism have not only shaped our society but have also powerfully contributed to making our common public day schools what they are; in particular, they have in various ways made it almost impossible for these common schools to inculcate an ethic — a way of living that is of ethical import. Let me now carry on with this already gloomy analysis by pointing to another social factor that powerfully shapes the American common public school and places before it intractable dilemmas whenever it proposes to teach its students how they should live. Or strictly, what I shall be calling to your attention is a pair of social dynamics coupled with a strong traditional preference for a particular way of structuring society in response to those dynamics. Let me speak first of the dynamics and then of the preferred structure.

I have in mind here the dynamic of increasing religious diversity in our society coupled with the somewhat halting and erratic, though nonetheless powerful, dynamic toward granting the representatives of that diversity equal freedom to exercise their religion. Typical of traditional societies was the presence of just one religion within the society; to be a member of the society was to be a participant in the religion. Such religious monolithicism was ruptured in Greco-Roman society of middle and late antiquity; it was, however, in good measure recovered by the "Constantinianism" of medieval European and Near Eastern society. But then it was ruptured again, and as we now know, destroyed for good in the West by the Protestant Reformation. Since the Reformation the various states of the West have all had to cope with an ever-increasing diversity of religions among their citizenry. They have experimented with a variety of strategies of coping with such diversity. But it is clear, in retrospect, that in all of them there has been a powerful dynamic toward giving equal legal standing to an increasingly large range of religious groups and religious convictions — and indeed, to an increasingly large range of antireligious groups and irreligious convictions.

A good many features of modern Western society are the consequence of this phenomenon of increasing religious diversity, coupled with the pressure toward giving the various representatives of this diversity equal freedom. One consequence is that religious groups, especially in America, see themselves as working in a marketplace competing for clients. Another consequence is that religious persons, confronted with alternatives to their own religious convictions, regularly feel it necessary either to explain and justify themselves, or to turn in the direction of subjectivism. Yet another consequence is that we have had to adopt other strategies for achieving social consensus and have had to appeal to dynamics other than shared religious convictions for securing social loyalty. It is especially at this point that nationalism and patriotism enter the picture. Still another consequence is that what we each care most deeply about is increasingly removed from public discussion as being irrelevant to the goals of the discussion. Another consequence is that religion is increasingly removed from public life to one's private life after work — a result, as we have seen, also provoked by the dynamics of capitalism. And, to end our list, a final consequence is that ecclesiastical and other religious bodies enjoy less and less by way of legally sanctioned privilege and voice, thus yielding an increasingly secularized society in the strict sense of that term. In my own view, it is not primarily the cultural phenomenon of secular humanism, but rather the social phenomenon of religious diversity, that has led to the removal of officially sanctioned prayers and other forms of religious activity from the American public schools. (I do not deny that secular humanism,

21

heavily concentrated in the intellectual elite of modern American society, may not only continue to have a voice in American culture out of proportion to its representation in the populace, but may also begin to have an influence on the structure of American society out of proportion to its representation.) As Peter Berger puts it:

> While the presence of religion within modern political institutions is, typically, a matter of ideological rhetorics, this cannot be said about the opposite "pole." In the sphere of the family and of social relationships closely linked to it, religion continues to have considerable "reality" potential, that is, continues to be relevant in terms of the motives and self-interpretations of people in the sphere of everyday social activity. . . . Such private religiosity, however "real" it may be to the individuals who adopt it, cannot any longer fulfill the classical task of religion, that of constructing a common world within which all of social life receives ultimate meaning binding on everybody. Instead, this religiosity is limited to specific enclaves of social life that may be effectively segregated from the secularized sectors of modern society. The values pertaining to private religiosity are, typically, irrelevant to institutional contexts other than the private sphere. For example, a businessman or politician may faithfully adhere to the religiously legitimated norms of family life, while at the same time conducting his activities in the public sphere without any reference to religious values of any kind. . . .
>
> The over-all effect of the afore-mentioned "polarization" is very curious. Religion manifests itself as public rhetoric and private virtue.[15]

Incidentally, I think it is appropriate to see the social and political liberalism espoused by John Stuart Mill as a generalization of the way that English and American society had developed for coping with religious diversity. Live and let live was the emerging practice when it came to religion. Mill generalized this by proposing that no matter what vision of the good a person set for himself or herself, be it religious or not, and no matter what goals he or she adopted, we should adopt a policy of live and let live. There is a line of influence from the plea of the Puritans for toleration to the liberalism espoused by Mill.

15. Peter Berger, *The Sacred Canopy: Elements of a Sociological Theory of Religion* (Garden City, NY: Doubleday, 1967), pp. 132-33.

If we are fully to understand the impact on our schools of the dynamic of increasing religious diversity and of freedom for all, one more factor must be brought into the discussion. It would be entirely possible for a modern society in which these dynamics were operative to adopt toward the various religious communities in its midst a policy of *equal support if any support* when it comes to education. That is to say, the society might decide to support equally and impartially the efforts of the various religious and nonreligious communities in its midst to educate their children as they see fit. Furthermore, there is nothing in the language of the First Amendment of the U.S. Constitution to prohibit such a policy. It is not, however, the policy that we in our country have followed, nor is it the policy that the U.S. Supreme Court has enjoined. We have instead adopted and been enjoined to adopt a policy of *no public support for any religious orientation to which anyone objects;* and as our society has become more diverse religiously, that policy has come to coalesce with a policy of *no public support for any religious or antireligious orientation whatsoever.* No religious community will be supported in the education of its children into its own way of life; the education supported by the society as a whole will have to be neutral among all the religions (and irreligions) present in society.

It's not hard to see why, historically, the United States has adopted such a policy. Among those who fled here from the religious intolerance they experienced in Europe were some who not only spoke for freedom and toleration but also insisted that here, unlike the lands from which they fled, no one should be forced to support the endeavors of any religion with which he or she disagreed. All support of all religion was to be entirely voluntary. It was this line of thought that Jefferson captured in his famous metaphor of "a wall of separation"; and the U.S. Supreme Court has always decided its cases as if the Constitution itself said that there must be a wall of separation between religion and the state — whereas in fact it says nothing of the sort.

Seeing the full picture requires recognizing that public school education has never entirely fit the policy of no support for any religious orientation with which anyone in society disagrees; when one reads documents from the past, one gets the impression that rhetorical flourishing of the principle often functioned more to conceal than to shape reality. When public schools first emerged in the nineteenth century the stated policy, at least in urban centers, was to provide a nonsectarian religious orientation in the schools. Not only would such an education supposedly be neutral among all the religious groups in society; it also fit nicely with the Enlightenment practice of distinguishing between natural religion and revealed religion. The schools would teach natural religion, which was supposedly rationally grounded; the churches would teach revealed religion. From the very beginning, however, Catholics protested that they did not find the schools to be nonsectarian; they found them to be Protestant. And eventually Jews spoke up and said that they found them to be Christian. Eventually both these protests were heard, both in the schools and in the courts. By this time, however, there was a significant number of persons present in American society who were not adherents to any religion at all; for them, supporting even the most vapid manifestations of theism in the common schools was a violation of conscience. This whole dynamic — over and over again new communities emerging who felt themselves excluded from the religious consensus then operative in the schools, and speaking up to say this — has generated a long succession of court cases; and the U.S. Supreme Court, with remarkable consistency, has declared the protesters right. Of course, while some citizens have felt that the schools were too slow in rubbing out manifestations of religious commitment that they found offensive, others have been offended by that very "rubbing out." Such people have never received satisfaction before the high court.

Some of those dismayed by this "rubbing out" were simply betraying their failure to keep up with the times. I think certain Baptist groups are the best example of this. The Baptists have typically been ardently committed to the "wall of separation" principle; many, however, have found it difficult to accept that America has really become as non-Christian as it has and that the wall of separation principle, accordingly, leads to the exclusion of all manifestations of Christianity from the common public schools. The position of certain others who were dismayed has been more interesting, however; for their position confronts the American practice with a dilemma that the Court in particular and Americans in general have done all they can to resist acknowledging. Let me develop this point.

Various religious groups, as they watched the emergence and progress of the common public schools in America, began to have doubts about them that were grounded in their religion and focused not on the remnants of some form of sectarianism but on the very strategy that Americans had hit on so as to make a system of public education a fair and equitable arrangement in a religiously diverse society — the arrangement of teaching only what no one in the community disagreed with, a policy that led eventually in most areas to an education confined entirely to secular matters. Various groups — some Catholics, some Lutherans, some Calvinists, some Jews — found that this strategy violated their conscience. They believed that the education of their children should be religiously integrated, not divided up into two pieces, a secular piece and a religious piece. They believed that the study of nature, for example, should be set within a religious context. The more reflective of these protesters attacked the Enlightenment understanding of learning that they saw as embodied in the public school system. Some of them worked out what we can now see to have been, in effect, a post-Enlightenment, or as some would call it, a postmodern, view of science. The enterprise of science, they said, is unavoidably shaped by values, including religious values. With these convictions in mind, they then started their own schools as a form of protest against the fundamental tenets of the public school strategy for dealing with religious diversity. However, they were not thereby released from the obligation to pay taxes for the support of the public school system.

By now a true dilemma is beginning to emerge. (In respect for the etymology of the word *dilemma* I should say that it is, strictly, a "quintilemma"!) Suppose that a society contains groups of people of at least the following two sorts: One group is such that their conscience requires an education for their children devoid of religious expression, and another group is such that their conscience requires an education for their children that is not only religiously committed but also integrated. Suppose further that the decision has been made to have a system of tax-supported schools. Suppose lastly that this society is bequeathed a constitutional provision, which says that the government shall do nothing to infringe on the free exercise of anyone's religion, and a provision of constitutional interpretation, which says that nobody shall be required to pay money that goes to the support of someone else's (or even his own) religion.

Here is the dilemma: If the government taxes for a school system that is enjoined to avoid all affirmation of religious conviction, it patently infringes on the free exercise of those whose conscience requires a religiously committed and integrated education for their children. Such parents, if they decide to educate their children in accord with their conscience, will have to start independent schools for which they will have to pay out of their own pockets — while nonetheless not being excused from paying the regular tax for the support of the public school system. This, to put it mildly, is an "infringing" effect of a governmental arrangement. But if the government goes in the other direction and funds all schools impartially, then somebody's tax money will go for the support of a religion with which he or she disagrees; and that will violate one of the principles of constitutional interpretation.

From this dilemma there is no escape, short of eliminating one of the five components producing the dilemma: elimination of one of the two groups, elimination of our tax support for schools, elimination of the no-support reading of the Establishment Clause in favor of a no-preference reading, or elimination of the demand that religious belief and exercise shall not be infringed on. There is no way out of the dilemma other than that of giving up one of these five components.

The serpentine character of the sequence of Supreme Court decisions concerning religion and the schools is in good measure due to the Court's confrontation with this dilemma. The Court has consistently decided to give up the demands of the Free Exercise Clause when it comes to the conscience of those who want religiously committed and integrated education for their children. Its squirmings are due to its wish to minimize the impact of those decisions.

To me it seems clear that overall the best way to escape from the dilemma is to give up the no-support reading of the Establishment Clause in favor of a no-preference reading. Why has the Court not chosen that option? For two reasons, so far as I can tell. One we have already considered: the Court has embraced that strand of thought which goes back to the days of colonial America and which was formulated in the Virginia Statute in the words, "no man shall be compelled to . . . support any religious worship, place, or ministry whatsoever. . . ." Though the First Amendment of our federal constitution says nothing at all about tax moneys not supporting religion, the Court has always read the Establishment Clause as if it were only another way of stating the provision from the Virginia Statute.

But there is a second reason. A good many citizens — including members of the Court — have felt it to be a matter of great social importance that most of our students attend a common school system that inculcates the values of the American system. Justice Frankfurter, for example, emphatically insisted that this was indispensable to our unity as a people. This then is an accommodationist argument. When it comes to chaplains in the armed forces, we accommodate the demand of no establishment to the preservation of our tradition as a religious people; when it comes to religion and the schools, we accommodate the demand of free exercise to the social good of having most students attend a common school inculcating the American Way. Of course there is great irony in the offering of this argument. A society founded on the principle of liberalism, that everybody shall be allowed to pursue his or her own vision of the good, thinks its continuance depends on pressuring parents into sending their children to schools where something other than their vision of the good is taught.

Let me summarize my argument. My general thesis has been that the fundamental features of public school education in the United States are a reflection of deep features in American society and culture; and that complaints about, and proposals for the improvement of, such education regularly border on the silly in their assumption that the schools can be changed without changing those features of society and culture that have made the schools what they are. More specifically, I have argued that the proposal that the schools inculcate the ethic of the citizen, minimalist though it be, fails to take into account why the schools are not doing that and the deep difficulties in their trying to do so — not to mention the obstacles in their succeeding. More specifically yet, I have argued that the present system imposes a severe infringement on the free exercise of those who believe that the day-school education of their children should occur in a religious context. The present system profoundly favors the secularist, along with the person who sees no special difficulty in dividing life into secular and sacred components.

This having been my argument, you will not expect me now to offer solutions to the ills of American education. I have pointed to capitalism as a phenomenon that has profoundly shaped American society, and thereby our schools. I do not expect the disappearance of capitalism in the foreseeable future; neither I nor anybody else knows of any serious alternative. As to the ideology of individualism, philosophers and intellectuals can of course develop alternatives; in my view they *should* develop alternatives. But capitalism lends to individualism such enormous social plausibility that I do not expect these alternative ideologies to win the day. Thirdly, I do not expect the phenomenon of religious diversity to disappear in Western societies; and while I believe that some elements in this diversity are treated unjustly, I sincerely hope that the various elements of that diversity can continue to live in such peace and harmony as we enjoy here in the United States. If I have to choose, give me the United States rather than Iran or Lebanon!

By contrast, it seems to me that the hope of moving from a *no support* policy to an *equal support* policy when it comes to religion and the schools is a realistic hope. I am well aware of the strength of the traditional conviction that no one should be taxed to support anyone else's religion; and I know the power of precedent in the law. Yet it seems to me possible to persuade the American people that the present system is unjust, unfair, and inequitable, and to get the Court to see that its interpretation of the First Amendment as enjoining *no support* has over and over forced them into infringing on the free exercise of the religion of a large number of people in our society.

The United States has been an Enlightenment experiment. Let us, we have said, get down to what we all share in common, to what Reason tells us to be true, and base our life together on that; let us then, in our private lives and our subcommunities, add whatever peculiarities we wish to that commonality of Reason. More and more it is recognized that the Enlightenment vision was an illusion. We cannot base our life together on what Reason tells all of us to be the case. But fortunately it is not necessary for living and talking together that we set all our distinct traditions and all our distinct visions of meaning on the shelf, and base our discussion solely on that which we all agree on. As persons with different traditions and different visions of meaning we can talk together, and in that very encounter we can find out where we agree and where we don't. Within our distinct communities we can pass on the traditions of that community; within our commonwealth we can encounter each other across our diverse communities and traditions. We do not have to be a melting pot. We can be a nation of nations. And we can have a school system that expresses that alternative image for our common life.

Let us not be naive. Capitalism eats away at all traditions and all subcommunities. It powerfully pushes all of us toward the melting pot. Yet there do remain within American society, so it seems to me, distinct subcommunities in which the conditions are still present for cultivating ethical sensitivity and developing moral character on an institutional basis. Here, moral categories continue to be used. Here, reflection on moral principles remains alive. Here, moral reasons still energize action. Here, an answer can still be given to the question "Who requires this of me?" — an answer that many students will accept. Here, social expectations remain effective.

28

Knowledge, Character, and Community

MARK SCHWEHN

What can we know? How should we live? In what or whom should we hope? A historian might fruitfully divide Western intellectual life into periods or cultures according to which one of these three questions was the central and controlling one for them. But this imaginary (and ambitious!) historian would find that she could not apply this principle of organization to the time after about 1980. Something astonishing appears to have happened. For the first time in history the answers to all three questions seem, for a large number of intellectuals at least, to depend completely upon the answer to the following prior question: "Who are *we*?"

I find this development disturbingly problematic, but it does provide, I believe, the most relevant and urgent context for the consideration of questions that address the prospective relationships between religion and higher learning or spirituality and education today. I shall accordingly try in the essay that follows to do four things. First, I will outline more fully my own sense of our present predicament. Second, I will reflect upon how we arrived at this situation. Third, I will address some of the difficulties that attend communitarian accounts of knowledge and truth. Finally, I shall argue that in order to realize its own best aspirations, the modern academy must seek to retrieve and revivify within its communal life certain virtues that arose originally within religious communities.

29

I

Of the three basic human questions posed above, the epistemological question (What or how can we know?) was the last to be superseded by the question of community (Who are *we?*). Since the seventeenth century and until very recently, both the ethical question (How should we live?) and the religious question (In what or whom should we hope?) were superseded by the epistemological question.[1] Thus, for example, before addressing the ethical question, moral philosophers felt obliged to demonstrate that ethical discourse really was cognitively meaningful. In a similar manner, theologians often felt obliged to show how knowledge of God was possible before they proceeded to address religious questions whose answers presupposed the existence of a deity. Epistemology was thought to be foundational for all other inquiries. A more exact way of formulating the distinctiveness of our present situation would be to say that the community question has, in the last decade or so, replaced the epistemological question as foundational for all other inquiries — epistemological, ethical, and religious.[2]

As a way of both documenting and deepening our sense of this decisive shift in the current climate of opinion, I shall consider briefly two very influential books that appeared within four years of one another: Richard Rorty's *Philosophy and the Mirror of Nature* (1979) and Parker Palmer's *To Know As We Are Known* (1983). Although the two books differ from one another in several important respects, they both concern themselves centrally with epistemological matters, and they converge from strikingly different directions upon the question of community. Rorty, an avowed secular humanist, writes from a position at the very center of the academic establishment; yet his book, in spite of its sometimes very

1. I am not altogether satisfied with the three labels "epistemological," "ethical," and "religious"; I have used them here for rhetorical convenience. Questions do not arise in such a departmentalized fashion.

2. Alasdair MacIntyre's *After Virtue* (Notre Dame: University of Notre Dame Press, 1982) is the best-known recent instance of the supersession of the ethical question by the community question. After critiquing the Enlightenment project, the effort to ground morality in the universal character of reason itself, MacIntyre proceeds to argue that every ethic presupposes a community or society that warrants it and gives it meaning. The religious question was perhaps the first to be subsumed under the community question. Here I have in mind any number of semiotically oriented cultural anthropologists; see, e.g., Clifford Geertz, "Religion as a Cultural System," in Geertz, *The Interpretation of Cultures* (New York: Basic Books, 1973), pp. 87-125.

technical discourse, is still widely discussed outside the academy. Palmer, a committed Christian, writes from a position peripheral to the academic establishment; yet his book continues to find large and receptive audiences within the secular academy as well as outside it. Thus the two books together both evince and advance the community question as the most vital theme within contemporary intellectual life.

Both Rorty and Palmer develop powerful arguments against the epistemological scheme that has dominated Western thought since at least the seventeenth century. Rorty, who refers to this scheme as the "mirror of nature" or "foundationalism," criticizes it from within the tradition of professional philosophy. Most of his book is a history of the unavailing efforts of philosophers, since the time of Descartes, to find certainty, to discover a set of sensations (raw feelings or clear and distinct ideas) or terms (analytical truths, the symbols of mathematical logic) that would provide a secure foundation for all human inquiries and activities.

According to Rorty, philosophers have hoped to find a way of securing an absolute fit between our knowledge of the world and the world itself, to show that in at least *one* area of intellectual endeavor human knowledge really does "mirror" reality. And for most of the last three hundred and fifty years this effort to ground all human knowledge has focused upon the physical sciences; indeed, "since the period of Descartes and Hobbes, the assumption that scientific discourse was normal discourse and that all other discourse needed to be modeled upon it has been the standard motive for philosophizing."[3]

Rorty not only demonstrates that the foundationalist project has in its own terms failed, he also shows how it led philosophy to abandon its proper subject. Through arguments that are too intricate and extensive to summarize here, Rorty shows how a series of philosophers, including especially Dewey, Wittgenstein, and Heidegger, but also including Wilfred Sellars, Hilary Putnam, and Thomas Kuhn, have exposed foundationalism as a fundamentally misguided effort. But Rorty is even more interested in the baleful effects of foundationalism than he is in charting its collapse. "The Cartesian change from mind-as-reason to mind-as-inner-arena," he writes, "was not the triumph of the prideful individual subject freed from scholastic shackles so much as the triumph of the quest for certainty over the quest for wisdom. From that time

3. Richard Rorty, *Philosophy and the Mirror of Nature* (Princeton: Princeton University Press, 1979), p. 387.

31

forward, the way was open for philosophers either to attain the rigor of the mathematician or the mathematical physicist, or to explain the appearance of rigor in these fields, rather than to help people attain peace of mind. Science, rather than living, became philosophy's subject, and epistemology its center."[4]

Palmer, to some extent like Rorty, begins with a critique of the dominant epistemological scheme of the last three centuries. Palmer calls this scheme "objectivism," and he describes it not so much in terms of a history of ideas or a group of thinkers as in terms of a set of pedagogical practices that characterize the contemporary academy.[5] Thus Palmer's focus remains in one respect broader and in another respect narrower than Rorty's. Its comparative breadth consists in Palmer's attention to the way in which most teachers teach, regardless of whether they are teaching philosophy, literature, religion, or physics. Thus Palmer's critique extends to practices far beyond the narrower confines of professional philosophy. On the other hand, Palmer's "objectivism" refers to the dominant strain or to an amalgam of two strains (empiricism and a certain kind of pragmatism) within the larger epistemological project that Rorty calls the "mirror of nature." These distinctions are important, because they help in part to explain why Rorty finally argues for an abandonment of epistemology altogether, whereas Palmer seeks to replace or supersede objectivism with another epistemology.

The sources of Palmer's critique of modern epistemology are very different from Rorty's. Whereas Rorty relies exclusively upon philosophical writings that have subverted the foundationalist project, Palmer draws primarily upon Christian classics and upon a tradition of Christian spirituality that he traces back to the desert fathers. Moreover, Palmer's indictment of objectivism stems from his insight that epistemologies have moral trajectories, that ways of knowing are not morally neutral but morally directive. Objectivism, he demonstrates, places the would-be knower in an alienated, even an antagonistic position over and against the known world. Impelled by curiosity and the mania for control, objectivism fractures the bonds of community and tends inherently toward violence.[6] In view of this violent trajectory of

4. Ibid., p. 61.
5. Parker Palmer, *To Know As We Are Known* (New York: Harper & Row, 1983), p. 29.
6. Ibid., p. 26.

objectivism, "we must," Palmer argues, "recover from our spiritual tradition the models and methods of knowing as an act of love."[7]

Yet another apparent difference between Rorty and Palmer reveals, upon closer scrutiny, the presence of a common spirit or at least a common undertaking between the two men, one that manifests itself most fully in something of a quest for community. Palmer always uses the term *objective* to describe the antagonistic posture of the isolated, active knower who seeks to grasp, through the scientific method and for purposes of manipulation and control, the passive objects of the world in such a way that the knowledge that results "will reflect the nature of the objects in question rather than the knower's whims."[8] Rorty, on the other hand, observes that we use the term *objective* sometimes to mean "representing things as they really are" and at other times to designate "the presence of, or the hope for, agreement among inquirers."[9] He argues that these two meanings of *objective* are by no means co-extensive, and he decidedly prefers the latter to the former designation. Indeed, according to Rorty's own preferred view of knowledge — "epistemological behaviorism," as he somewhat unfelicitously calls it — "we understand knowledge when we understand the social justification of belief, and thus have no need to view it as accuracy of representation."[10]

Though this view is by no means identical to the one that Palmer advocates, some of the affinities between the two are quite striking. Thus, for example, Palmer insists that both knowledge and truth are communal terms. Knowledge is not the result of the isolated individual's efforts to mirror the world; it is instead a form of responsible relationship, even a "means to relationship," with others.[11] Knowing "becomes a reunion of separated beings whose primary bond is not of logic but of love"; truth is the name of this "community of relatedness."[12] For Rorty, once we see knowledge as a matter of conversation and of social practice, rather than as an attempt to mirror nature, truth is "what is *good for us* to believe" rather than privileged "contact with reality."[13]

7. Ibid., p. 9.
8. Ibid., p. 27.
9. Rorty, pp. 333-35.
10. Ibid., p. 170.
11. Palmer, p. 53.
12. Ibid., pp. 32-33.
13. Rorty, p. 176. Emphasis mine.

However much they may differ on other matters, both Rorty and Palmer understand knowledge and community as correlative terms.

They also both absorb aspects of the projects that they criticize into the fabric of the enterprises that they promote. Thus Palmer recognizes that the objectivist project has "helped to untangle some very twisted strands of the human soul."[14] And he retains in his own epistemological scheme objectivism's honorable opposition to self-centeredness. Rorty wishes to retain epistemological behaviorism's understanding of objectivity, even as he argues for the abandonment of epistemology-centered philosophy in favor of hermeneutics.

Rorty's description of the hermeneutical or edifying philosopher resembles Palmer's description of the knower-in-community. Instead of passing judgment upon which discourses are rational and which are not, or seeking to "ground" all discourse in a common set of terms or procedures, the hermeneutical philosopher "sees the relations between various discourses as those of strands in a possible conversation, a conversation which presupposes no disciplinary matrix which unites the speakers, but where the hope of agreement is never lost so long as the conversation lasts. This hope is not a hope for the discovery of antecedently existing common ground, but *simply* hope for agreement, or, at least, exciting and fruitful disagreement."[15] Above all else, the edifying philosopher takes responsibility for keeping this conversation alive, not by "finding the proper set of terms into which all the contributions should be translated," but by being willing "to pick up the jargon of the interlocutor rather than translating it into one's own." The participants in this conversational endeavor — this *societas* — are "persons whose paths through life have fallen together, united by civility rather than by a common goal, much less by a common ground."[16]

Rorty and Palmer do not finally share a "common ground" (a matter that I shall reconsider at a later point). I have nevertheless tried to discern here, by tacking back and forth between them and noting certain revealing points of intersection, the shape of the conversation that provides the current context for discussion about religion and higher education. The most important feature of that context seems to be the very recent but very striking ascendancy of the community question over all others. Before attempting to advance the discussion about religion and higher

14. Palmer, p. 26.
15. Rorty, p. 318.
16. Ibid.

education within this context, and because the context itself seems so novel, I think it is important to enlarge the historical perspective upon our present situation by way of providing some correctives to the historical accounts that are either supplied or implied by Rorty and Palmer. Developing these correctives will also sharpen the features of some of the problems that are peculiar to our present situation.

II

Let me begin by stating as succinctly as I can the story of how we came to this present pass. The outlines of what Rorty calls foundationalism and what Palmer calls objectivism were developed during the seventeenth century by thinkers such as Descartes, Hobbes, and Locke. But two centuries elapsed before these ideas attained cultural dominion in the West (or at least in the Anglo-American portion of it). That dominion was completed by four concurrent and overlapping developments: the rise of professionalism, the emergence of the academic disciplines as we know them today, the making of the modern research university, and the shift from a mechanistic (because based upon physics) to a developmental (because based upon Darwinian biology) view of knowledge and culture.

During this same period (roughly 1870 to 1900), however, there arose several powerful critiques of the dominant — because recently institutionalized — epistemology. Nietzsche inaugurated one line of criticism that has continued through the works of Heidegger and Gadamer. Charles Peirce and William James began another line of criticism that has continued through Dewey and the Chicago pragmatists to Quine and Rorty. These various lines have by now threatened to undermine foundationalism altogether, but the institutional superstructures that secured foundationalism's triumph remain intact. We stand in something of the same position relative to anti-foundationalism as was once occupied by early nineteenth-century American colleges relative to foundationalism. We are, to speak in sociologese, in a period of culture lag; or, to speak more poetically, we are "wandering between two worlds, one dead, the other powerless to be born" (Matthew Arnold).

It is important to stress that the two dominant lines of criticism noted above began during the 1870s and 1880s at precisely the same time that the modern research university emerged as a new institution of higher learning in America. Palmer recognizes the appearance of significant dissent from the objectivist position, but he suggests that it has been only recently developed and voiced.[17] And partly for this reason he amalgamates one of these dissenting lines, pragmatism, with empiricism in order to describe objectivism.

But pragmatism, at least the pragmatism of William James, actually arose as a sharp protest against the kind of thinking that Palmer calls objectivism but which was called *positivism* at the time that James was writing in the 1870s and 1880s. Thus, for example, James's earliest writings contain detailed attacks against what he called the "correspondence theory of truth."[18] He always insisted that we are "coefficients" of the truth we seek to know, neither alienated from nor antagonistic to the world of which we are a part. He argued, moreover, that "the whole man within us is at work" — our feelings, our faiths, our intuitions, and our hopes, as well as our thoughts and theories — when we seek knowledge.[19] He was, as all of his writings attest, an unrelenting enemy of the objectivist or positivist account of knowing as a mere matter of logic and dispassionate reasoning.[20]

Palmer ignores this Jamesean strain of pragmatism because his own

17. Palmer, pp. 27-29.

18. William James, "Remarks on Spencer's Definition of Mind as Correspondence," *Journal of Speculative Philosophy* 12 (1878): 1-18.

19. The entire passage is worth quoting: "Pretend what we may, the whole man within us is at work when we form our philosophical opinions. Intellect, will, taste, and passion cooperate just as they do in practical affairs; and lucky it is if the passion be not something as petty as a love of personal conquest over the philosopher across the way." And again, from the same essay: "If we survey the field of history and ask what feature all great periods of revival, of expansion of the human mind display in common, we shall find, I think, simply this: that each and all of them have said to the human being, 'The inmost nature of reality is congenial to powers which you possess'" (William James, "The Sentiment of Rationality," in *The Writings of William James*, ed. John J. McDermott [Chicago and London: University of Chicago Press, 1977], pp. 334, 331).

20. James was, in my judgment, the most trenchant critic of positivist epistemology, but he was only one of several such dissenters from what was fast becoming the epistemological orthodoxy of his day. See, for example, James Kloppenberg's analysis of the four intellectuals who, along with James and Dewey, sought to develop what Kloppenberg calls an epistemology of the *via media:* Wilhelm Dilthey (1833-1911), whose father and grandfather were Calvinist ministers; Thomas Hill Green (1836-1882), whose father was also a clergyman; Henry Sidgwick (1838-1900), another clergyman's son who, along with Green, was among the founders of the Free Christian Union; and Alfred Fouille (1838-1912), whose goal was "to establish philosophy as the fusion of what is true in science, accompanied by an awareness of its limits, and what is true in religion, the experience of something beyond" (Kloppenberg, *Uncertain Victory: Social Democracy and Progressivism in European and American Thought, 1870-1920* [Oxford

thinking was shaped, as he tells us in one of the most powerfully confessional portions of his book, by a different strand of the pragmatic tradition. He came to believe that knowledge emerges through the imposition of order upon the chaos of experience, and that truth is just a name for whatever "works" to solve certain problems, for whatever eventuates in a satisfactory manipulation of the world.[21] This vulgarly practical and relativistic theory of truth perhaps most closely approximates the current, popular sense of the word *pragmatic,* and one can find warrants for it in the writings of all the pragmatists, even including some of James's.

Nevertheless, as Richard Bernstein has observed, the American pragmatists — especially Peirce, James, and Dewey — had already thematized an anti-foundational approach to philosophy before the First World War. In addition, they had emphasized the "social character of the self and the need to nurture a critical community of inquirers." What Peirce wrote long ago about philosophers applies today to all of those who seek to discover knowledge and truth, because according to Peirce our understanding of matters is invariably fallible and partial — both in the sense of being biased and in the sense of seeing only a part: "we individually cannot reasonably hope to attain the ultimate philosophy which we pursue; we can only seek it, therefore, for the *community of philosophers.*"[22]

In sum, we should not permit the cultural ascendancy of a vulgar strain of pragmatism during most of the twentieth century to obscure the very promising alternatives to objectivism that were developed by Peirce, James, and others as early as 1880. One strain of pragmatism has combined with logical positivism to produce objectivism. But another strain of pragmatism — its most original strain, and one that is still discernible in Rorty — is very congenial to Palmer's own critique of objectivism.

There is, however, another and better reason why Palmer ignored James and other late nineteenth-century critics of objectivism: he did

---

and New York: Oxford University Press, 1986], pp. 26-46). For consideration of an exclusively American set of thinkers who dissented from positivism in various ways during this same period — Charles Peirce, James Mark Baldwin, Edward A. Ross, G. Stanley Hall, and Josiah Royce — see R. Jackson Wilson, *In Quest of Community: Social Philosophy in the United States, 1860-1920* (London and New York: Oxford University Press, 1968).

21. Palmer, pp. 3-4.

22. Richard J. Bernstein, "Pragmatism, Pluralism, and the Healing of Wounds," *Proceedings and Addresses of the American Philosophical Association* 63, 3 (1989): 9.

not set out to write a piece of intellectual history. Rather, as noted earlier, he derived objectivism from current pedagogical practice, and he never intended to suggest that objectivism, in the complete sense of the word, could be found in the writings of any given thinker or set of thinkers. Yet if Palmer is correct, as I think he is, in taking objectivism to be *the* epistemology that informs the practices of the modern university, and if I am correct in suggesting that James and others had already fashioned powerful alternative theories of knowledge as early as 1880, a vital historical question arises. How, given the presence of several conflicting epistemologies, did one of them come to dominate the modern university?

We might expect to find an answer to this question from Rorty, who is explicitly and deliberately historical in a way that Palmer is not. Rorty's history is, however, purely "internalist" by design. He attends only to the development of ideas within the discipline of philosophy, not to external considerations — social, economic, technological, and political — that impinged in various ways upon that development and doubtless propelled it in certain directions. Though a complete historical explanation of the ascendancy of objectivism or foundationalism would require an analysis of all of these conditions, only one of them — the political factor — is crucially relevant to my present purpose.

That purpose is to issue an emphatic historical reminder to all of us who criticize the ethos of objectivism in the name of communitarian accounts of knowledge and truth. The principal danger inherent in communitarianism is tribalism and the subsequent violence that often arises among rival tribes, each of them inflexibly wedded to their respective versions of the truth. I would argue that objectivism initially arose and that it subsequently attained cultural dominion primarily because it was intended by its architects as a way of *avoiding* violence. We must at least add the desire for civil peace to the two desires that Palmer has identified as the motives for objectivism — curiosity and control.

Hobbes and Descartes manifested this pacific motive most vividly of all the seventeenth-century advocates of objectivism or foundationalism. "Fear and I were born twins," Hobbes said, remarking upon the fact that his birthday fell on the same day that England trembled under the onslaught of the Spanish Armada. When he developed the objectivist epistemology that encompassed the first part of *Leviathan*, arguing contrary to all of the ancients that nature "dissociates," he did so — against

38

the background of civil war — primarily to secure a rational foundation for politics so that such wars could be avoided in the future.[23]

While Hobbes was brooding over the growing civil strife in England, Descartes was in winter quarters with the French army in Germany where the "fortune of war" had taken him. There he retreated alone into a stove-heated room "to look for the true method of attaining knowledge of everything [his] mind could grasp." Again, as we can see from the autobiographical account Descartes gave us in his seminal *Discourse on the Method of Rightly Directing One's Reason and of Seeking Truth in the Sciences,* the quest for certain and secure foundations began, as it had with Hobbes, in part as a stay against the confusion and violence born of religious conflict.[24]

Objectivism as the best *alternative* to violence — both Rorty and Palmer ignore this important truth about the epistemological tradition they criticize, though they do so for different reasons. Rorty ignores it because he is concerned only with the internal history of modern philosophy. Palmer ignores it because he believes that in order to account for the violent trajectory of objectivism he must find exclusively egoistic motivation — idle curiosity and the desire for control — as the basic impetus behind it.

I do not mean to suggest here that Rorty and Palmer ignore the virtues of the Enlightenment altogether, much less that either man is antagonistic to them. Indeed, as noted earlier, they both incorporate some elements of objectivism into their own prescriptions. Palmer, moreover, openly insists that we must not romanticize the life of "the earlier [pre-modern] world [which] was often little more than a reflection of the passions and prejudices of those who claimed to know."[25] And Rorty states flatly that "the preservation of the values of the Enlightenment is our best hope."[26]

But by ignoring or at least underestimating the extent to which objectivism's vices are precisely the defects of its virtues, both Rorty and Palmer are more sanguine than the historical record warrants in believing that one can persuasively disentangle the sinister strands of objectivism from its more humane strands within the academic conscience

23. Thomas Hobbes, *Leviathan* (New York: Penguin Books, 1981), pp. 186-87.
24. Descartes, *Discourse on the Method,* in Elizabeth Anscombe and Peter Geach, eds., *Descartes' Philosophical Writings* (Indianapolis: Bobbs-Merrill, 1971), p. 19.
25. Palmer, p. 26.
26. Rorty, p. 335.

of the West. Any radical alternative to foundationalism or objectivism will seem to open up the prospect of renewed violence among different communities who would seem to have no *rational foundation* on the basis of which they might adjudicate the disagreements that will inevitably arise among them.

There may very well be a way to assuage successfully this fear of violence, and I think that Palmer at least has partially succeeded in doing so. But those who welcome the supersession of the epistemological question by the community question need to recognize how deep-seated and how historically well-founded are the fears of foundationalists who believe that if objectivism disappears, force, not some new epistemology, will take its place. This fear of tribalism and violence is perhaps the foremost difficulty that most communitarian accounts of knowledge must face.

III

Though I myself welcome the recent cultural ascendancy of the community question, I need to admit and then to face honestly three further difficulties that have attended this development before I can proceed to demonstrate the need for the cultivation of certain religious virtues within communities of higher learning. These three difficulties should already be apparent from my brief account of Palmer and Rorty. First, the concept of community needs further specification. Second, the relationship between community on the one hand and knowledge and truth on the other hand needs further elucidation. Third, the communitarian impulse needs to be freed from hopelessly nostalgic yearnings. In the course of addressing these difficulties, I will anchor my discussion firmly within the actual experiences of common life within the present-day academy.

Much of the discussion of community today is marked by a degree of imprecision that borders on obscurity. Most parties to the discussion exhibit a terminological wavering of the sort that once characterized the discussion of culture among anthropologists. In the latter conversation, some thought of Culture (invariably with a capital C) as a unitary concept of an ideal and then proceeded to determine how much Culture any given group possessed. Others insisted that the topic could only be fruitfully pursued if one spoke of cultures, always in the lowercase plural and always designating empirical realities, to refer to all groups that shared a common language and a common past or identity.[27] Still others oscillated between the grand ideal of Culture (variously described) and the actual diversity of groups, all of them cultures but possessing no discernible "essence" in common.

Conversation about community over the course of the last century has paralleled the conversation about culture. Thus Dewey, one of the philosophers who has most influenced Rorty, sometimes spoke of publics or communities in the plural to refer to any group of people that recognizes itself as having some common problem or another. Under this description communities are kaleidoscopic, evanescent entities, assuming temporary shape and then dissolving once the problems that gave them their original purpose have disappeared or been resolved. On the other hand, Dewey spoke of the search for the "Great Community" or "Public," and these were terms that designated his special sense of democracy itself.[28]

Rorty's own notions of community are much more obscure than Dewey's. He never actually uses "community" as a significant analytical category, but he constantly refers to collectivities of one sort or another in his effort to substantiate what he takes to be the only defensible understanding of knowledge (what is warrantably assertible by us) and truth (whatever is good for us to believe). Thus he speaks of the subjective conditions of inquiry of any kind as "just the facts about what a given society, or profession, or other group, takes to be good ground for assertions of a certain sort." Rorty then refers to all of these collectivities as "disciplinary matrices."[29] This bewildering parade of names indicates that the dialectics of Dewey (his movement back and forth between the ideal and the reality of community) has degenerated, in Rorty's hands at least, into sheer obscurantism.

Let me begin to demystify matters here by articulating some obvious truths. Academies are places of learning. Students and faculty come together because they seek knowledge and understanding. It may well be

27. The best account of the shift from Culture to cultures is George W. Stocking, Jr., "Matthew Arnold, E. B. Tylor, and the Uses of Invention," in Stocking, *Race, Culture, and Evolution* (Chicago and London: University of Chicago Press, 1982), pp. 69-90. Cf. also Stocking, *Victorian Anthropology* (New York: The Free Press, 1987), pp. 302-30, and Clifford Geertz, "Thick Description: Toward an Interpretive Theory of Culture," in *The Interpretation of Cultures*, pp. 4-5.

28. John Dewey, *The Public and Its Problems* (Chicago: Swallow Press, 1954), pp. 143-84.

29. Rorty, p. 385.

that many, perhaps most, students go to colleges and universities for other purposes; nevertheless, the two constitutive functions of academies are teaching and learning. These functions in turn include a variety of activities — reading, writing, computing, memorizing — that purport to advance disciplined thinking about important matters of human concern.

All disciplined thinking, even when it proceeds — as most of it does — in the solitary confines of the study, derives from and therefore depends upon social processes like language and tradition. Moreover, disciplined thought is itself often dialogical (involving two inner voices), more often conversational (involving many such voices). The eminent British philosopher of education R. S. Peters has put this latter and by now commonplace point as elegantly as anyone:

> Plato once described philosophy as the soul's dialogue with itself. It is a pity that this clue was not followed up. For the notion would not then have developed that reason is a sort of mental gadget that can be used by the individual, or, as Hume described it, a "wonderful and unintelligible instinct in our souls." The ability to reason, in the philosophical sense of thinking critically about one's beliefs, develops only as a man keeps critical company so that a critic is incorporated in his own consciousness. The dialogue within is inseparable from the dialogue without.[30]

This image of the individual disciplined thinker as engaged in a process that is in a derivative sense communal outlines some of the central and ideal features of *academic* community. First, this community is intentional in that it aims at knowledge and truth. Second, just as the voices within converse with one another in an intimate, critical, and engaging manner, so too must students and faculty treat one another with critical respect and concern. Like disciplined thought itself, community flourishes or perishes depending not only upon the critical acumen of the various voices that comprise it but also upon the extent to which and the manner in which they respect and listen to one another.

Of all the gatherings on a university campus, classroom meetings would seem most closely to approximate the ideal features of academic community just outlined. Like Dewey's emerging publics, these meetings arise around a set of questions or problems or subject matters. And

---

30. R. S. Peters, *Ethics and Education* (London: George Allen & Unwin, 1968), p. 51.

they are surely evanescent. But unlike Dewey's publics, classroom meetings end not when a given problem has disappeared or been resolved but when a bell rings or a term concludes. Like the internal conversation that is disciplined thought, classroom meetings do aim at knowledge, truth, and understanding. But many, perhaps most, classroom meetings do not include much conversation, nor is there, for the most part, much intimacy and engagement among the several members of the group.

It therefore seems strained at best to speak of most classrooms as communities; perhaps they are best described, to borrow a term from Erving Goffman, as "focused gatherings." Yet they are nevertheless the single most important element in the overall assemblage of groups that constitutes the academic community, for the classroom is the place where students learn the disciplines and the virtues that are necessary to participate in a community of learning. In short, every teacher is teaching at least two things in every classroom — his or her subject and the manners of learning. I use the term *manners* here deliberately to capture both the sense of *methods* and the sense of *virtues*.

Flourishing beyond the classrooms are a bewildering number of academic assemblies: faculty groups, sometimes defined along departmental lines, sometimes not; informal gatherings of students in residence halls and other locations; and any number of groups, comprised of both students and faculty, who congregate for the purpose of learning together. Faculty members are the most crucial element in this assemblage of groups, because they, more than the students, give shape and substance to the entire configuration of groups, because they are relatively more permanently rooted within any given academy, and because they are charged with the task of initiating the students into the discourses and the disciplines, the subjects and the manners of higher learning.

In brief, any academic community is itself an assemblage of groups that can be designated "communities," not because they possess a common essence but because they display a certain family resemblance to one another. Even so, there are some basic outlines that circumscribe academic communities: their face-to-face quality; their common pursuit of knowledge and understanding; and their integral character, the sense in which the quality of the individual's thought and the quality of the communities' thinking are mutually dependent upon one another. The excellence of "the dialogue within is inseparable from the [excellence of] the dialogue without."

When Palmer claims that knowing is a "reunion of separated beings

43

whose primary bond is not of logic but of love" or that knowledge is itself a form of responsible relationship, he intends, I think, to call attention to this integral character of the community of learning. When Rorty argues that "we understand knowledge when we understand the social justification of belief," he too means to emphasize the irreducibly communal dimension of thought. Even so, both Palmer and Rorty occasionally mystify and perplex readers who need greater clarity about the exact connections between community on the one hand and knowledge and truth on the other. I will therefore turn now to this second difficulty that has arisen recently in the context of the community question.

Academic community does not refer to some sort of metaphysical entity that is prior to the individuals comprising it and free from its own history and traditions. It is instead, as I have been suggesting, a configuration of plural communities with their own conventions, disciplinary histories, standards of evidence and argument, and patterns of discourse. So we need not conjure up, in thinking through the relationships among community, knowledge, and truth, assortments of alchemists or flat-earthers as plausible examples of communities of inquirers within the contemporary academy. Inquiry takes place within academic communities that are themselves embedded within an epistemic context, and this context conditions in large part the justification of belief. To know something is just to hold beliefs about it that are justified. Justification of belief is itself a communal endeavor, the outcome, if you will, of disciplined inquiry.

Though communal inquiry secures knowledge through internal processes of justification, it does not insure truth. Inquiries can go wrong in many ways and for many reasons. Even so, as Jeffrey Stout has said well in *Ethics After Babel,*

> truth is a property of interpreted sentences, and interpreted sentences belong to languages which are human creations. The world-as-it-is-in-itself is, by definition, the world apart from the application of interpreted sentences by human beings — the world described for epistemological purposes as undescribed. It therefore includes no truths. To accept or discover the truth about something is to have acquired a language in which interpreted sentences can be applied in a certain way. It is therefore to make use of human artifice, to possess certain habits, beliefs, and so on. That is the only road to truth about anything.[31]

31. Jeffrey Stout, *Ethics After Babel: The Languages of Morals and Their Discontents* (Boston: Beacon Press, 1988), p. 54.

Academic communities are interpretive and self-critical. But though they aim at knowledge and truth, their capacity really to discover the truth about any matter will depend, as Stout here suggests, in part upon their possession of certain vocabularies, skills, and virtues. In other words, precision about truth and knowledge is itself contingent upon the understanding of the particular contexts within which these terms are used. For this reason, Parker Palmer is correct when he argues that community and truth are correlative terms.

In our present circumstances the clarification of the concept of academic community and the elucidation of knowledge and truth are therefore closely related enterprises. To ask about the meaning of truth is to raise questions about context, about the boundaries, the vocabulary, and the virtues that collectively define the shape and the substance of a particular community of inquirers whose primary intention is to discover the truth. Once the epistemological center of gravity has shifted to a place outside of the self, questions about communal ideals and questions about knowledge and truth are, though not identical to each other, ineluctably convergent.

Some contemporary thinkers, however, suspect all such references to communal ideals, regardless of whether or not these ideals are advanced within epistemological contexts, and this brings me to the third and final difficulty that attends current conversation about community. Michael Ignatieff, in his book *The Needs of Strangers*, has framed this last and fairly widespread critique of communal ideals as forcefully as anyone:

> Words like fraternity, belonging and community are so soaked with nostalgia and utopianism that they are nearly useless as guides to the real possibilities of solidarity in modern society. Modern life has changed the possibilities of civic solidarity, and our language stumbles behind like an overburdened porter with a mountain of old cases. . . . Our task is to find a language for our need for belonging which is not just a way of expressing nostalgia, fear and estrangement from modernity.[32]

Jeffrey Stout has discerned some of these same nostalgic impulses at work among several communitarians, and on that basis he has suggested

32. Michael Ignatieff, *The Needs of Strangers* (New York: Viking Press, 1985), pp. 138-39.

that many of them suffer from "terminal wistfulness."[33] And Jeremy Waldron, who has himself been persuaded by Ignatieff's critique among others, has noted repeatedly that terms like *brotherhood* and *community* are now merely codewords that timid or estranged souls use to protest modernity.[34]

Though all three of these critics are speaking about civic life, their misgivings about community apply as well to my discussion of academic life in communitarian terms. Ignatieff continues his critique of communitarians with a question: "Our political images of civic belonging remain haunted by the classical polis, by Athens, Rome, and Florence. Is there a language of belonging adequate to Los Angeles?"[35] I might well ask, given my present purposes, "Is there a language of community adequate to UCLA?"

No and yes. No, because UCLA, along with any number of other large research-oriented universities, embodies in its practices and in its language a Weberian conception of the academic vocation. And when Max Weber, in his famous address *Wissenschaft als Beruf,* sought to shape the self-understanding of the modern academy, he did so by insisting that the academic realm, like the political and economic realms, had become and would remain governed by means-end rationality and by impersonal constraints. Like Ignatieff, Weber believed that talk of friendship, community, and a sense of belonging was best consigned to private life. Up to a point, Weber and Ignatieff would surely be right: UCLA *as a whole* cannot be adequately analyzed by the language of community.

But matters are more complicated than this. One of UCLA's own faculty members has written a historical study of civic life in early modern Philadelphia that is directly germane to my own analysis of his and others' academic lives at UCLA. Gary B. Nash has noted that in pre-Revolutionary days, Philadelphia was in some sense a single community. But over time its population increased, its class divisions became more pronounced, its ethnic composition became more diverse, its neighborhoods changed their configurations, and its economic system became more geared to the impersonality of the marketplace. Unlike

33. Stout, pp. 220-42, esp. p. 229.
34. Jeremy Waldron, "Particular Values and Critical Morality," *California Law Review* 7 (May 1989): 582.
35. Ignatieff, p. 139.

some historians who, in view of these developments, proclaim the loss of community in Philadelphia, Nash argues for another analytical strategy. "Rather than nostalgically tracing the eclipse of community," he writes, "we need to trace the continuously evolving process of community." Nash then proceeds to write about craft organizations, working-class taverns, benevolent societies, free black churches, and reform associations. Instead of dismissing these structured organizations as mere *Gesellschaft*, Nash assigns to them a leading role in the creation of genuine urban community, of what he calls "*Gemeinschaft* of mind — the mental life of community."[36]

Although analogies drawn between civic and academic life are far from perfect, I would insist that something like Nash's analysis of Philadelphia better captures the fabric of his and others' academic lives at UCLA than does the language of *Gesellschaft*. UCLA is simply less than the sum of its parts. Its intellectual vitality arises not at the level of the university as a whole but from the myriad of communities whose assemblage we designate UCLA. And these communities are marked in turn by features I have already outlined as circumscribing the family of communities that constitutes any college or university — face-to-face engagement, aspirations to knowledge and truth, and integral relationships between individual thought and communal conversation.

Neither the language of *Gesellschaft* nor the language of *Gemeinschaft* can adequately describe the modern academy. The two vocabularies arose initially, in the writings of Ferdinand Tönnies, in a kind of dialectical opposition to one another. Indeed, it would be a subtle historical task indeed to determine whether the language of community arose as a protest against modernity or whether the language of modernity arose as a protest against what were taken to be the utopian impulses behind the language of community. At any rate, Tönnies, who first coined the word *Gemeinschaft* as a sociological category, used the term in both a descriptive and a critical sense. "His images of *Gemeinschaft*," Harry Liebersohn has shown, "were not an inducement to nostalgia so much as a powerful reminder of things that once had been and could return."[37]

36. Gary B. Nash, "The Social Evolution of Preindustrial American Cities, 1700-1820: Reflections and New Directions," *Journal of Urban History* 13 (Feb. 1987): 119, 133. I thank my colleague David Paul Nord for first drawing my attention to Nash's analysis.

37. Tönnies and Weber were part of a constellation of thinkers, including Ernst Troeltsch, Georg Simmel, and Georg Lukacs, for whom the terms *Gemeinschaft* and *Gesellschaft* were not only sociological categories but also terms with which they charted

To criticize communitarian thought simply because it deploys images drawn from a real or imagined past as criticism of the present is to dismiss arbitrarily much of modern social and political theory. Are we simply to disregard Rousseau's *Discourse on the Origins of Inequality* because of his invocation of a state of nature and a subsequent state of nascent civil society? Are we to dismiss Thomas Paine because he takes us back to Eden on the road to establishing the rights of man? If thinkers as diverse as Rousseau, Paine, and Tönnies are all to be understood as utopian insofar as they criticize the present from the standpoint of a real or imagined past, then utopianism is an honored mode of cultural criticism.

IV

Communitarian accounts of knowledge and truth have been vulnerable to charges of tribalism, imprecision, and nostalgia in part because communitarians have been insufficiently attentive to the affections and the virtues that sustain disciplined communal conversation. So, for example, even though Richard Rorty does not think of himself as a communitarian, he repeatedly insists that we must focus upon the "social justification of belief" if we are first to understand and then to pursue knowledge and truth. Yet Rorty's understanding of communal processes is weak in part because he lacks a spiritual tradition within which he can articulate it. By contrast to Rorty, Parker Palmer is quite lucid on

---

"the shift from a religious to a social framework of meaning. . . . To explain how man's social fate had replaced his religious fate was one of the chief ambitions underlying their work and remains a powerful, though seldom acknowledged, source of its enduring interest" (Harry Liebersohn, *Fate and Utopia in German Sociology, 1870-1923* [Cambridge, MA, and London: Massachusetts Institute of Technology Press, 1988], p. 10). Liebersohn points out that Tönnies was uncertain "whether *Gemeinschaft* referred to an actual historical example or to an abstract model more or less approximated by empirical social orders." I need also to stress that the German word was originally more restricted in its use than the English word *community*. The latter term can refer either to an *involuntary* social grouping like a network of families "bound together by a unity of wills and creating cooperation prior to its members' conscious choice [*Gemeinschaft*]," or, more often, to *voluntary* "ethnic or religious groups, whose members are free to join or leave" (Liebersohn, p. 7). Clearly, academic communities are voluntary, but they are bound together by, among other things, a unity of purpose — the discovery of knowledge and truth.

the subject of community precisely because he, unlike Rorty, is rooted in a spiritual tradition. And unlike many of his fellow communitarians, Palmer consistently connects his analyses of knowledge and community to his understanding of character, to what in his terms might be called spiritually grounded habits of mind.

Indeed, I shall venture farther than Palmer to suggest that the practice of certain spiritual virtues is and always has been essential to processes of higher learning, even within the secular academy. I have tried thus far to demonstrate that the secular part of Western culture has itself raised the community question with unprecedented urgency and that the religious are best situated to address the question with authority based upon both tradition and experience. Here, however, I wish only to make a more restricted suggestion regarding the relationship between religion and communities of higher learning. I believe that the most promising argument for an integral relationship between them can be made through a demonstration that genuine learning has always entailed the exercise of virtues that arose initially within communities that were self-consciously religious in character. I want now briefly to consider three such virtues — humility, faith, and self-denial — and to show how each one of them is arguably indispensable to the process of genuine learning.

Much of what passes for laziness or the proverbial "lack of motivation" among today's students really involves a lack of humility, stemming in part from a lack of piety or respect for that aspect of God's ongoing creation which manifests itself in works of genius. During the last term, I asked my students why they had not thought through a particular passage from St. Augustine on friendship and loss. I knew, because I had by that time grown to know these students very well, that they cared very much about the matters that Augustine was examining. I had not realized, however, that some of my students were easily convinced, based upon a quick reading of the text, that Augustine was simply mistaken or overly agitated about these matters. Others complained that Augustine was unnecessarily obscure. All of them dismissed the passage in a peremptory fashion.

Current educational theory would suggest, in the face of these student comments, that I had failed properly to motivate them to want to learn about friendship and loss, or that I had not managed to make Augustine accessible to them. I *had* probably failed in these ways. But my students could have overcome my failings had they been sufficiently

49

humble, had they presumed that Augustine's apparent obscurity was *their* problem, not his, and had they presumed that his apparent inconsistencies or excesses were not really the careless errors they took them to be.

Humility on this account does not mean uncritical acceptance: it means, in practical terms, the *presumption of wisdom and authority in the author.* My students are far too often ready to believe that Kant was simply, in a given passage, murky or that Aristotle was pointlessly repetitive or that Tolstoy was, in the battle scenes of *War and Peace,* needlessly verbose. Such quick, easy, and dismissive appraisals preclude the possibility of learning from these writers. Yes, some of these judgments might turn out to be warranted, but the practice of humility at least prevents them from being made summarily. *Some* degree of humility is a precondition for learning.

As is faith. James Gustafson has recently argued in an address delivered at Valparaiso University that "if the university is to be a fruitful location for exploring larger issues of life, perhaps we need to acknowledge, each of us as scholars, teachers, and students, that all our knowing involves 'faith,' human confidence in what we have received."[38] The point seems indisputable. We all rely upon the work and the thought of others, and we cannot possibly think well in an atmosphere of mistrust. Again, as in the case of humility, trusting the research and the theories of others does not mean uncritical acceptance. It means, as Gustafson has said, that we typically believe what we are questioning and at the same time question what we are believing.[39] Faith then is a persistent beat in the rhythm of intellectual life. Without it, we would not be able to learn. All of us in some sense or another really do believe in order to understand.

Finally, and perhaps fundamentally, the virtue of self-denial is indispensable to learning. By self-denial I mean the capacity first to risk and then to give ourselves up if necessary for the sake of the truth. The Italian Renaissance philosopher Pico della Mirandola argued that the conflicts that arise within a community of inquiry are "peculiar in that here it is a gain to lose. Consequently, anyone very weak can and should not only not disparage them [the struggles], but also seek them volun-

38. James Gustafson, "Human Confidence and Rational Activity," *Cresset,* September 1988, p. 17.
39. Ibid., p. 16.

tarily, since the loser truly receives benefit and not injury from the winner, for through him the loser returns home richer."[40] I would prefer to say that truth is always the victor in these struggles. All participants lose, in the sense that they all surrender a part of themselves in the process of growing into the truth together.

Humility, faith, and self-denial — these practices do not exhaust the list of spiritual virtues that are indispensable to learning, nor do they represent a list of *distinctively* Christian virtues. Indeed, the virtues I have touched upon here did not originate from the example of Jesus of Nazareth. They arose instead from the practices and the teachings of the ancient Hebrews, a people whose deep and widely celebrated commitment to learning was and still is informed by an epistemology that is profoundly communal in character. To say with Parker Palmer that we must "recover from our spiritual tradition the models and methods of knowing as an act of love" is to direct us to the roots of that tradition in ancient Israel in which knowledge and intimacy were one and the same thing.

Nor should we limit our understanding of religious virtues to the Judeo-Christian strand of the Western tradition. Plato — whose academy, Josef Pieper reminds us, regularly performed religious sacrifices — understood very well the integral relationship between virtue and knowledge, character and learning.[41] He chose the dialogue form, I believe, because it was the vehicle best designed to dramatize the movement of inquiry as an act of life, involving characters in conversation, not intellects in isolation. The *Meno,* Plato's only dialogue on the subject of education, features a title character whose failures to learn are more frequently the results of flaws in his character than they are the results of lapses in his logic. Meno needs to change if he is to come to know the truth, and insofar as the truth comes to Meno, he does change — not just his ideas but his way of living.

Indeed, whether we look to the teachers of ancient Israel or the Platonic academy or to Augustine at Cassiciacum or to the medieval university or to Pico's disputatious Florence or to the small colleges of early nineteenth-century America, we find learning flourishing in communities formed by the conscious practice of spiritual virtues. Over the

40. Pico della Mirandola, "On the Dignity of Man," trans. Charles Glenn Wallis, in *On the Dignity of Man and Other Works* (Indianapolis: Bobbs-Merrill, 1981), p. 20.
41. Josef Pieper, *Scholasticism* (New York: McGraw, 1960), p. 155.

course of the last century, the modern university has ceased to attend to character formation — or it has imagined that such attention should be an "extra-curricular" enterprise having little or nothing to do with knowledge. From this perspective, the current ascendancy of the community question may be Western culture's way of awakening from a comparatively brief slumber induced or at least maintained by objectivism. If so, the "problem" is not to explain, much less to justify, the relationship between religion and higher learning. The "problem" is to account for how we could ever have lost sight of it.

This blindness to the relationship between spirituality and learning has been in part the fault of the "enlightened" secular establishment and in part the fault of religious bigotry and obscurantism. David Hume insisted that some of the very virtues I have just discussed are inimical to learning. He understood very well that the Christian religion was not merely a set of teachings but a way of life. And in his *Inquiry Concerning the Principles of Morals* he insisted that "monkish" virtues like humility and self-sacrifice "stupefy the understanding and harden the heart, obscure the fancy and sour the temper."[42] For all of its remarkable achievements, the Enlightenment rationalism of Hume and others always had the potential to corrode the very virtues that made enlightened inquiry possible.

On the other hand, the religious bigotry and superstition that Hume assailed so mercilessly have persisted long after his critiques of them. At the very moment at the end of the nineteenth century that the universities were consolidating the triumph of objectivism, many of the religious were claiming that religion meant dogmatism based upon a peculiar reading of the Scriptures (Genesis as a geology text, for example). If the current ascendancy of the community question really does mark something of a rediscovery, we might expect that the religious will rediscover the ethical dimension of their spirituality at the same time that the academicians rediscover the spiritual dimension of their ethos.

To speak in such abstract and exalted terms is to engage the language of hope, not optimism. For it is one thing to suggest that the life of learning will always be in some sense dependent upon the exercise of spiritual virtues in however attenuated a form, and quite another to

---

42. David Hume, *An Inquiry Concerning the Principles of Morals* (Indianapolis: Bobbs-Merrill, 1976), p. 91.

imagine that the universities will turn to the practice of those spiritual disciplines, such as prayer, that give those virtues meaning and strength. I do not therefore expect any grand restructuring of academe in the near future, and I would myself shrink back from participating in such a venture. Again, I think that Palmer is correct. He argues that the place to begin to counter the objectivist epistemology that still grips the academy is in individual classrooms where teachers, having disciplined themselves first, create spaces "where obedience to truth is practiced."

I also agree with Palmer that the state of relatedness or wholeness that was present "in the beginning" constitutes the horizon of our hopes. But I read Genesis a bit differently from him, and I am therefore less sanguine, I think, than he is about the penultimate prospects of our knowledge under any description, even the description of knowing as an act of love. I noted earlier the ironic and paradoxical fact that the violent trajectory of objectivism was impelled in part by the desire for civil peace. I believe that Genesis teaches us that all *human* knowing is paradoxical in character — paradoxical because limited, limited because human.

Indeed, the first disobedience involves something like a "fall" *into* humanity. Mortality and self-consciousness (in the double sense of self-awareness and embarrassment) emerge from the knowledge of good and evil. And the sources of the most profound human achievements seem thereafter bound up inextricably with the sources of human shame and misery. Since this is so, the ultimate grounds for our hope must lie somewhere beyond ourselves and our knowing. Perhaps the pivotal point of relation between higher learning and religion lies somewhere between the deepest human sense of the limits of our knowing and the cultivation, in the midst of such chastening wisdom, of the spiritual virtue of hope.

Teaching as Drama

JEAN BETHKE ELSHTAIN

Clearly I have something dramatic in mind. As I thought further about the title I had given my talk, I got a bit queasy. I didn't want to come before you suggesting that teaching involves a bag of tricks — a dramatic entrance, a fake gun, smoke and mirrors, high or low melodrama with clear-cut bad guys and good guys. Nor did I have in mind classic tragedy, with deepening angst and mounds of bodies left on the floor at play's end. Nor was I thinking of "living theater" where the performers move out and harangue the audience or demand their involvement. I did have in mind a touch of the theater of the absurd, for from time to time, invariably and unavoidably, the ironic voice prevails in teaching, or must if one is to keep one's sanity. But none of this quite captures my intention. What, then, *did* I have in mind?

I must beg the indulgence of any serious students of the theater for what may be my clumsy analogies and analyses. In order to focus my meandering thoughts, I checked out "drama" in the *Oxford English Dictionary* and found the following: "a composition adapted to be acted in prose; a story related by means of dialogue and action represented with gesture, costume, scenery; or actions involving a course of events having dramatic unity and leading to a final catastrophe." Hopefully, a final catastrophe is not where teaching as drama winds up. But a story

---

This essay began life as a presentation at Vanderbilt University for a series on teaching excellence. I have maintained the informality and spontaneity of the discussion for inclusion here.

related by means of dialogue and action, if you count speech acts as a form of action with words — then, yes, there is something in this standard definition that serves my purposes. I didn't and don't have anything like a technique or a worked out or worked through method in mind. Rather, I'm trying to capture a sensibility, to create in the classroom an ambiance of anticipation, an aesthetic construction that is itself or that exudes an ethics.

An ethics of respect for the views of others, for the possibility of keeping multiple perspectives in play and in mind and, at the same time, focusing those perspectives, drawing out themes and imperatives, refusing to bring an artificial unity to the whole — this is the challenge. Let me home in on concrete examples and exemplars. As I remember my years as a student, it seems clear to me that the most effective teachers were those with a heightened sense of drama. Not those who came in, furrowed their brows, pounded their foreheads, and put on display their own quivering inner selves. I have no patience whatsoever with capitulation to the cult of personal experience. But we do bring ourselves to the teaching enterprise. Teaching, in part, is about the cultivation of character, which involves an openness to new possibilities as well as a recognition of stubborn realities. One's own past enters the classroom, but formed and shaped in such a way that it is fit for public presentation.

What this involves is, first, a sense of form, by which I mean a recognition that *how* material is presented is inseparable from what is being proffered; second, respect for the intelligence of one's audience, here one's students; and third, a conviction that the audience, too, appreciates the crafted by contrast to the clumsy, the dramatic by contrast to the didactic. The classroom drama I am attempting to give you a sense of is neither a vision of "let it all hang out" or "just say whatever is on your mind," on the one hand, nor a passive, orderly reception of instruction, on the other. It is, to be sure, responsorial. Whether there is much discussion or not, the classroom *must* be responsorial. The classroom is an arena within which the teacher engages those before her in recognition that what is being imparted is not simply that which she has come to know but how she has come to know it and the difference this knowing makes.

Education to me is captured by the classic word *Bildung,* a coming into being, an education of the moral sensibilities, the creation of a self. Bear in mind that the world of political thought I inhabit was shaped very early on by the dialogue form. As one recent commentator put it, "Dialogue was and remains the vehicle best designed to dramatize the movement of inquiry as an act of life, involving characters and conversation, not intellects in isolation."[1]

What sort of theater is the classroom? As a student and teacher of political thought, the classroom for me is an arena within which interlocutors engage one another from a stance of mutual respect. I'm not sure I'm always successful in this, but when a student asks a question I attempt to put the best construction on that intervention. I craft the question, if it has been put rather clumsily or has been awkwardly cast or proffered with great reticence. If it is ill-formed, I give it form so that it might engage others. This I take to be an instance of the respect for students central to teaching as drama.

A civic space, an arena for engagement, a drama with many voices. But one voice, my own, proffers the underlying theme, the *cantus firmus,* open to many variations. When this drama is at its most effective, I learn things I didn't know before. And it's not so much that I have taught myself something, but that the arena within which I am teaching has, on that particular occasion, offered up something surprising, a new beginning, a new way of thinking about a particular issue. The possibility of that epiphany — "I learned something I hadn't known before" — that moment of recognition, is much enhanced as one frees oneself to be experimental. Not out of control, not rambling, but experimental.

For example, a challenge or a question is presented by a student and I'll say, "Now, okay, I'm not sure where this is going or if the argument will work, but let's try this," and then go on to spin it out, to spell it out. I often wind up looking to my students and saying, "That's not quite it, is it? That doesn't quite work, does it? Let's try something else." And then I move to other suggestions and recraft the theme or the issue in such a way that it comes closer to the mark of what is required in order to sharpen up an important distinction or in order to create something coherent out of a potpourri of elliptical hints. Student "lines" and student attentiveness, including that which is offered silently as well as that which is proffered verbally, are essential to this process.

What sort of drama, then? A democratic drama, not as interest group politics, but as respect for those interlocutors with whom one is engaged. Respect for the process of dialogue and debate. Respect for the

1. Mark Schwein, from a paper delivered to the Faculty Forum, Vanderbilt University, March 16, 1991.

need — not only in intellectual life but also in political life, on certain issues, at certain times — to compromise. Recognition that neither in *this* classroom nor in *that* civic world is there a moral consensus on a variety of highly charged issues. One cannot always get what one wants.

When I read student/teacher evaluations of my teaching, the comment that most pleases me is "respect for and openness to a variety of different points of view." I do not believe it is the job of the teacher to proselytize, to push one perspective, to make all sorts of grandiose and false claims, including the hubristic claim that the world can be brought to heel if we just find the right method, or that we can predict or control events when we have no such control and can honestly offer no such predictability.

When I was in Prague, Czechoslovakia, I was told by many of those I met that the democratic ideal was a very difficult one for people who had lived more than forty-five years in the highly ideological world of authoritarian politics. For it was difficult to move into a way of thinking that was not totalistic. And one former dissident, now a member of parliament, told me, "You know, democracy is a very tricky ideal because it embeds in its heart the ideal of compromise." Which is to say a limit on control. We live in a world in which there are other voices. We live in a world in which we either respect the limits set by the existence of others with whom we must engage, or we construct for ourselves a politics, a method of teaching, a perspective that wishes them away, bowls them over, or silences them so that an engagement is no longer necessary. In a democratic society, a teacher of political thought has the responsibility to exemplify democracy not as watery tolerance, not as a shrinking back from offering up hard truths and sharp claims, but as a way of proffering hard truths and sharp claims that does not demolish those with whom one disagrees.

What sort of drama is this? It is a drama that attends to the obligation the teacher has to both the living and the dead. The living are those before one in the classroom, those who, for a short four years, are blessed to have been given a precious space within which their primary task is engaged thinking, the cultivation of character. It is an extraordinary gift. That it should be seen by some as an entitlement of privilege is a pity indeed.

What about an obligation to the dead? There's a lot of careless talk these days about our dead forebears, usually cast as dead white European males. One really can't help being either dead, or white, or European, or male, so I'm not quite sure what kind of critique this is. The worst feature of vulgar assaults on the past is not only that they sever our connection to the past but that they enjoin and legitimate a willfulness of the present moment. That is not what the drama of democracy and of teaching political thought in a democratic society is all about. What is it about? It is about permanent contestation between conservation and change, between tradition and transformation. To jettison one of these two sides is to live either in a sterile present-mindedness or in an equally sterile reaction. Let me offer up as an example of what I have in mind some words from a novel by Willa Cather, *A Lost Lady*. Her protagonist, Neil Herbert, discovers the classics and the classics provide him a way into a new world and a way out of the town of Sweetwater, Nebraska. Cather describes Neil Herbert's discovery of the past:

> There were philosophical works in the collection, but he did no more than open and glance at them. He had no curiosity about what men had thought; but about what they had felt and lived, he had a great deal. If anyone had told him that these were classics and represented the wisdom of the ages, he would doubtless have let them alone. . . . He did not think of these books as something invented to beguile the idle hour, but as living creatures, caught in the very behaviour of living — surprised behind their misleading severity of form and phrase. He was eavesdropping upon the past, being let into the great world that had plunged and glittered and sumptuously sinned long before little Western towns were dreamed of. Those rapt evenings beside the lamp gave him a long perspective, influenced his conception of the people about him, made him know just what he wished his own relations with these people to be.[2]

In novels Herbert finds a living, breathing, socially embodied tradition. This is the excitement I hope to convey about the tradition of political thought. The dead not only come to life in and through these texts, they help to forge the conception of the people about us.

We are invited into the drama and the dislocation promised by a heady tradition. *Tradition* comes from *traditio*, to be led out. We are always already part of a tradition or part of the fragments of many traditions. A tradition can lead us out of ourselves, out of previously unthought perspectives into worlds at once more self-aware and less

2. Willa Cather, *A Lost Lady* (New York: Alfred A. Knopf, 1923), pp. 81-82.

predictable. To think a tradition is to bring matters to the surface, to engage with interlocutors long dead, protagonists who never lived save on the page, and through that engagement to elaborate alternative conceptions through which to apprehend one's world and the way that world represents itself. What could be more dramatic than that? An expansive set of conceptual possibilities — I take these to be essential to a university.

Students come to us and rightly ask, "What sort of new world is this?" Ideally, it is a world rather like the one Cather's protagonist finds in a long tradition of great works that reveal how people unlike ourselves, from different times and places, lived and felt. It is a place in which students are invited to eavesdrop on the past and to become attuned in critical, interpretive ways to the present. We hear a lot these days about diversity. We are bombarded with celebrations of diversity, but often this bombardment is rather harsh, even accusatory. We are accused of ignoring this perspective or that, this group or the next. Now don't get me wrong. I hope I have conveyed to you already my insistence that we must open up our conceptual and ethical perspectives to those previously unrecognized or underrepresented. But this should not yield diversity of the sort in which hostile groups, defined exclusively by their racial, sexual, or religious identities, refuse to make common cause with or enter into meaningful dialogue with others, and are legitimated in that refusal, even encouraged to it, by faculty. Genuine diversity does not consist in a dozen groups issuing a dozen manifestos, but in men and women debating, discussing, and revealing themselves through speech and communication in a manner respectful of the identities of others.

Confronting diversity — the one and the many — is one of the great dramas of political thought. It is an issue that has vexed political thought from its beginning. This helps to account for that dialogue form with which political thought in the West was first given shape and life. It also accounts for why at least part of the drama of the American founding was the founders' awareness of the vexations attendant upon the creation of a new political body. Was it possible to create a "we" that enabled those thus united to recognize one another in and through their differences as well as in what they shared in common? That was the great challenge. And that remains the great challenge for contemporary American society, as well as the contemporary American university. We require others to help us to define ourselves. We require an arena within which to explore, in a disciplined atmosphere, our own convictions and enthusiasms; hence the drama of the classroom. Through innovative speech and action we show who we are, we reveal identities that are not reducible to race, or gender, or region of birth. Teaching as drama, then, embodies and embeds what might be called a communicative vision of community.

I fear I have not been as dramatic as I had hoped in conveying to you some sense of teaching as drama. Let me offer, finally, a sense of how a crafted drama can probably be used to convey complex political ideas for our time. My examples are two plays by Albert Camus — *Caligula* and *The Just Assassins* — and there are a couple of moments I want to draw to your attention in order to demonstrate the ways in which ideas embodied in the words of protagonists can help to score powerful ethical and philosophical points.

In *Caligula,* a play based upon the story of the Roman emperor drawn from a reading of Suetonius's *Twelve Caesars,* we find Camus facing the aftermath of the fascism of World War II — the growth of Stalinism. He poses questions of collaboration and of vengeance in the wake of collaboration, creating a drama in which the problem revealed is that of an idealism that knows no limits. Thus we find one Roman patrician, when he is asked to join a conspiracy against Caligula, saying, "If I join forces with you, it's to combat a big idea — an ideal, if you like — whose triumph would mean the end of everything. . . . I cannot endure Caligula's carrying out his theories to the end. He is converting his philosophy into corpses and — unfortunately for us — it's a philosophy that's logical from start to finish."[3]

Caligula is a dangerous man, a tyrant, because he insists on carrying out a theory to the end, because he insists that there should be one voice, one perspective only that is triumphant — his own. The play emerges as a cautionary tale of a politics without limits. The tyrant is a man who sacrifices a whole nation to his ideal and his ambition. I dare say there are in our ranks teachers who are prepared to sacrifice a classroom to similar ambition — the ambition to push a single perspective with no limits, and with no appropriate sense of humility. A morality play? Yes. But life is a morality play, and Caligula's crime is to embrace absolute freedom for himself, which means denying any freedom to

---

3. Albert Camus, *Caligula and Three Other Plays,* trans. Stuart Gilbert (New York: Alfred A. Knopf, 1958), p. 21.

others. You will recall that I mentioned the "other before me" as an interlocutor who necessarily limits my ability to control and shape the world through my words and my perspective alone. It is always striking for American students, for whom the word *freedom* prompts a rousing three cheers in unison, to learn that freedom without limits becomes terror.

A final example from Camus' play *The Just Assassins,* in which a band of Russian anarchists, terrorists if you will, plot to assassinate a grand duke, someone who is a member — in our current lingo — of the ruling establishment. The plan is for one of the conspirators, Kaliayev, to throw a bomb into the grand duke's carriage as it moves past in a processional, but at the last moment he finds that he cannot do this because he sees that the grand duke's children are in the carriage with him. "How sad they looked! Dressed up in their best clothes, with their hands resting on their thighs, like two little statues framed in the windows on each side of the door. . . . My arms went limp. My legs seemed to be giving way beneath me. And, a moment afterwards, it was too late." This is the conspirator, Kaliayev, speaking.

In the aftermath of this failed assassination attempt the band gets together — Stepan, Kaliayev, and Dora, among others — and Stepan is outraged that Kaliayev could not carry out the deed. This prompts Dora to initiate the following dialogue, a drama within the drama:

Dora: You, Stepan, could you fire point blank on a child, with your eyes open?

Stepan: I could, if the group ordered it.

Dora: Why did you shut your eyes then?

Stepan: What? Did I shut my eyes?

Dora: Yes.

Stepan: Then it must have been because I wanted to picture . . . what you describe, more vividly, and to make sure my answer was the true one.

Dora: Open your eyes, Stepan, and try to realize that the group would lose all its driving force, were it to tolerate, even for a moment, the idea of children's being blown to pieces by our bombs.

Stepan: Sorry, but I don't suffer from a tender heart; that sort of nonsense cuts no ice with *me*. . . . Not until the day comes when we stop sentimentalizing about children will the revolution triumph, and we be masters of the world.

61

Dora: When that day comes, the revolution will be loathed by the whole human race.[4]

Teaching as drama. Not a world of special effects but a world of special engagements. Not a theater of self-indulgent first-person soliloquies, but a theater of crafted and shaped interventions that tap, at one and the same time, that which we are coming to know and that which we are learning to be.

•

4. *The Just Assassins,* in ibid., pp. 254, 256-57.

THE COMMON SCHOOL

Living by Principle in a Complex Social Order

JAMES SKILLEN

Christianity: A Way of Life

Christians who take seriously their allegiance to the one who claims that all authority in heaven and on earth now belongs to him cannot help but seek to follow his commandments in all areas of life — no matter what the outcome. That is called obedience. Furthermore, they will often experience this way of life as antithetical to other ways of life — those that honor someone (or something) other than God as highest master.

In the face of this simple confessional truth, one of the key questions about contemporary American society — for both Christians and non-Christians — has to do with the extent to which the Christian way of life is compatible with the "American way of life." Should Christians act on the conviction that their way of life is somehow normative for non-Christians as well as for Christians, offering something constructive to American society with regard to family well-being, educational progress, economic stewardship, social welfare, and public justice? Or is the Christian way of life such a peculiar and at times perhaps not even sufficiently progressive impulse that its adherents should abide by the judgments of those who believe that it ought to be confined in narrow straits to keep its advocates from disturbing the peace? If, in particular, the Christian way of life sometimes stands in antithetical juxtaposition to other ways of life, should it even be tolerated publicly in a society built on the supposedly tolerant conviction that there is room in the public square for only a single democratic, public consensus, not for antithetical ways of life?

The argument of this paper is that Christians should, indeed, act consistently as Christians — in accord with the demands of their Master — and in so doing they should act with the conviction that behavior that accords with principles of the Christian life *does* lead to social health and well-being as salt and light for the whole world. The "principles" that bind human beings are not, from this point of view, the subjective projections of one group in society, but are the normative standards of the Creator-Redeemer himself. At the same time, however, due to the sinfulness that Christians acknowledge in themselves and in others, they should recognize that "Christians" have not always exercised their influence according to Christian principles; thus, the process of distinguishing normative principles from positivized action is difficult and complicated. Moreover, Christians should not assume that they alone have been entrusted with the responsibility to enforce or impose normative standards of practice in all areas of life.

From this it follows both historically and logically that the nature of the antithesis between Christian and non-Christian ways of life may at times be difficult to discern, and it certainly cannot be discovered simply by pitting those who call themselves Christians over against those who refuse that identity. Even when they *intend* to live lives of obedience to their Lord, Christians often exhibit disobedience to his precepts. Nevertheless, despite sinfulness and cloudy vision, and with all due humility in acknowledging that their actual behavior should not be mistaken for divinely normative principles, it would be contradictory for Christians to believe that the Christian way of life may be legitimately relativized, sidetracked, or entirely privatized by an antithetical way of life. Thus the challenge for Christians is to learn how to live self-critical, loving, and modest lives as they seek to contribute to the health of the larger social order (all their neighbors) by standing for Christian principles and against other patterns that appear to lead to the destruction of social health, justice, stewardship, truth, and love.[1]

---

1. I have argued some of what this implies in *The Scattered Voice: Christians at Odds in the Public Square* (Grand Rapids: Zondervan, 1990), and in "Going Beyond Liberalism to Christian Social Philosophy," *Christian Scholar's Review* 19, 3 (March 1990): 220-30. I am especially indebted to the wide-ranging philosophical work of Herman Dooyeweerd, including his *Roots of Western Culture: Pagan, Secular, and Christian Options*, trans. John Kraay, ed. Mark Vander Vennen and Bernard Zylstra (Toronto: Wedge Publishing Foundation, 1979), and his *A Christian Theory of Social Institutions*, trans. Magnus Verbrugge, ed. John Witte, Jr. (La Jolla, CA: The Herman Dooyeweerd

To face this challenge of living fully and consistently out of Christian conviction in the world today, Christians should persist in trying to develop a principled Christian philosophy of society. If the world truly belongs to and is governed by the God whom Christians profess, then the Christian way of life necessarily entails acknowledgment of the heteronomous normativity (the binding authority) of God's creation-order principles, which have been reaffirmed and freshly illumined through the incarnation, death, and resurrection of Jesus Christ — the one in and through whom all things were created.[2] To bow before the Creator and Redeemer in this way entails something more complicated than simply calling for the development of separated Christian communities, over against the fracturedness of a secularized society shaped in many respects by antithetical, liberal/individualist norms. My argument will point to the need for a normative Christian understanding of many differentiated institutions, communities, and organizations such as families, schools, churches, business enterprises, and the state. With respect to the state and its public laws in particular, I will argue that from a Christian point of view normative justice for a pluralistic, differentiated society is antithetical both to the liberal ideal of tolerance and to classical ideals of a hierarchical or undifferentiated community.

The Crisis of Enlightenment Liberalism

As a point of departure, let's take up Alasdair MacIntyre's critique of liberalism. According to MacIntyre, the "liberal project" is intended to emancipate individuals from the tyranny, contingency, and particularity of tradition "by appealing to genuinely universal, tradition-independent norms."[3] Its aim is to create a society in which people "who espouse widely different and incompatible conceptions of the good life" can "live

---

Foundation, 1986). For an introduction to Dooyeweerd, see L. Kalsbeek, *Contours of a Christian Philosophy,* ed. Bernard and Josina Zylstra (Toronto: Wedge Publishing Foundation, 1975), and my doctoral thesis, "The Development of Calvinistic Political Theory in the Netherlands" (Duke, 1974).

2. See generally Oliver O'Donovan, *Resurrection and Moral Order: An Outline for Evangelical Ethics* (Grand Rapids: Eerdmans, 1986), and Lesslie Newbigin, *Foolishness to the Greeks: The Gospel and Western Culture* (Grand Rapids: Eerdmans, 1986).

3. Alasdair MacIntyre, *Whose Justice? Which Rationality?* (Notre Dame: University of Notre Dame Press, 1988), p. 335.

together peaceably within the same society, enjoying the same political status and engaging in the same economic relationships."[4] Evidence that this project is a failure appears from the fact that in the course of history (which liberalism has not been able to escape), liberalism itself has been transformed into a tradition, defined in part by the interminable debate over what those tradition-independent norms really are.[5]

> Every individual is to be equally free to propose and to live by whatever conception of the good he or she pleases, derived from whatever theory or tradition he or she may adhere to, unless that conception of the good involves reshaping the life of the rest of the community in accordance with it. Any conception of the human good according to which, for example, it is the duty of government to educate the members of the community morally, so that they come to live out that conception of the good, may up to a point be held as a private theory by individuals or groups, but any serious attempt to embody it in public life will be proscribed. And this qualification of course entails not only that liberal individualism does indeed have its own broad conception of the good, which it is engaged in imposing politically, legally, socially, and culturally wherever it has the power to do so, but also that in so doing its toleration of rival conceptions of the good in the public arena is severely limited.[6]

The antinomy or inner contradiction described here is that a particular conception of society is actually imposed, often quite intolerantly, in the name of opening up the possibility for every individual to live without subjection to any forced imposition from outside his or her own autonomy. Another way to put it is that in a liberal society those who are most free, both in public and in private, are those who live by liberal convictions despite the inner contradictions. Others may enjoy some freedom in private circles, but they are not necessarily free to live out their convictions in public. Liberal toleration is toleration of non-liberals on liberal grounds.

MacIntyre then moves to expose liberalism's failure to achieve an "overall ordering of goods" because its ideal of "order" is one of subjectivistic diversity, not of coherence. The "order" that liberalism im-

4. Ibid., p. 336.
5. Ibid., p. 335.
6. Ibid., p. 336.

poses on society is one that insists that there can be no overriding good. "The recognition of a range of goods is accompanied by a recognition of a range of compartmentalized spheres within each of which some good is pursued: political, economic, familial, artistic, athletic, scientific." A "just society," from this point of view, then, is little more than rules "to set constraints upon the bargaining process" so that individuals can have as much freedom as possible "to implement their preferences" in a variety of compartmentalized spheres.[7]

> The liberal norm is characteristically, therefore, one according to which different kinds of evaluation, each independent of the other, are exercised in these different types of social environment. The heterogeneity is such that no overall ordering of goods is possible. And to be educated into the culture of a liberal social order is, therefore, characteristically to become the kind of person to whom it appears normal that a variety of goods should be pursued, each appropriate to its own sphere, with no overall good supplying any overall unity to life.[8]

MacIntyre's critique of liberalism is part of an exploration to discover the truth about the inescapability of tradition in both philosophy and society, and thereby to learn where and how to take one's stand in a coherent and noncontradictory tradition rather than in an incoherent and contradictory tradition. "We, whoever we are," MacIntyre concludes, "can only begin enquiry from the vantage point afforded by our relationship to some specific social and intellectual past through which we have affiliated ourselves to some particular tradition of enquiry, extending the history of that enquiry into the present: as Aristotelian, as Augustinian, as Thomist, as Humean, as post-Enlightenment liberal, or as something else."[9]

Advancing beyond Liberalism

While MacIntyre's inquiry unveils his affinity for the Thomist/Aristotelian tradition, I would like to take off from his critique of liberalism

7. Ibid., p. 337.
8. Ibid.
9. Ibid., pp. 401-2.

to show why I am led to affiliate myself more closely with the Augustinian/Calvinist tradition.

MacIntyre has demonstrated convincingly, I believe, that liberalism lacks a coherent vision of an "overriding good." Or rather, one might say that the overriding good for liberalism — namely, individual freedom — lacks any embracing coherence as a *social* vision. "Society" or "political community" — if those words can even be used in connection with liberalism — amounts to little more than rule-making procedures, utilitarian calculations, bargaining processes, contractual agreements, and so forth, as the *means* by which individuals seek to protect their freedoms and to advance in the direction of ever more complete individual autonomy and self-expression. This way of life and thought, however, has now become another tradition rather than an achievement that surpasses all traditions. And it cannot escape the internal contradictions that MacIntyre and others have shown it to display.

But is MacIntyre correct in assuming, as he apparently does, that the differentiation of society into a range of "compartmentalized spheres" is chiefly, if not solely, the result of the impact of liberalism? Does the emergence of distinguishable political, economic, familial, artistic, athletic, scientific, and educational spheres of life follow only as a consequence of the rejection of any "overall ordering of goods"? And does the differentiation of society run antithetically against the Christian way of life, which calls for coherent, integral, well-ordered obedience to a single, sovereign Creator-Redeemer? Is the best antithetical Christian alternative to liberalism to be found in Aristotelian Thomism? I'm not persuaded.

From the viewpoint of Aristotelian Thomism, the overall ordering of goods in society goes hand in hand with a certain conception of practical rationality, as MacIntyre has so ably explained. In fact, human nature and the nature of society *are* rational in the sense that reason is identified with normativity as an order-giver — as the rational natural law. Society's overall natural order is understood to be rational in character. Among other things, this means that it should be possible to conceive of every social differentiation as "part" of the larger rational, social "whole." Liberalism fails then not simply because its conception of a "political order of autonomously free individuals" is internally contradictory (an "imposed" order of "freedom"), but also because it accepts the differentiation of society without expecting or desiring society's rational ordering into a coherent and just whole. This means not only that society will inevitably become more chaotic than coherent, but also that human life will be unjustly impoverished because the very nature of rational-social creatures requires for their fulfillment the experience of the rational ordering of all parts of society in a coherent whole — toward a rational *telos*. From MacIntyre's point of view, liberalism then is unjust as well as self-contradictory.

I would contend, however, that MacIntyre's appeal to Aristotelian Thomism keeps him from seeing something important about the nature of creation's differentiation and the manner of its coherence. Look for a moment at MacIntyre's discussion of Aristotle's conception of the *polis*.[10]

On the one hand, Aristotle conceives of the individual human being as part of the *polis*. This is also his conception of the family — it too is part of the *polis*. Human beings achieve their highest purpose *(telos)* in the *polis* because it represents the whole in which human nature finds the just and rational ordering of all its functions. Different classes of people perform different functions in the *polis* in order for it to reach its *telos*. But in achieving fulfillment as a *polis*, human nature is also thereby fulfilled.

On the other hand, Aristotle and Plato both conceive of human nature as reaching its *telos* in rational experience and insight that transcend the experience of the *polis*. Ultimately, the right order of the human soul is to be found in its attunement with cosmic reason, which amounts to more than a political ordering of social functions. To gain fulfillment through the philosophical quest is to become wise — to achieve the rational ordering of mind, passions, and bodily functions, including insight into the normative mode of one's participation in a *polis*. The *polis* is somehow subordinate to the larger cosmic order of reason. To reach a truly human *telos*, the individual should become wise through philosophy. Human nature cannot be reduced to a particular function in a *polis*. The *polis* exists for the individual, not the individual for the *polis*.

The tension between these two incompatible conceptions of the *telos* of human nature manifested itself very starkly in Plato's and Aristotle's actions to create the Academy and the Lyceum. These intellectual or spiritual institutions were clearly differentiated from (and within) the larger whole of the Athenian *polis*. Part of the motivation behind

10. Ibid., pp. 97-108.

their founding was Socrates' (and Plato's and Aristotle's) experience of an unjust *polis* that was not rationally well ordered. The experience of philosophy (both before and after the founding of those schools) allowed the participants to transcend the existing *polis* at least in some spiritual or intellectual way. The Academy or the Lyceum was, in the conception of its founder, something like a *polis* of philosophers or a *polis* composed of those who thirsted to know the true, rational meaning of life, in contrast to the *polis* of Athens governed by those with other motives and standards.

But the use of analogical language in this fashion obscures the differentiation process. The school was not the government of Athens, even though Plato and Aristotle wanted reason to govern the *polis*. Athens as a whole was not a school, even though the city was conceived of as performing an educational function for all its citizens. MacIntyre comments that it is not unimportant to recognize that "the Academy or the Lyceum could to some degree at least discharge the functions which Aristotle ascribes only to the *polis*" — military, merchants, slaves, etc. — and the *polis* was not merely a school. The school was a mind-ordering institution; the *polis* was a more complex society-ordering institution.[11]

Plato's and Aristotle's functional conception of the *polis* allows that some classes of people will function as the means to the fulfillment of the *polis* without experiencing either citizenship or personal fulfillment through philosophy. From this point of view, the *polis* really is conceived as a whole destined to reach fulfillment regardless of the rational fulfillment of every human creature. And yet, when Socrates, Plato, and Aristotle judged that an unjust *polis* was not permitting the fulfillment of human nature, they were ready to die or to start schools in order to reach the rational fulfillment that the *polis* did not permit. We must ask, therefore, whether intellectual/spiritual fulfillment through philosophy is the highest good of a human being in terms of which even the *polis* should be ordered? Or is philosophy (along with many other arts and labors) a means to the fulfillment of the *polis*? What kind of order is correct and prior here? In the final analysis, are human beings rational or political animals? Do all human beings share a common nature destined for the same *telos,* or do they have different natures defined by their different functions in the *polis* so that all find their fulfillment only

11. Ibid., p. 99.

72

through the multifunctional fulfillment of the *polis?* Should the authorities of the *polis* have the right to determine the function, curriculum, and limits of any academy or lyceum within its borders because by definition everything belongs to (is a function of) the *polis,* existing for its fulfillment, even if that means death for Socrates and political interference in the practice of true philosophy at Plato's Academy or Aristotle's Lyceum? Or should the *polis* be organized as a more limited or restricted community with a peculiar, differentiated purpose, serving as one among many expressions of human beings whose *telos* transcends the order of the *polis?*

MacIntyre says,

> What therefore remains so far at least unscathed in Aristotle's account of the best kind of *polis* is the thesis that a political constitution which is designed to promote the exercise of virtue in political life will need to concern itself with the occupational structure of the *polis.* It is also clear that although Aristotle's account of the hierarchical ordering of the best kind of *polis* rests on certain mistakes, the best kind of *polis* will have an hierarchical order. This is because it has to school its citizens in the exercise of the virtues. The hierarchy of the best kind of *polis* is one of teaching and of learning, not of irrational domination.[12]

It seems to me, however, that Aristotle's account of the well-ordered *polis* is integrally problematical and not merely partially mistaken, in large part because its hierarchical order, thought to be an all-embracing whole, turns out to be internally ambiguous and even contradictory.

Does the *polis* have the character of an academy in which leaders "school its citizens in the exercise of the virtues"? If so, then why allow academies to become differentiated from the government within the *polis?* Any such differentiation would seem to violate the very identity of the *polis* as educational institution. On the other hand, if education is not identical with political rule, and if political rule is not exhausted in education, then a better understanding of societal differentiation must be obtained. Is the *polis* a lover and trainer of children? If so, then why the need for families? Are political leaders, by their very nature, qualified to school citizens in every kind of virtue? Is it the political leader, *qua* political leader, who teaches the virtue of parenting, or of

12. Ibid., pp. 105-6.

wine production, or of sailing? Given the differences between these kinds of virtues, what makes them political virtues at all? If, to the contrary, parenting is a virtue carried on in families, and teaching is a virtue carried on in academies, and wine growing is a virtue practiced in the vineyards, then what is it that distinguishes the peculiar virtues of citizenship and political leadership? Or to ask it in a somewhat different way, how shall we account for the multiple, simultaneous functions (or roles) played by many people — both in ancient Athens and in our own day? A single individual can be a citizen (and perhaps even a town council member), a spouse, a parent, a philosopher, a sailor, a gardener, and much more — all at the same time. What is it that orders this panoply of functions? Is it the *polis* of which all these are political parts? Or do political life, family life, education, art, science, and the rest find their meaningful coherence in something larger than a political hierarchy? Why should we even think that an overall ordering of goods has to be a *political* ordering of all parts in a political whole? It seems apparent to me that the individual is not a *polis* writ small, nor is the *polis* an individual writ large; and the cosmos is neither a *polis* nor an individual writ large. The analogies finally break down.

When MacIntyre says at one point, "What matters for my present argument is the claim that it is not merely the *polis* but the *cosmos* itself, the very order of things, which provides the context within which justice and practical rationality are related," he opens the door to these larger questions.[13] But why should our conception of *cosmic* order be built on the analogy of an Aristotelian political order? In fact, I believe that the biblical tradition is antithetical to Aristotle at this point and that the Thomist synthesis therefore is also internally problematic. But is there a better way to conceive of the order of creation to avoid the antinomies of liberalism and Aristotelianism?

A Short Detour through Jeffrey Stout's Stereoscopic View of Society

Jeffrey Stout in his *Ethics After Babel* does not argue the case that I want to make for a Christian social philosophy, but he does engage MacIntyre in a way that helps to point to where I want to go. While appreciating

13. Ibid., pp. 101-2.

MacIntyre's illuminating critique of liberalism, Stout fears that Mac-Intyre's approach also obscures some of the reality before our eyes.

> MacIntyre sees our society as an expression of Enlightenment philosophical ideas gone wrong. If he is right, and the Enlightenment project was bound to fail, then our way of life was bound to fail too, and we should not be surprised to find it in ruin. On MacIntyre's view, our society is as radically individualistic and unconcerned with the common good as liberal philosophers have always wanted it to be, and this is the clue to its moral downfall.[14]

The truth is, however, that our society is not merely a reflection of liberal intentionality, according to Stout. American society displays degrees of social agreement about the nature of the common good and about different virtues needed in diverse spheres of social life. The differentiation of society has not been produced solely by individualist motives, nor does it lack coherence outside and among its many "compartmentalized spheres."

Stout, along with Michael Walzer, believes that our contemporary American agreement to build the political order on a "thin" rather than a "deep" consensus about the nature of the common good is something healthy. It represents a rational consensus and not merely an agreement to disagree. It provides relatively peaceful support for the creative differentiation of social spheres. It is not a sign of the complete rejection of any "overall ordering of goods." To the contrary, not conceiving of the political community as a single, hierarchical whole makes room for a "complex equality" among many social spheres in which people may nurture their agreements about many different virtues appropriate to schooling, family life, health care, worship, etc. Stout is not naively optimistic about the future of such a society because there is plenty of evidence of mistaken interference of one sphere in another, and of the imposition of norms in one sphere that are appropriate only in another. But he believes that our social order *as a whole* is more rational and less fractured than MacIntyre fears.

Stout wants a "stereoscopic" view of society in which the *political* common good is understood to guarantee the integrity of diverse social spheres as well as the relative freedom of individuals. While this is more liberal than Aristotelian, Stout thinks it is something different than the

14. Jeffrey Stout, *Ethics After Babel* (Boston: Beacon Press, 1988), p. 220.

highly individualistic and relativistic liberalism that MacIntyre criticizes. Stout also wants to comprehend society as a whole, but not as a simple unity of which all functions and institutions are political parts. A stereoscopic view accepts more differentiation than does a hierarchical view.

> We can make good use of Aristotelian and civic republican talk about the virtues and politics as a social practice directed toward the common good without supposing that this sort of moral language requires us to jettison talk of rights and tolerance. We can use this talk by thinking of liberal political institutions as oriented toward a provisional *telos* — a widely shared but self-limiting consensus on the highest good achievable under circumstances like ours. But this *telos* justifies a kind of tolerance foreign to the classical teleological tradition. And it rightly directs our oral attention to something our ancestors often neglected, namely, the injustice of excluding people from social practices because of their race, gender, religion, or place of birth.[15]

Stout identifies his approach as a form of pragmatic social criticism. But he rejects the charge of relativism. "The language of morals in our discourse are many, and they have remarkably diverse historical origins, but they do not float in free air, and their name is not chaos. They are embedded in specific social practices and institutions — religious, political, artistic, scientific, athletic, economic, and so on."[16]

But we must stop here to ask how well Stout's argument addresses the questions raised by MacIntyre about the crisis of liberal society. Granted that society has become highly differentiated institutionally, is there any normative basis for accepting the diversity of "specific social practices and institutions" as we find them? On what basis do we decide what makes for a good school, a loving family, a stewardly business enterprise, a true religion, a just political order? The truth is that we find in our society not simply the differentiation of social spheres but also an active competition within each of them among antithetical views of life about the normative well-being of each. Christians, Muslims, Marxists, liberals, libertarians, and others often disagree about the normative nature of family life, education, politics, and business. If the complex array of institutions does not "float in free air," then what order

15. Stout, p. 292.
16. Ibid., p. 291.

of reason, nature, or divine creation holds them together and provides the norms for their healthy differentiation and the interrelation of their complexity? Can Stout, in fact, provide any ontological grounding for his stereoscopic view of society that lies deeper than positivist description, personal preference, or pragmatic social criticism? Stout helps to illuminate the factual nature of our structurally differentiated society, but he does not do enough to account for the antithesis between competing traditions of rationality and ethics. And he has not made a sufficiently strong case for the trans-subjective normativity of a "thin" agreement about the political order's "provisional *telos*." He seems still to be operating with what MacIntyre would describe as the liberal hope of achieving a universal rational agreement (however thin) about the nature of the common political good that holds society together.

The Differentiation of an Integral Creation Order

The failures and internal contradictions of liberalism, I would contend, are rooted in its rejection of the creation's manifold, heteronomous normativity. That rejection grows from liberalism's mistaken (antithetical) conviction that individuals are (or can be) autonomous. The ideal of individual freedom functions both as the normative standard for all action and as the identity of the subject. Conflating the "norm" and the "subject" in this fashion is part of what leads to the antinomies that MacIntyre and countless others have struggled with — namely, a social order that is no order, built on asocial individuals, and the necessity of imposing a political order on all individuals in the guise of autonomous self-rule.

Liberalism — both as an ideology and as a subsequently "structured" society — flows along to some degree with the differentiation of society because it contains within itself a centrifugal tendency. But if liberalism is fundamentally in error (and internally contradictory) about the nature of reality and human identity, then we need to look elsewhere for an account of the ontological basis of societal differentiation.

That which makes possible the actual differentiation of society, I would argue, is not arbitrary self-expression and self-creation *(ex nihilo)* by autonomous individuals, but the manifold creation order upheld by the providential grace of God. The God who created all things is the order-giver, the law-giver, the norm-giver who binds all human (and nonhuman) subjects by his creation norms, which allow and command human development along the lines of our creaturely potential and generational unfolding. For human beings this includes the creaturely characteristics of language, love, thought, culture, a multitude of institutional differentiations, and much more.

All anti-normative (disobedient) actions on the part of human subjects (e.g., acts which are unloving instead of loving, irrational instead of rational, uneconomical instead of economical, unjust instead of just, etc.) do not truly succeed as autonomous projects but rather exhibit the historically deforming contradictions and antinomies that we have witnessed. At the same time, the relative order, coherence, and goodness that exist in human experience are due to actions, behaviors, and institutions that comport with what is creationally normative. Therefore, both the critical analysis of individual and social deformation and the exploration of how human beings *ought* to live in this world should be part of a single quest to discern the normative demands of the Creator-Redeemer whose creation mandates (laws, statutes, standards, principles) bless obedience and curse disobedience.

On this account, history does not really manifest an array of equally legitimate though incompatible human traditions, each freely standing on its own foundations as a subjective project. Rather, history reveals the unfolding of God's creation, which brings to light (and to judgment) both human obedience and human disobedience to the norms of his creation. History displays both order and disorder, both integration and disintegration, both good and evil. But both are judged by the same norms. Human beings are not free to create or to synthesize anything they choose. Every way of life that stands antithetical to divine normativity will inevitably exhibit and lead to further deformity, contradiction, injustice, and evil.

From this point of view, the problems inherent in the Aristotelian/Thomist tradition are rooted in an attempted synthesis of incompatible Greek and biblical convictions about the basis of normativity. If, as the biblical tradition attests, the creation's order is in God's hands and all humans are subject to his norms, then reason or rationality (as articulated by Plato and Aristotle) is *not* that order. The creation does manifest normative standards for thinking (logical laws), but they do not exhaust the creation's order, nor should those standards be confounded with the rational function of the human subject. The creation's order is a manifold of ethical, juridical, rational, economic, aesthetic, social, and other norms, which all cohere as the heteronomous demands upon human subjects to love and obey God — the God who transcends all that he has created and who holds his creatures accountable to his normative standards in all spheres of life. On biblical grounds, reason is not the "divine" element in humanity. It is not the norm-giver that unites God and humanity by a shared attribute.

From this point of view, it also becomes clear that the order of the cosmos may not be confused with any particular human institution on earth. The model of order, therefore, is not a political hierarchy as developed in the ancient *polis* or in imperial Rome. The creation's order is not that of a family or a school or a marketplace. All of these differentiated "orders" — whether relatively well-formed or relatively malformed when measured by the Creator's normative standards — are developments of the creation's diversity, which coheres not in any one of them (even by analogy) but only in the integral fullness of the creation by means of God's creating and redeeming grace. Just as the *telos* of human nature is not to be found in philosophy (rational fulfillment), so also its *telos* is not to be found in the fulfillment of the *polis* or political community. Moreover, it will not do simply to add to this Aristotelian vision a supranatural *telos* via the church. The creation is not an Aristotelian political or rational whole in need of a *donum superadditum*. Rather it is a single manifold complexity that coheres in and through the Son of God, with no single function or institution being able to serve as its unifying or teleological whole. The church is not a community or institution established alongside or above nature; rather, it is a community of the regenerated and restored creatures of the original creation. The church of God in Christ is the normative community of believing, obedient creatures (the "new man") following a way of life *in all spheres of society* that is antithetical to the disobedient ways of life followed by the "old man."

To grasp this point of view, we need to pursue the meaning of the creational/redemptive antithesis against sin in every sphere of human life, and not merely point to the existence of a particular community or institution that exists above or alongside a supposedly natural, rational, political world in which human beings supposedly share all things in common on the same terms. What binds people together is God's creation order; what divides them is fundamental disagreement (different ways of life) in response to the norms of that order. Some disobedient ways of life actually claim to have the freedom and ability to proceed apart from God and in disregard of his norms altogether. The antithesis between obedience and disobedience, therefore, exists in the shaping of all spheres of the creation even while God holds all creatures together within his one and only world.

Examining American society from this critical standpoint yields a different view of reality than does either liberalism or Aristotelian Thomism. The new view accepts and relishes the historical differentiation of society as a normative consequence of the creation's manifold character — as an expression of the Creator's design. It condemns both collectivizing and individualizing excesses spawned by the mistaken convictions that human beings are either communally fulfilled or individually liberated by means of autonomous self-creation in this world. From a Christian perspective, human beings are expected to live in each differentiated sphere of society in obedience to God's creation ordinances. The political order is one among many such differentiated spheres of life, and it ought to function as a public-legal integrator (not a complete social/moral/religious unifier) of society in accord with creationally differentiated standards of public justice. The political order should not be mistaken for a total hierarchical "whole" of which all other social spheres are "parts." Rather it should be recognized as a public-legal order of citizens and rulers, differentiated from the orders of family life, educational life, business life, ecclesiastical life, etc. The same people live in all (or most) of these spheres of society simultaneously. But they have different obligations in each one depending both on the different nature of each sphere and on the role that they play in each one.

The political order of any given state, and ultimately the international political order governed by interstate relations and transnational institutions, should be judged by standards of justice that must be articulated for that differentiated realm. Political order is one kind of human community and notes merely the contractual rules for coordinating the free actions of autonomous individuals. But political order is not a societal totality that defines and unifies all of human nature as its parts. Other spheres of human society are not "parts" of the political order; rather, all spheres of society, including the political order, are parts of the creation that coheres in God alone as the domain of his sovereign rule. An "overall order of goods" is not to be found, therefore, within any of the institutions that human beings organize. The various modes of practical rationality are necessarily dispersed according to the responsibilities of the differentiated spheres of life in which human beings find themselves. But this does not mean that human life and society have no coherence or that they are nothing more than the free and contractual expressions of autonomous individuals, as liberalism claims. Human life in all its complexity coheres in the integral creation order upheld by God. In seeking to love God and neighbors obediently in every sphere of life (in antithesis to every disobedient way of life in those spheres) human beings may experience the integrality of life in Christ — now by faith, and one day by sight.

The mode of human action by which social order is achieved is not that of practical rationality ordered toward political unity, but rather that of obedience to God's commands simultaneously within all spheres of life. Different forms of practical rationality will unfold in science, art, family life, pedagogy, manufacturing, etc., in conformity with the creation's own manifold character. A single form of integrative rationality is not the order-giver of the cosmos; rather, all forms of human reasoning — and all forms of sociability, love, stewardship, and justice — cohere in the loving obedience that human beings should render to God himself. God is the only order-giver and unifier of the entire creation.

What does this mean for contemporary family life, education, and the church? Perhaps the best way to illustrate the consequences of this point of view is to sketch out a practical example. Partly because many of the questions in dispute here have to do with the identity of the political community, and partly because we are, in this volume, focusing attention on the meaning of education and family life in American society, the illustration I will offer deals with public policy for education. Here, then, is a normative argument — grounded in the kind of Christian philosophy hinted at in the paragraphs above — for what *ought* to be the structure of government policy for education.[17]

17. The argument that follows is developed in detail in my "Religion and Education Policy: Where Do We Go From Here?" *The Journal of Law and Policies* 6, 3 (Spring 1990): 503-29; and in my "Changing Assumptions in the Public Governance of Education: What Has Changed and What Ought to Change," in *Democracy and the Renewal of Public Education*, Encounter Series 4, ed. Richard John Neuhaus (Grand Rapids: Eerdmans, 1987), pp. 86-115; and in Rockne McCarthy, James Skillen, and William Harper, *Disestablishment a Second Time: Genuine Pluralism for American Schools* (Grand Rapids: Eerdmans; Washington, DC: Christian University Press, 1982).

JAMES SKILLEN

Toward a Christian Philosophy
of Public Justice and Educational Equity

To speak of public policy is to speak of government laws and programs. If we assume that the government of a political community (such as that of the United States or of one of its several states) is the authority of a particular, differentiated realm of responsibility, then our concern for its legally enforceable policies is that they should be just in at least two respects. First, they should be just in the sense of meeting the normative criteria for public law itself — that is, they should be fair and equitable laws properly belonging to the jurisdiction of a political authority that is governing citizens in political community. Second, the policies should be just in the sense of giving the proper recognition due to each nonpolitical institution and realm of responsibility. In other words, in face of what I am referring to as the creationally normative differentiation of society, the distinguishable and limited identity of the political order itself must be recognized in relation to all other differentiated spheres of life. In the case of education this means a proper and just relation of government to families, schools, and churches.

Now, any political order (consisting of its fundamental law or constitution structuring the normative relationship of citizens to the legislative, executive, and judicial branches of government in its federated or administrative parts) is of necessity an *imposed* order. The liberal ideal of individual autonomy not subject to any imposed order is a myth. The key question is simply what kind of imposed order is a normatively just one.

MacIntyre, among others, is correct that no neutral, universal, rational basis can be found to answer this question. There are different antithetical conceptions of political order, and there always have been. Christians should take seriously the binding and universal norms of the creation order by recognizing that the kind of political order they should contend for is one that will be normatively just for everyone. They should not accept the idea that a political order is simply an expression of the will of the people who create and maintain it.

For reasons of both the creation's structural differentiation and the antithetical ways of life expressed within that structural diversity, Christians should work for a political order that gives proper due to the contending ways of life expressed in the different spheres of life. This is not a liberal argument for the maximum tolerance of individual freedom (which ends up discriminating against non-liberals), but rather is an argument for public-legal recognition of the full range of human responsibilities and authorities that God holds directly accountable — parents in their homes, teachers in schools, and so forth. Since God himself is the gracious one who continues to allow both the wheat and the tares to grow up together, and since only he and his angels will discharge final judgment (see Matt. 13:24-30, 36-43), public laws that govern entire public territories should treat equitably (with the same civil rights and freedoms) the antithetical expressions of citizens in the various spheres of life.

This is not the same as saying "anything goes," because many things should not be permitted in a just public order. I am making a normative argument, not trying to make everyone happy. A normative argument for justice must be made at every policy juncture, and obviously my point of view will conflict at many points with that of a Marxist, an Aristotelian, a liberal, and others.

As a matter of public-legal principle, mine is an argument for both a "structural" pluralism and a "confessional" pluralism. In other words, I am contending for the imposition of a particular kind of non-neutral political order that disallows other forms of political order. To take the simplest and most familiar American example, a political order that recognizes constitutionally the independence of churches from the state and that refuses to establish any single church as the true or privileged one does impose a pluralism that excludes a state church and will forever disappoint those who believe that a government-established church is normative. From a constitutional standpoint, my view recognizes both the "structural" diversity of social spheres (churches and states) and the "confessional" diversity of religious convictions within the public order.

From a Christian point of view this should be understood as a normative *political* order that is in keeping with God's gracious patience in upholding his structurally diverse creation while withholding final judgment against those ways of life that run antithetical to his commandments. This is not, however, an argument for the relativity of ecclesiastical or any other truth. By means of persuasion in every sphere of life, Christians ought to contend for the universal recognition of the truth of God's revelation, and therefore should use their religious freedom not only to worship the true God but also to contend publicly against the errors of those who deny God and his standards for life. But at the same time, according to this argument, this includes the fight for a pluralist state (as defined above), both because the political order is not the exhaustive, all-encompassing Kingdom of God and because only a pluralist state in its own sphere of responsibility can do justice to the diverse range of institutions and responsibilities that God has given his creatures. In other words, Christians should contend against non-pluralist states and in favor of a state that can be normatively just in accord with God's final revelation in Christ. There is no neutral option.

This means, among other things, that as citizens we should be seeking to conserve those elements of the American political order that are just (on terms sketched above) while seeking to eradicate or to reform those elements that are unjust. My example of the reform of education policy will illustrate both of these tendencies.

To whatever degree our political order has been thought to be liberal, it continues to carry forward some characteristics of the classical *polis*. One of those characteristics is the idea that education is a department of state, or that governments are principally responsible for educating their citizens. Government, in other words, is the "principal" in education. I would argue that this assumption should be challenged and that American educational policy should be changed to recognize *parents* as the proper principals in the education of their children. And following from this, public law should also recognize that government has no right of monopoly over the "agencies" of education — the schools. What government *should* have a monopoly over is the enforcement of public justice — the fair and equitable treatment of all citizens in a context that displays full respect for the independence of families and schools.

What are the policy implications flowing from this change of assumptions? First, it would mean that public law would treat all families with the same equitable respect, recognizing them as the principal parties responsible for raising and educating their children. Diverse parental decisions regarding where and how their children should be educated would be recognized in public law. Those choosing a Catholic or Quaker school would not be treated better or worse than those who choose a secularized liberal school or a Muslim school or a Jewish school. If through public-legal processes the government promotes education (for the proper political purpose of strengthening *civic* virtue), and if this entails taxation to pay for some or all of the costs of schooling, then the tax system should be fair, and the distribution process should be equitable for all families — fully respecting diverse parental choices of schools. The consequence of this change in policy would be that public monies would flow with proportionate equity to self-confessed religious schools as well as to secularized schools, to schools not related to the government as well as to government-run schools.

The second obvious consequence is that government-run schools would no longer be treated as the only legitimate agencies of public education. If government no longer presumes that it is the principal in education and if it no longer claims a monopoly over the agencies of education, then its recognition of the independence of schools, with their own authority in their own sphere, means that all schools would be treated as having public legitimacy to perform the public service of educating children. Schools that are not run by the government would no longer be disadvantaged by being excluded from proportionate public funding, for example.

Third, it follows from this argument that government should no longer be allowed to make the secularized liberal claim that it is nonsectarian, nonreligious, and neutral. The kind of structural and confessional pluralism presented here begins with the recognition that people are religious through and through — in all areas of life — even if their religion is fully humanistic. No one is neutral. No government can stand on neutral foundations. Thus, the only *just* way for a government to treat its citizens is to recognize that their religious differences do express themselves (often antithetically) in all spheres of life, including the family, the school, and the state. True freedom of religion (as guaranteed in the First Amendment), then, will mean the freedom of all citizens to work out their "ways of life" in family life, education, business, journalism, and politics. Those who wish to raise their children in a Christian way of life should be treated with the same public-legal fairness as those who choose to raise their children in a secularized liberal way of life. This fair and equitable public-legal treatment of all families and schools is not neutral — but if one makes the assumptions we've made here, it is just.

Conclusion

In respect to all three of the consequences for education policy outlined above, this view of the public order allows for greater tolerance than does liberalism since it gives the same room to liberals as it does to Christians. Liberalism, on the other hand, wants to lock away non-liberal religions (including Christianity) in private quarters so that it can gain an advantage for its individualist, secularized rationality in the public arena. The pluralistic political philosophy for which I am contending makes full room for Christians to live open, public lives, not only in worship on Sunday but also in the education of their children, in political campaigning, and in every other sphere of life — but on the condition that the political arena itself meets the Christian standards of equitable justice for all. The pluralist state for which I am contending, in other words, tolerates liberals and everyone else on Christian grounds.

Christians should seek in every sphere to articulate and to obey God's creation norms for life. In that way, their lives should exhibit an integrity and coherence that accords with the truth. But this unity is not sought in an intra-mundane, whole-part hierarchy of institutional relationships. Human rationality does not comprehend or rule the creation as a whole, nor do all parts of earthly life find their place in a politically ordered hierarchy. The aim of a Christian political philosophy is to clarify the demands of public-legal justice in a differentiating world, knowing that obedience in the political realm will meet happily and coherently with obedience in every other realm and will bear witness to God's providential and redemptive purposes for his whole creation.

Stout is correct, I believe, in suggesting that our society manifests more coherence and testifies to a greater degree of sound practical rationality in its differentiated condition than MacIntyre allows. But the reason is not because liberalism or pragmatism works. Rather, it is because the creation order itself is differentiating and demands diverse kinds of human responsibility in multiple spheres. God is graciously upholding that order even as he patiently endures (for a time) the pretensions of those who disobediently misuse the creation and oppose his commandments.

This is where MacIntyre correctly points out that liberal reasoning runs against the creation order, for the creation order reveals a heteron-omous normativity incomprehensible to those who make individualist autonomy claims. Our society is not in good health because in many areas it is being shaped in ways antithetical to God's ordinances for creation. Radical reform is needed, not just hope for liberal progress. But MacIntyre credits liberalism with more negative power and influence than it deserves, while mistakenly (in my opinion) reaching for Aquinas and Aristotle to find a tradition of rationality that can comprehend the good of the whole.

My argument therefore has been that we should distinguish more radically the biblical tradition of creation order from both Aristotle's conception of an integral, rational hierarchy and the liberal Enlightenment tradition. The result will be a further exposure of the meaning of the antithesis among competing religious/philosophical traditions and, at the same time, a recognition of the dominant reality of God's creation order that drives every form of human disobedience to contradiction and antinomy.

Seeing life from this perspective should provide new energy for Christians to go forward in articulating and living out a way of life that they will recognize as antithetical to other ways of life. Though they may have to endure abuse and suffering as Christians have often done, they may contend in quiet confidence and with heartfelt concern for their neighbors. They will labor diligently for public policies that do justice to the independence of all the diverse spheres of life and to all the antithetical ways of life exhibited by people within those spheres. Christian confidence will rest ultimately not in Christians themselves and not in a tradition of practical rationality, but in the God whose will remains firm, whose creation order cannot be destroyed, and whose curses and blessings fulfilled in Jesus Christ are deciding the entire outcome of history.

Making Room for Religious Conviction
in Democracy's Schools

CHARLES L. GLENN *and* JOSHUA L. GLENN

Starting with the Family

The socialization of children begins in the family, but what the family can teach is supplemented — in most societies — by some form of schooling that occurs outside the home. The existence of extra-familial provisions for schooling, however, does not, from the perspective of Christianity, Islam, and other religious traditions, replace the responsibility and authority of the family to shape the development of children, and especially the development of their character.

Catechism and other instruction in religious mysteries, apprenticeships, rites of passage, itinerant teachers of reading and writing, village schools, training in military skills, and — in our time — Berlitz and Arthur Murray classes are examples of extra-familial provisions for schooling that do not claim to replace the family.

It has become fashionable among educators and human service professionals to justify and enhance their professions by pointing to the collapse of the traditional family and — rather than supporting policies that would help to rebuild family life — to call for ever-expanding government and professional intervention in all aspects of the development of children.

The demise of the traditional family, it is safe to say, has been greatly exaggerated — though there is certainly much to be concerned about.[1]

---

1. See Allan C. Carlson and Bryce J. Christensen, "Of Two Minds: The Edu-

But what is cause and what is effect? Has the state expanded its role because of an abdication by the family, or has growing intervention by the state weakened the ability of the family to carry out its traditional responsibility of raising children into decent and useful adults?

"[F]undamental among all the 'emancipations' of modern history has been the emancipation of the State from the restrictive network of religious, economic, and moral authorities [to which we might add the family] that bound it at an earlier time."[2] Universal public schooling has been provided under the state's supervision precisely in the name of emancipating children from the tutelage of their benighted families. As one author notes approvingly, "for most of this century education was thought to be the means by which upwardly mobile children could escape the crippling confines of their family's culture."[3]

But what if they were simply emancipated into the state? Randall Jarrell put it well in his poem "The Death of the Ball Turret Gunner": "After my mother's sleep I fell into the State . . ." After all, "children are small, weak, and inexperienced; adults are big, strong, and shrewd. There is no way to send an 8-year-old child out of the sovereignty of the parent and into a world of liberty. He will be projected instead into a new sovereignty of one kind or another."[4]

And what of the fundamental rights of parents? "The right to form families and to determine the scope of their children's practical liberty is for most men and women the primary occasion for choice and responsibility. One does not have to be rich or well placed to experience the family. The opportunity over a span of fifteen or twenty years to attempt the transmission of one's deepest values to a beloved child provides a unique arena for the creative impulse. Here is the communication of ideas in its most elemental mode."[5]

---

cational and Cultural Effects of Family Dissolution," *The Family in America* 2, 8 (Aug. 1988); and Ann M. Milne, "Family Structure and the Achievement of Children," in *Education and the American Family: A Research Synthesis,* ed. William J. Weston (New York: New York University Press, 1989).

2. Robert A. Nisbet, *The Quest for Community* (London: Oxford University Press, 1953), p. 89.

3. Abigail Thernstrom, "Is Choice a Necessity," *The Public Interest* 101 (Fall 1990): 128.

4. John E. Coons, "Law and the Sovereigns of Childhood," *Phi Delta Kappan,* Sept. 1976, p. 22.

5. John E. Coons, "Intellectual Liberty and the Schools," *Journal of Law, Ethics & Public Policy* 1 (1985): 511.

One of the arguments commonly used against providing public funding so that moderate-income parents, as well as those more affluent, will be able to select the schools their children will attend is that such parents will inevitably make bad choices since they are so messed up in their personal lives. While there can be no denying that this description fits some poor (and some middle- and upper-class) parents, the senior author's thirty years as an active member of inner-city churches has given him an unshakable conviction of the abundant grace evident in the lives of poor families — and their responsible approach to child-rearing and to decisions about schooling. This observation is supported convincingly by anthropological research into the actual family practices of poor black parents in Chicago.[6]

The content and purpose of schooling can vary widely. The distinction made in French between *instruction* and *éducation* is useful. *Instruction* refers to the teaching of skills and information, while *éducation* refers to the formation of character and values, the development of the person. In practice, of course, instruction always has an element of education, and education of instruction. Nevertheless, the distinction is useful, and the discussion that follows is concerned exclusively with *éducation* in this narrower sense. It is also important to note that there can be no true education that does not automatically entail a preconception about "the Good," even if the preconception is that there is no such thing. Education is always based upon a worldview — even if it is one that merely rejects the significance of ultimate questions — and thus perforce excludes other worldviews. It is impossible for education, or for a school that seeks to provide education, to be value-neutral.[7]

The State and Education

It has only been in the past two hundred years that the state has made the schooling of children an essential part of its program for interven-

---

6. See Charles L. Glenn, "Letting Poor Parents Act Responsibly," *Journal of Family and Culture* (1987); and Reginald M. Clark, *Family Life and School Achievement: Why Poor Black Children Succeed or Fail* (Chicago: University of Chicago Press, 1983).

7. See Richard A. Baer, Jr., "American Public Schools and the Myth of Value Neutrality," in *Democracy and the Renewal of Public Education,* ed. Richard John Neuhaus (Grand Rapids: Eerdmans, 1987); and Stephen Arons, "The Myth of Value-Neutral Schools," *Education Week,* 7 Nov. 1984.

tion in and shaping of civil society. The Roman Empire did not make provision for schooling children, while in Babylon and Egypt boys who learned to write did so at temple schools. Sparta, described by Plutarch as taking boys from their mothers to raise them for the state, was always seen in antiquity as exceptional — a utopia or dystopia according to taste. The state schooling described in Plato's *Republic* is the exception that proves the rule.

Assumption by the state of a *mission éducatrice* has been intimately associated with "nation-building," as a means of bypassing "mediating structures" and extending the influence of the state and its governing elites directly over the rising generation.

Historian Jan Lewis suggests a "division of labor worked out by nineteenth-century Americans — which gives to parents, and particularly to mothers, the responsibility for the development of character and to the schools the responsibility for teaching content,"[8] but none of the reformers who shaped the development of public education throughout the century, from Horace Mann to John Dewey, would have agreed. For them, the primary purpose of the common school was to play a major role in shaping the character, and indeed the worldview, of its pupils.

In the United States and in other Western democracies (with the partial exception of Great Britain), state intervention to provide and to regulate schooling antedates development of state activism in other dimensions of social services. Historical evidence suggests that the primary impetus was less a concern with *instruction* than with *éducation*, that civic education rather than literacy for its own sake was central, as has been the case in more recent "literacy campaigns" in China, Cuba, and Nicaragua.[9]

Totalitarian regimes are characteristically most concerned with the control of schooling, but democratic regimes (especially those with massive immigration or large indigenous minority populations) are deeply concerned as well, while traditional and authoritarian regimes tend to be little concerned about popular schooling.

For a totalitarian regime, the control and content of popular ed-

---

8. Jan Lewis, "Mothers As Teachers: Reconceptualizing the Role of the Family as Educator," in Weston, p. 131.

9. See Charles L. Glenn, *The Myth of the Common School* (Amherst: University of Massachusetts Press, 1988).

ucation poses no problems; indeed, it is a fundamental means of imposing uniformity and adherence to the regime.[10] The child belongs to the state rather than to his or her family, a claim articulated for the first time since Sparta by the French Jacobins during the 1790s. The possibility that parents would seek to nurture in their children a commitment to a religious tradition or indeed to any other entity in the civil society is seen as a direct threat to the state's authority.

> To achieve their aims, governments established through revolution frequently attempt to offset conservative family socialization influences by setting up new educational forms for inculcating desired attitudes. Thus the Communist Revolution in Russia led quickly to edicts limiting parental power while insisting on parental responsibility to further the objectives of the revolution through the rearing of children. . . . Pedagogues committed to communism were given responsibility both for guiding parents and for reshaping the school system to the ideals of the revolutionary regime.[11]

The true scope of the educational program of totalitarian regimes (which characteristically includes the "re-education" of adults) can only be understood as comparable to that of a religious community. Thus a study of Poland notes that "planned secularization and anti-religious policy, key features of atheist totalitarianism, are themselves a secular version of the millennial fantasy: planned secularization is typically described by its proponents as a means to the realization of those values which Christianity itself postulates but is unable or unwilling to implement . . . planned secularization is very much oriented in its theory towards the realization of the secular fantasy and in its practice towards the establishment of a system of total control."[12]

Catholic theologian John Courtney Murray found evidence of the same "Jacobin revolutionary principle which abolishes all social insti-

10. See, e.g., Martin J. and Penelope P. Croghan, *Ideological Training in Communist Education: A Case Study of Romania* (Lanham, MD: University Press of America, 1980); and Samuel Northrup Harper, *Civic Training in Soviet Russia* (Chicago: University of Chicago Press, 1929).

11. John A. Clausen, "Perspectives on Childhood Socialization," in *Socialization and Society*, ed. John A. Clausen (Boston: Little, Brown, 1968), p. 154.

12. Maciej Pomian-Srzednicki, *Religious Change in Contemporary Poland: Secularization and Politics* (London: Routledge & Kegan Paul, 1982), p. 184.

tutions intermediate between the individual and the state"[13] in postwar efforts to banish religion from American public life, including schools.

The Inevitable Conflict

For a democracy, popular education is the focal point of a dilemma inherent in the democratic system itself: how to accommodate at the same time the system's need for a certain solidarity among its members based upon shared values, and the divergent values of groups within the society.

It has come to be accepted, at least among social scientists and educators, that the family cannot be trusted to shape the values and worldview of its children unassisted. "In any democratic society where social origins are associated with grossly varying cultural orientations, the attainment of responsible citizenship by the bulk of the population is largely dependent on the educational system. The assimilation of ethnic and other minorities requires that agents from outside the family provide orientation to the larger society and its values."[14]

But are we sure that this is an unmixed blessing for a society that prizes freedom and diversity? "Even the well-intentioned state," writes legal philosopher John Robinson, "tends to homogenize its citizens, delegitimizing all loyalties except those that bind the individual to the state. . . . The family is a natural antidote to the state's totalitarian tendencies. As does a church, it generates loyalties that rival in intensity those that the state evokes, and it conveys beliefs that can undermine the ideology that the state is purveying."[15]

Democratic government — especially when newly established — poses in an acute form the problem of its own legitimacy and the willing participation of its constituency. It reaches instinctively toward the possibility of shaping its future citizens, even though freedom from being shaped should presumably be one of the benefits of life in a free society.[16]

13. Quoted in A. James Reichley, *Religion in American Public Life* (Washington, DC: The Brookings Institution, 1985), p. 287.

14. Clausen, p. 154.

15. John H. Robinson, "Why Schooling Is So Controversial in America Today," *Notre Dame Journal of Law, Ethics and Public Policy* 3, 4 (1988): 529-30.

16. See Stephen Arons, *Compelling Belief: The Culture of American Schooling* (Amherst: University of Massachusetts Press, 1986).

The rhetoric that surrounded the establishment of state-provided popular education in the United States, France, and other democracies often reached for religious images — the teacher was a "preacher" or a "priest," the schoolhouse a "sacred place" — suggesting that, here too, there was an effort to realize a "secular fantasy." Horace Mann was quite clear about his belief that the common school taught a purer form of Christianity than did the churches.

There is no liberal democracy that has not experienced the tension between its educational mission and that of the family, and it has often been the source of major conflict, as in the early 1980s in France and Spain. Dutch political scientists commonly attribute the mobilization (*emancipatie*) of the common people to the "school struggle" that persisted through most of the nineteenth century.[17]

Nor should we expect that our own society could be immune from such tensions. As Richard Baer has pointed out, "a government monopoly school system with a captive student audience — a system which in significant curricular matters is no longer locally controlled, and which, especially at the pre-college levels, is no genuine market-place of ideas — will almost always be experienced as coercive and oppressive by various dissenting minorities."[18]

Since (as we have argued) education is always value-laden, the question arises inexorably: which or whose values will be taught? Those that the state considers most conducive to social order and progress, or (to the extent that they differ) those considered central by communities and individuals of faith?

For Horace Mann and his allies in American educational reform, as they created the state systems of public schooling, there was no doubt that schools could teach values and a worldview "on which all reasonable men [*sic*] agree." Those groups within society who held different views (Shakers, Calvinists, Roman Catholics) were thereby demonstrating their own unfitness to make decisions about the content of schooling. "What an unspeakable calamity," Mann wrote, "a Calvinistic education is."[19]

17. See Charles L. Glenn, *Choice of Schools in Six Nations* (Washington, DC: U.S. Department of Education, 1989); Gerard Leclerc, *La bataille d'école: 15 siècles d'histoire, 3 ans de combat* (Paris: Denoël, 1985); and D. Langedijk, *De Schoolstrijd* (The Hague: Van Haeringen, 1935).

18. Richard A. Baer, Jr., "Censorship and the Public Schools," typescript (Cornell University, 1984).

19. Quoted in William Kailer Dunn, *What Happened to Religious Education? The*

Given the homogeneity of most local communities in nineteenth-century America, the reformers were close enough to being right — and the deviant groups were sufficiently marginal — to make this a sustainable proposition.

While never absent (since even in a traditional society or a local community controlling its own schools there are nuances of commitment to the prevailing values), this question of whose values will be taught becomes acute only as the state seeks centrally to impose the values of the dominant elite upon what may in fact be a majority of the population: examples include the educational agenda of the French Revolution after 1792 in relation to a predominantly Catholic population, or the conflict between liberal regimes and Protestant evangelicals in the nineteenth-century Netherlands and the contemporary United States.

"Worldview minorities" (to coin an awkward phrase) are particularly likely to become aggressive about the ways in which they differ from the majority after the institution of compulsory schooling. Roman Catholics, for instance, are in tension with the state's school both as a majority under a secularized government (in Poland) and as a minority (in Australia). Many Moslems are currently alienated from public schooling in Western Europe and seek Islamic schooling.[20]

This tension is implicit in the nature of religion itself. _Religion, as we use the word here, is the set of beliefs and stories — the "narrative" — about the nature of existence by which an individual or community derives moral values (the Good) and a definition of proper action in the world._ In discussing which values should be taught in schools, and how, it is essential to make a basic decision about whether or not experience _does_ have the inherently narrative quality assumed by traditional religions. If not, then it should be possible (as Horace Mann and John Dewey believed) to define a "common faith" of those beliefs and values most useful to social harmony. If, on the other hand, experience/life does have an inherently narrative character and we derive values and justifications for action from the particular narrative to

---

Decline of Religious Teaching in the Public Elementary School, 1776-1861 (Baltimore: Johns Hopkins University Press, 1958), p. 124.

20. See Mervyn Hiskett, _Schooling for British Muslims: Integrated, Opted-out or Denominated?_ (London: The Social Affairs Unit, 1988); and Gilles Kepel, "L'école laïque et l'Islam," _Hommes et Migrations_ (Strasbourg, 1988).

which we adhere, then the debate concerns justice: how do we accommodate differing narratives within democracy fairly? From this perspective, Horace Mann and John Dewey articulated not a common faith but worldviews deriving directly from the narratives (social and intellectual milieux, personal experience) to which they adhered.

Neutering the Public School

In the United States over recent decades there has been an attempt to render public schools inoffensive to all parents by progressively removing from curriculum and school life any elements to which there could be objections from any quarter — preeminently including discussion of religion as other than a historical curiosity.[21]

Although often traced to the post–World War II rulings of the Supreme Court on religious observances in school, this process in fact began in the mid-nineteenth century. In an attempt to meet the objections of Roman Catholics to public schooling (in order more effectively to socialize their children and thus to reduce the "papist threat"), many communities voluntarily reduced the religious content of that schooling to vestigial observances empty of doctrinal content.[22]

The "neutralization" of the common school has been considered, by those who articulate the "official" educationist position, the only solution to the oppressiveness of single-value education. If a particular conviction causes tension for those who don't share it, then the complete absence of conviction — a lowest common denominator — should resolve the tension.

No educator would explicitly endorse "value-free" education, of course. Honesty, consideration, and above all tolerance are commonly

21. See Paul C. Vitz, *Censorship: Evidence of Bias in Our Children's Textbooks* (Ann Arbor: Servant Books, 1986); Robert Bryan, *History, Pseudo-History, Anti-History: How Public-School Textbooks Treat Religion* (Washington, DC: LEARN, n.d.); and Charles L. Glenn, "Religion, Textbooks, and the Common School," *The Public Interest* 88 (Summer 1987).

22. See Samuel Windsor Brown, *The Secularization of American Education* (New York: Teachers College Press, 1912). On the Supreme Court's rulings, see Robert T. Miller and Ronald B. Flowers, *Toward Benevolent Neutrality: Church, State, and the Supreme Court* (Waco, TX: Markham Press, 1982), and Frank J. Sorauf, *The Wall of Separation* (Princeton: Princeton University Press, 1976).

endorsed as traits that public schools should seek to develop in their pupils, and to which no right-thinking person should object. In very much the same way, in the 1840s Horace Mann insisted that schools could and should teach "the pure religion of heaven" (strongly resembling his own Unitarian beliefs) and that only the most bigoted fanatic could possibly object.

To many in the society, however, an education that declines to take positions on what seem to them to be fundamental aspects of human life as they wish their children to understand and live it is by no means neutral; they perceive it as directly hostile to the convictions by which they live. Thus books are published with such titles as *Your Children: The Victims of Public Education* and *Schools: They Haven't Got a Prayer,* and there has been a tremendous growth in the number of (mostly very small) Protestant alternative schools. Enrollment in evangelical and Assemblies of God schools increased from 113,410 in 1965-66 to over one million (attending 8,400 schools) in 1988-89.[23]

Parents who select such schools for their children — or who protest against the worldview that serves as the basis for education in the public schools their children attend — are often dismissed as "sectarian." The use of this term has, since Thomas Jefferson, implied that citizens with strongly held religious beliefs that exclude the equal validity of other modes of understanding the world are "bigoted, narrowminded, and unorthodox" in relation to the prevailing consensus of reasonable people.[24]

The same attitude toward those whose religious beliefs include absolute truth-claims was expressed by Justice Douglas in *Lemon v. Kurtzman,* when he wrote that, while it was the purpose of public schools to educate, it was that of Catholic schools to indoctrinate. James Hitchcock notes in this connection that "it sometimes appears in court decisions that there exists a constitutional right on the part of nonbelievers to be protected from unpalatable impositions of religious beliefs, but no corresponding right on the part of believers to be protected from ideas which they find offensive."[25]

There is good reason to question whether the bigotry and intoler-

---

23. Bruce S. Cooper and Grace Dondero, "Survival, Change, and Demands on America's Private Schools," typescript (Fordham University, 1990).

24. See Richard A. Baer, Jr., "The Supreme Court's Discriminatory Use of the Term 'Sectarian,'" *The Journal of Law and Politics* 4, 3 (Spring 1990).

25. James Hitchcock, "Church, State, and Moral Values: The Limits of American Pluralism," *Law and Contemporary Problems* 44, 2 (Spring 1981): 13.

ance are all on one side, and whether it is indeed possible for a school to be as truly "value-free" or "neutral" as has been claimed. As Richard Baer has put it, the position that secularism and humanism are religiously neutral and hence fit to serve as a civil religion is "philosophically naive and politically unfair." Secularism is no more "reasonable" than religious conviction.[26]

If experience does have an essentially narrative character, then the imposition of one narrative on diverse "narrative-groups" is tyrannical. The only rational basis for demanding a state-sanctioned, centrally imposed narrative is the assumption that there is, in fact, no authentic narrative quality to experience. In this view, the diversity of worldviews is irrational and societally counterproductive, and the imposition of one rational, productive central narrative — whether a civic religion or a set of nation-affirming myths — upon the fanatics who persist in maintaining their own distinctive narratives and versions of reality is justified by *raison d'état.*

When the convictions that make it possible to take seriously a non-rooted civic religion or to assert confidently a national myth have been shaken, as occurred in the United States during the sixties, educators may be placed in the position of denying significance to *any* narrative.

There is a strange affinity between this position of the American education establishment and that of Sartre in his philosophical novel *Nausea.* Roquentin, the main character, decides that the intrinsic narrative quality of human experience in which he had always believed is in fact merely an artificial structure imposed on an essentially structureless existence. Humans have a basic need for existential orientation, he concludes, so they invent one. Roquentin decides that, in order to have "existential integrity," he must cease to believe that life has any inherent structure from which to derive meaning, values, and action justifications. Because of his integrity, Roquentin becomes "nauseated" by the meaninglessness of any experience or action. But he believes that exile from humanity and paralysis of action are what integrity demands.

Alasdair MacIntyre, arguing against Sartre/Roquentin, claims that Sartre's truth-claim about the non-narrative character of experience is in fact part of Sartre's own narrative.[27] MacIntyre faults Sartre's conclusion

26. See Richard A. Baer, Jr., "Agricultural Ethics at State Universities," *Agriculture and Human Values* 2, 4 (Fall 1984).

27. Alasdair MacIntyre, "The Virtues, the Unity of a Human Life and the Concept

that in order to have integrity one must be disassociated from humanity. This is a diminished concept of integrity, for to be human is to be inextricably involved with other humans. And to be involved with other humans is to be part of many narratives. While Sartre/Roquentin may choose to author his own narrative to the effect that there is no such thing as narrative (or author), he is inescapably an actor in other narratives. To be human, then, is to be "intelligible" to other humans, and intelligibility assumes a coherent narrative quality of experience. According to MacIntyre, an unintelligible action is in fact not an action at all. For whether or not a particular action is intelligible to one narrative, it is always intelligible to some narrative. Thus even Roquentin's non-action is an action, intelligible within Roquentin's particular anti-narrative narrative.

MacIntyre faults the premise that "*either* we can admit the existence of rival and contingently incompatible goods which make incompatible claims to our practical allegiance *or* we can believe in some determinate conception of *the* good life," but that these are mutually exclusive alternatives. There are better and worse ways for an individual to "live through the tragic confrontation of good with good." One cannot opt out of this confrontation by insisting, with Sartre/Roquentin, that there is no such thing as the Good.

The attempt of Horace Mann and his allies in American educational reform and of Ferdinand Buisson and other educators of the French Third Republic to create a common civic education that would evoke in the young a "higher loyalty" to the nation-state, to the exclusion of particularistic loyalties, showed signs of renewed popularity in the 1980s. Secretary of Education Bennett was perhaps unaware that his Socialist counterpart in France, Jean-Pierre Chevenement, shared his interest in a common civic education for all.

This position seems to want — without success — to have it both ways. On the one hand, the enthusiasts for civic education seem to believe with Sartre/Roquentin that there is no such thing as an inherently stubborn narrative quality to experience; thus a common myth can be invented (by a selective use of history) that will serve to foster national unity. But when they seek to impose a utilitarian narrative upon schoolchildren, they fail to live up to the logical conclusion of their own assertion of the nonsignificance of existing narratives, because a utili-

---

of a Tradition," in his *After Virtue* (Notre Dame: University of Notre Dame Press, 1981), pp. 190-209.

tarian narrative is just as meaningless as any "religious" narrative from the perspective of Sartre/Roquentin (and according to our definition of religion, utilitarianism is itself a religion). If, on the other hand, they believe that life *does* have an inherently narrative quality, then they fail to be just, for the imposition of one narrative/religion upon the public is tyrannical (and illegal under the First Amendment).[28]

The fact that "neutrality" has not led to universal support for the common public school causes genuine bewilderment to members of a secularized elite for whom religiously based truth-claims are a relic of an earlier stage of human development. Thus the organization People for the American Way warns of the collapse of public education if religiously based concerns are accommodated in any way.[29]

Is it fair to characterize as "The American Way" the exclusion from the schools that children attend of the values that are most important to their parents?

Reintroducing Explicit Moral Education

Over the past several years there has been an emerging chorus of support for curriculum revision that would do justice to the values by which most Americans live. In 1987, for example, a broad spectrum of distinguished Americans endorsed a Statement of Principles stressing that "students need an honest, rigorous education that allows them to penetrate Orwellian rhetoric. . . . Such a goal is compromised when the drawing of normative distinctions and values is frowned upon as a failure of objectivity . . . it is absurd to argue that the state, or its schools, cannot be concerned with citizens' ability to tell right from wrong, and to prefer one over the other in all matters that bear upon the common public life. That would be utterly to misunderstand the democratic vision, and the moral seriousness of the choices it demands of us."[30]

Two related but distinguishable challenges are involved: doing jus-

28. As argued by James Skillen, "Public Justice and True Tolerance," in *Confessing Christ and Doing Politics* (Washington, DC: Association for Public Justice Education Fund, 1982).

29. See Anthony T. Podesta, "The Tennessee Decision: Wider Debate," *Religion and Public Education* 14, 1 (Winter 1987).

30. *Education for Democracy: Guidelines for Strengthening the Teaching of Democratic Values* (Washington, DC: American Federation of Teachers, 1987).

tice to morality and character development, and doing justice to religion and spiritual development. Though both are difficult under present conditions, the first is likely to be easier to address in a satisfactory manner than the second.

Moral education in American public schools went astray in the late 1960s, as schools lost conviction about their mandate to shape the character of their pupils.[31] In response, many educators sought pedagogical strategies that would make it unnecessary for the teacher to take a position on right and wrong ("values clarification"). Kevin Ryan comments that "discussing these topics without having to study what the culture had learned about them proved very popular with students. The techniques of values clarification were easy to learn and required little of teachers — except, perhaps, the ability to remain neutral in discussions that were often highly charged and riddled with misinformation."[32] Others hoped that Lawrence Kohlberg had developed an approach to moral development that was scientifically objective and thus not based upon inappropriate "value judgments."[33]

There seems to be an emerging agreement, however, that society has a right, through its schools, to teach commonly accepted virtues necessary for the functioning of the political order and the civil society. The United States Catholic Conference, for example, insisted recently that "a renewed shared moral vision within the public schools is possible." These qualities, it is argued, can be developed through stories (historical and fictional), service projects, and recognition of virtuous behavior.[34]

31. See Robert L. Hampel, *The Last Little Citadel: American High Schools Since 1940* (Boston: Houghton Mifflin, 1986).

32. Kevin Ryan, "The New Moral Education," *Religion and Public Education* 16, 3 (Fall 1989): 373. See Sidney B. Simon, Leland W. Howe, and Howard Kirshenbaum, *Values Clarification: A Handbook of Practical Strategies for Teachers and Students* (New York: Hart, 1972); but see also Richard A. Baer, Jr., "Values Clarification as Indoctrination," *The Educational Forum*, Jan. 1977.

33. See, for example, Lawrence Kohlberg, "Moral Education, Religious Education, and the Public Schools: A Developmental View," in *Religion and Public Education*, ed. Theodore R. Sizer (Boston: Houghton Mifflin, 1967), and Kohlberg, "Stages of Moral Development as a Basis for Moral Education," in *Moral Development, Moral Education, and Kohlberg: Basic Issues in Philosophy, Religion, and Education*, ed. Brenda Munsey (Birmingham, AL: Religious Education Press, 1980), pp. 15-98.

34. See, e.g., the following articles in *Religion and Public Education* 16, 3 (Fall 1989): Marilyn Braveman, "Moral Education in the Life of the School"; the Administrative Board of the United States Catholic Conference, "Value and Virtue: Moral Education in the Public Schools"; and Kevin Ryan, "The New Moral Education."

To the extent that morality can be reduced to negotiated rules of behavior and qualities of character, without dealing with the convictions and worldview on the basis of which most human beings decide and act, this strategy could produce modest but real improvements in the effectiveness of public schools. There is reason to believe that schools that are morally coherent tend to be more effective in providing *instruction* as well as *éducation*.[35]

It would be naive to assume, however, that attention to the explicit moral content of instruction in terms of commonly accepted rules of behavior — however desirable — would be sufficient to put education back on the right track. Harriet Tyson comments that "a new push for values education that focuses on a narrowly drawn core of citizenship values will not be enough. We need to strengthen the humanities, because only there do students learn that an inner life exists. Only there are students exposed to the complexities of the human dilemma and to the language of heart and soul, right and wrong, good and evil."[36]

The Continuing Dilemma of Religion and Schooling

Nor would lowest-common-denominator moral education be likely to satisfy parents for whom religion and moral decision making based upon religion are of fundamental significance. As Baer notes, "when it comes to the *Big Questions* — questions regarding the meaning and purpose of life, who we are, and how we ought to live in light of our deepest religious and metaphysical commitments — Americans today hold very different views about reality and what is appropriate belief and behavior."[37]

Why is it that people of particular strongly held views on such matters (i.e., faith) often refuse to accept a lowest-common-denominator

35. See James S. Coleman and Thomas Hoffer, *Public and Private High Schools: The Impact of Communities* (New York: Basic, 1987); Peter L. Benson et al., *Catholic High Schools: Their Impact on Low-Income Students* (Washington, DC: National Catholic Educational Association [NCEA], 1986); and Michael J. Guerra, Michael J. Donahue, and Peter L. Benson, *The Heart of the Matter: Effects of Catholic High Schools on Student Values, Beliefs and Behaviors* (Washington, DC: NCEA, 1990).

36. Harriet Tyson, "The Values Vacuum: A Provocative Explanation for Parental Discontent," *Religion and Public Education* 16, 3 (Fall 1989): 393.

37. Baer, "The Supreme Court's . . . ," p. 465.

version of religion that stresses only what most faiths hold in common? Aren't all religions about the same things when you get down to the basics?

Stanley Hauerwas and David Burrell argue that the attempt to secure a rational foundation for morality by ignoring or rejecting religious narrative rests upon a distorted account of moral experience. The move away from narrative towards a more universal, abstract notion of Truth, the Good, etc., results in part from the scientific ideal of objectivity. Stories are subjective, therefore irrational. Modern ethical theorists have tried to free objective moral reason from subjective narrative by claiming that everyone is logically committed to certain basic moral principles and procedures because of (take your pick) the "categorical imperative," the "ideal observer," "universalizability," the "original position," etc. This attempt to secure what Hauerwas and Burrell call "a 'thin' theory of the moral life" aims at the admirable goal of insuring "that what we owe to others as strangers, not as friends or sharers in a tradition, is nonarbitrary."[38]

The implication is, of course, that people whose ideas of morality are based on a nonobjective foundation (and are thus "sectarian") cannot be trusted to act morally towards those whose morality is not based on their narrow view. In this argument, all people are reduced to ultimately self-serving individuals, and all morals to mere rules by which to protect interest groups from one another.

But how, Hauerwas and Burrell ask, can we even speak of morality-as-decision-making when the decisions themselves are determined by one's character, a character that is formed not by objective decision but by subjective beliefs? This is where narrative comes in, for it is narrative "that provides the context necessary to pose the terms of a decision, or to determine whether a decision should be made at all."[39] Rationality itself is a notion determined by a particular narrative. Furthermore, an "objective" account of morality assumes that everyone has the same basic notions about the world in which we make decisions. This is untrue. Our moral notions are based on examples from narratives.

Any pluralistic society contains groups whose moral notions are formed by particular narratives. Just because many of those moral notions are on the surface identical does not prove that the narratives that give rise

38. Stanley Hauerwas and David Burrell, "From System to Story: An Alternative Pattern for Rationality in Ethics," in *Why Narrative? Readings in Narrative Theology,* ed. Hauerwas and L. Gregory Jones (Grand Rapids: Eerdmans, 1989), p. 162.
39. Ibid., p. 167.

to those notions are identical. The attempt to free moral notions from particular narratives proves to be "too monochromatic." The attempt to create a rational, scientific, secure system of morality is doomed to failure, since it assumes that rationality is itself objective and free of narrative.[40]

One aspect of doing justice to religion is to ensure that its role in history and in contemporary American life is presented fully and fairly. Historian Paul Gagnon and others have demonstrated that, because of a desire to avoid controversy, religion has been expunged from textbooks as an element of fundamental significance for many individuals and societies. This is simply a dishonest distortion of reality, a form of censorship no less objectionable than the earlier failure to mention the role of women and of members of minority groups.[41]

A number of groups have urged that history and social studies texts be changed to reflect our history more accurately. It is worth noting that this has changed in a very few years from a conservative to a mainstream position, and is even supported by the fiercely "separationist" People for the American Way (PAW). Most notably, an all-star cast of religious, civic, and political leaders endorsed the "Williamsburg Charter" and called for schools to do justice to the role of religion in American life.[42]

There are nuances in this support. PAW has chosen to stress teaching about "religious freedom," which may translate into presenting history as a series of protests against orthodoxy. Thus Roger Williams is portrayed as a dissenter from the Calvinism of Massachusetts Bay but not as devout Baptist.

Teaching about religion, although it raises issues of interpretation and emphasis, could be implemented in a relatively noncontroversial way. It is, however, subject to several objections, which may be illustrated from the British experience.[43]

The British Education Reform Act of 1988 requires religious ed-

40. Ibid., p. 169.

41. Paul Gagnon, *Democracy's Half-Told Story: What American History Textbooks Should Add* (Washington, DC: American Federation of Teachers, 1989). See also Tyson, "The Values Vacuum"; and Charles L. Glenn, "Why Public Schools Don't Listen," *Christianity Today,* 20 Sept. 1985.

42. *Education Week,* 15 April 1987; Ernest L. Boyer, "The School Curriculum Project of the Williamsburg Charter Foundation" (typescript, 20 October 1988). See also The Williamsburg Charter Foundation, *The Williamsburg Charter: A National Celebration and Reaffirmation of the First Amendment* (Williamsburg, VA, 1988).

43. The following discussion relies heavily on accounts appearing in issues of *The Times Educational Supplement* between 1988 and 1990.

ucation in all publicly supported schools; in schools run by local education authorities, this teaching is based upon a locally established syllabus which "must reflect the fact that religious traditions in the country are in the main Christian whilst taking account of the teaching and practices of other principal religions."[44]

Thus the religious education syllabus for the London borough of Ealing states, "Whilst our children need to understand that Christianity is a living faith which has shaped the history, institutions, art and culture of Britain, they also need to explore the other living faiths in our borough so that the richness of our religious experience can be shared and appreciated." The suggestion that the effect of Christianity is more appropriate for study than is its content has been attacked by some Christian parents in Ealing. They and others have urged that religious education in Britain should include more than vague traditions; if religious teaching is to be in the school at all, let it be explicit.

A school may teach about religion on such a superficial basis that nothing of its real power comes across. Reviewing American history texts, Tyson notes that "words such as *faith, love, heart, soul, sorrow, pain, pride, greed,* or *evil* are hardly ever used. One gets the impression that religion is nothing more than a fun spoiler, like parents and teachers."[45] And a comparative religions approach (such as the required course in "spiritual currents" in Dutch schools) threatens to trivialize each of the religious traditions discussed.

Should children be taught that all beliefs and values are a matter of opinion? Baer comments that "the position that the [elementary school] child should be exposed to a multiplicity of values . . . presupposes that, for the sake of what is viewed as a good cause, the state has the right to violate the parents' wishes for the child's moral and religious development. This position also prejudges the very difficult psychological question of how much exposure to diversity of values is good for the moral development of the child."[46]

An approach that relativizes all religions and value systems will satisfy no one but the historian — and those who wish to convey a

44. Department of Education and Science, *The Education Reform Act 1988: Religious Education and Collective Worship,* Circular 3/89 (London, 1989).
45. Tyson, "The Values Vacuum," pp. 386-87; see also Paul Gagnon, *Democracy's Half-Told Story;* and Charles L. Glenn, "Why Public Schools Don't Listen," *Christianity Today,* 20 Sept. 1985.
46. Baer, "Censorship and the Public Schools."

radical individualism that rests upon the rejection of those convictions that are shared. Thus Moslems in Britain have objected to teaching about Islam by a nonbeliever.[47] Equally objectionable to those for whom religious and cultural traditions have living power is their trivialization by a focus upon easily accessible customs and artifacts: "Jews have dreidles, Christian have manger scenes. . . ."

What many parents seem to be looking for is the presence of religion itself in the school. It is presumably not without advice from his pollsters that President Bush has continued to call for reinstituting "school prayer."

Schools could seek to express a generalized or a vaguely Christian religiosity, as in Great Britain. The fundamental charter of postwar education in England and Wales, the Education Act of 1944, required that all pupils attending government-supported schools (including "maintained schools" under nongovernmental management) take part in a daily act of collective worship. Over recent decades, however, under the influence of secularization and the growing religious diversity of Britain's population, the Christian content of such worship has been increasingly attenuated. As a senior producer at BBC School Radio wrote in a paper for teachers, "It is possible, through careful choice of themes, expressed in stories, songs and prayers which are not narrowly confessional, to plan assemblies which are based on broad principles of Christianity, but which can appeal to all children whatever their background or personal beliefs." This sort of "Cross and Crescent, Star of David, Sutra and psalm, turban and Torah" approach pleases neither Christians nor Muslims. Christian parents at the Sandal Magna First School, for example, objected to the school's multi-faith worship, insisting, "[w]e don't expect [our child] to go to school and celebrate other people's faiths."

In reaction to such objections, the Educational Reform Act of 1988 requires that such collective worship in schools be "wholly or mainly of a broadly Christian character, though not distinctive of any particular Christian denomination." The Act has been criticized by both Christians and Muslims. The head of one secondary school wrote, "I have no wish to compromise my position as a Christian by insisting that non-believers take part in a Christian act of worship." Another practicing Christian

---

47. See, e.g., Yaqub Zaki, "The Teaching of Islam in Schools: A Muslim Viewpoint," *British Journal of Religious Education*, Autumn 1982, pp. 33-38.

school headmaster said the Act "simply degrades true faith and adds stress. One cannot devise acts of worship for non-believers."

The General Secretary of the Association of Christian teachers has written that any school which adopts the ideology of agnostic secularism (in the interest of consensus) and adds to it a concern for "spiritual development" is in fact teaching "pantheistic tribalism" and should "give up any pretense of being multicultural." Other Christians have charged that the Religious Education (RE) content in many schools had become "'excessively secularized and politicized,' and took a multi-faith approach which trivialized all religions." Christian teachers are "not able to cope with multi-faith RE. . . . For reasons of conviction and tempera-ment . . . they cannot play the RE game to the revised rules which require a certain openness in the treatment of Christianity."

The 1988 Act makes provision for a local "standing Advisory Council on Religious Education," with representatives of local religious communities, to approve alternative forms of collective worship when warranted by a school's enrollment. As many as a quarter of the schools in the city of Bradford applied for such an exemption due to their large Muslim population. Some schools with large Muslim populations have begun holding non-Christian acts of worship without first applying for formal permission, stating that it is patently obvious that in a school with 90 to 95 percent Muslim pupils, a Christian act of worship would be completely inappropriate. The Muslim Educational Trust has pub-lished a booklet outlining what Muslim parents should do to avoid indoctrination (if they choose not to withdraw from the school system altogether).[48]

Parent choice activist Fred Naylor argues that any attempt to teach children to respect another faith as much as their own is impossible; it will demean both faiths as being completely relative: "It is impossible to believe truly in a faith — any faith — and to admit that it is no more worthy than others. And to pretend otherwise is dishonest." What we *should* respect is the right to have a different faith.[49] Moslems inter-viewed by Naylor saw apathy — rather than attacks by Christians — as the greatest threat to handing on their faith to their children. This helps

48. Ghulam Sarwar, *Education Reform Act, 1988: Compulsory Christian Collective Worship and Christian Religious Education in School; What Can Muslims Do?* (London: The Muslim Educational Trust, 1988).

49. Fred Naylor, *Dewsbury: The School Above the Pub* (London: Claridge Press, 1989), p. 96.

to explain the choice of many Moslem parents, in the Netherlands as well as Britain, to put their children into Christian rather than secular schools out of a preference for schooling that takes religion seriously.

According to one Christian married to a Muslim, "either [we] teach ethics and values, or we teach Christianity. We should not adopt the ingenuous Western attitude that rites, traditions and structures don't matter. They do matter, because they make us different, and they respect the values we hold dear; they should not be lightly shared, cheapened or trivialized in an attempt to promote multicultural understanding. That kind of understanding only begins with mutual respect."

The growing demand for Islamic schooling in Britain (as in the Netherlands, France, and elsewhere in Western Europe) has produced a response eerily reminiscent of that of Horace Mann and his contemporaries to the demand for Catholic schooling: accommodate the protesting parents by removing the vestiges of Christianity from the common school. A report issued by the Commission for Racial Equality (CRE) in July 1990, though entitled *Schools of Faith*, in fact urged that the denominational (mostly Roman Catholic and Anglican) schools in Britain were inimical to a multiracial society. "If Anglican, Catholic and Jewish schools continue, then Muslim and other ethnic minority faith schools will emerge."[50] On the other hand, the Commission predicted, parents would be satisfied with state schools if only elements were removed that were offensive to their beliefs.

Moslems' responses to this recommendation have been mixed. While progressive (and secularized) elements in the community have supported "the abolition of state funding for religious schools" and "the abolition of the compulsory act of Christian worship in state schools," others have charged that the CRE "ignores the religious needs of a community and treats the issue solely as a social and political matter. Along with other religions, what we are asking for is a less secular education for our children."

The Association of Christian Teachers, in response to the CRE report, conceded that many Moslem and Sikh parents regarded state schools as Christian, "but they are mistaken. It is because many Christian parents see mainstream state education as being increasingly intolerant of Christianity that in recent years there has been a significant

50. Commission for Racial Equality, *Schools of Faith: Religious Schools in a Multicultural Society* (London, 1990), p. 21.

growth in the number of independent Christian schools. . . . The idea seldom seems to occur to the Commission that religious parents ask for religious schools for religious reasons. On the contrary, we are all assumed to have voted at some time for what the Commission sees as normal, 'a secular democratic state.'" Assuming as the CRE does that Moslem parents will be satisfied with accommodation of their food and dress requirements "seems to see such religious phenomena as harmless cultural odds and ends instead of as expressive of a whole religious world view."

We can see, then, that the attempt to express religious faith and worship within a public school that serves all comers leads to tensions that work against the unifying intention. Both non-Christian and Christian parents are dissatisfied. Non-Christians fear that their children will be indoctrinated, and Christians dislike what they see as a distortion of their faith.

Neither the attempted exclusion of religion and values from schooling nor the imposition of a single form of spirituality and a single worldview — a civic religion that is not rooted in the life of any particular faith community — promises a satisfactory resolution to the dilemma of education in a democracy. The latter has been tried and found wanting; the former, which developed as a remedy, is equally unworkable. And those who urge a return to the earlier approach have not reflected sufficiently upon what history can teach us.

The Williamsburg Charter signatories, by contrast, agree that any hope of finding a religious lowest common denominator for the public schools can lead only to "the folly of endless litigation and further flight from public education" by those parents (and children) who can't accept that version of religion as representing fairly the stubborn particularity of their own faith. To respond adequately to this "new stage and new stress in America's public philosophy" requires an entirely new structure of public education.[51]

The unsatisfactory nature of attempts to come to terms with the place of convictions and values in American schools is a result of an ill-conceived attempt — beginning with Horace Mann and his allies in the 1830s — to avoid the conflict of ideas within society. Paul Gagnon points out that there is an inherent tension in education in a free society:

51. "Chartered Pluralism: Reforging a Public Philosophy for Public Education" (Washington, DC: The Williamsburg Charter Foundation, 1988).

"the aims of education for democratic citizenship are by their nature contradictory. . . . We seek to develop at one and the same time a taste for teamwork and a taste for critical, thorny individualism, at once the readiness to serve and the readiness to resist." This confusion of purpose leads to a fundamental weakness in how American history is presented in textbooks, as the authors seek to avoid confronting the ways in which Americans really differ. "In this long march of earnest, mind-numbing prose there is no hint of hard and costly choices, real sacrifices that underlie success, or possible failures to solve particular problems."

With regard to the presentation of religion in history textbooks, Gagnon asserts that "students are left with the impression that toleration is the only 'religious' idea worth remembering. . . . Modern readers, always ready to mistake their own indifference to religion for the virtue of toleration, could profit from better perspective. . . . The teaching of toleration, as with any other democratic virtue, must be done in relation to matters we feel strongly about." Gagnon concludes finally that, "without preaching or indoctrination, texts need to demonstrate, for example, that ideals and values are important."[52]

An important study sponsored by Connecticut Mutual Life Insurance found that Americans are deeply divided on a number of important questions that are very close to how they live and (presumably) how they want their children to live. The study concluded that "it is the level of our religious commitment which . . . is a stronger determinant of our values than whether we are rich or poor, young or old, male or female, black or white, liberal or conservative."[53]

Two Possible Solutions

One possible response to the existence of real differences would be to make the exploration of these differences a central element in instruction. The Dutch are talking about creating "encounter schools" in which Christian and Islamic and secular humanistic convictions would be fully expressed in a climate of mutual respect.[54] This educational strategy has

52. Gagnon, *Democracy's Half-Told Story*, p. 198.
53. John Crothers Pollock et al., *The Connecticut Mutual Life Report on American Values in the '80s: The Impact of Belief* (Hartford, 1981).
54. See J. Gerritsen, "De ontmoetingsschool," *Bulletin: Unie School en Evangelie* (1985).

much to recommend it, especially in comparison with present practice, though its effective implementation poses difficulties. Maintaining a balance among teachers who are expressing different convictions (and, inevitably, who differ in their ability to convey and to convince) would be enormously sensitive. And creating the unified staff vision essential to an effective school would be difficult.

The recent First Amendment rulings about religious expression in schools assume that different practices are appropriate depending upon the level of maturity of the students. A balanced encounter among religious and moral perspectives seems essential to higher education (though in practice neither traditional faith nor traditional virtues seem to be treated with much respect), and it would be worthwhile to find ways of exposing secondary students to the conflict of convictions without trivializing those convictions.

In elementary education, however, an emphasis upon how groups and individuals in the society differ in their convictions and loyalties does not seem appropriate. Developmentally, the more important learning at this stage is that convictions and loyalties are important, and that people whom the children respect are morally responsible actors. "The most liberated adult," John Coons suggests, "could turn out to be one who, throughout his school life, has experienced the steady and uncompromising faith of his fathers — religious or secular. . . . A strong value position defended by intelligent and committed adults could prove an exhilarating and toughening experience for a young person weaned on Fred Flintstone; it might do more for the possibility and practice of liberty than even a prolonged immersion in socratic dialogue."[55]

Children need not share the convictions by which their teachers live in order to learn that such convictions are important. Parents often select religiously based schools for their children even though they are not adherents of that religion. A recent study in the Netherlands has found that "denominational schooling receives some support from the youngest as well as the oldest generation. The process of secularization . . . has evidently had no effect on the preference for a particular type of school."[56] Many inner-city Protestant parents in the United States send their chil-

55. John E. Coons, "Intellectual Liberty and the Schools," *Journal of Law, Ethics & Public Policy* 1 (1985): 521.

56. J. F. A. Braster, *School Struggle, Pillarization and Choice of Public and Private Schools in the Netherlands* (Rotterdam: Erasmus University, 1990), p. 13.

dren to Catholic schools, and many Moslem parents in the Netherlands select Protestant rather than secular schools for their children.[57]

The only way to have elementary schools that can truly *educate* through dealing seriously with the profound stuff of life, while avoiding paralyzing conflict over the basis and content of this education, is to encourage a real diversity among schools, based upon parent and teacher choice among meaningful alternatives.

Teachers must be allowed to do their delicate work in schools that provide collegial support based upon shared values and goals. Parents must be allowed to select schools whose teachers share their own values. Parents, teachers, and children should form a community in support of real education. It is no coincidence that this is also the best formula for the fundamental reform that American public education so urgently requires.[58]

The solution is not simply a "disestablishment" of American public education in the interest of real freedom and energy for reform, though that has much to recommend it.[59] A carefully crafted *system* of educational provision is needed, with the state exercising its appropriate role as the guarantor of justice rather than insisting upon being the primary provider of schooling.

Such a system will require three elements that are not present as American schooling is now organized:

a. procedures to assure equal access to educational opportunities unlimited by race or place of residence (and thus ability to afford housing in affluent areas);
b. vigorous and effective outreach to low-income and minority parents to help them to become effective choosers of schools and advocates for and participants in the education of their children; and

57. See Charles L. Glenn, *Why Parents in Five Nations Choose Schools* (Quincy, MA: Massachusetts Department of Education, 1988).

58. See James S. Coleman, "Schools and the Communities They Serve," *Phi Delta Kappan,* April 1985; Coleman, "Families and Schools," *Educational Researcher* 16, 6 (1987); and Charles L. Glenn, "*Perestroika* for American Education," in *Rethinking Effective Schools,* ed. William Firestone and Craig Richards (Englewood Cliffs, NJ: Prentice Hall, 1990).

59. See Rockne M. McCarthy, James W. Skillen, and William A. Harper, *Disestablishment a Second Time: Genuine Pluralism for American Schools* (Grand Rapids: Eerdmans, 1982); and John E. Coons and Stephen D. Sugarman, *Education by Choice: The Case for Family Control* (Berkeley: University of California Press, 1978).

c. consistent encouragement of real diversity among schools, expressed in the preparation of teachers, the measurement of outcomes, and the provision of support for program development and for starting new educational alternatives.[60]

Rather than continue to deny the existence of fundamental differences among Americans on a variety of value-laden issues, while persisting in the impossible task of providing an education that engages real issues while offending no one, it would be appropriate to organize education in a way that would give full scope to the ingenuity and commitment of teachers and encourage the support and participation of parents.

The goal should be, not to suppress the conflict over ideas and values that is essential to a democracy, but to remove schools and children — especially at the elementary level — from the line of fire.

Why should we do so? Only for the sake of liberty and out of respect for parents? No, although those would be sufficient reasons. It is also important to encourage schools to educate with confidence by coming to grips with the profundity of human life, to expose our children to schools that are not constrained to trivialize. In too many schools the great mystery of our sexuality has been reduced to the mechanics of putting a condom on a zucchini!

Perhaps Glenn Tinder is right to warn us that democracy and the civic virtue that sustains it will not long survive the failure to wrestle with ultimate meaning. "Many would like to think that there are no consequences — that we can continue treasuring the life and welfare, the civil rights and political authority, of every individual without believing in a God who renders such attitudes and conduct compelling. . . . [O]ur position is precarious, for good customs and habits need a spiritual base; and if it is lacking, they will gradually — or perhaps suddenly — disappear. To what extent are we now living on moral savings accumulated over many centuries but no longer being replenished?"[61]

Our system of schooling will be part of the problem rather than

60. For a more detailed discussion of these points see Charles L. Glenn, "Putting Choice in Place," in *Public Schools of Choice*, ed. Joe Nathan (St. Paul, MN: Institute for Learning and Teaching, 1989).

61. Glenn Tinder, *The Political Meaning of Christianity: An Interpretation* (Baton Rouge: Louisiana State University Press, 1989), pp. 49, 51.

part of the solution so long as teachers are constrained to teach defensively a curriculum from which all the vital juices have been squeezed out. Well-organized diversity and parent and teacher choice of schools, by contrast, can create the space for real education.

A Call for Reform Schools

PATRICIA BEATTIE JUNG

In this essay I wish to develop a distinctively Christian argument for the development of many different kinds of reform schools. By "reform" schools I mean two things. On the one hand reform schools are profoundly traditional institutions willing to bear a solitary witness in the world if necessary to the truth of their traditions. On the other hand such reform schools are structurally open to the faithful reformation or reconstruction of those same traditions.

An argument for the development of such a framework for moral education must establish two contentions. First, it must uncover the inadequacy of the primary alternatives — that is, of either exclusively liberal or rigidly traditional forms of moral education. At present most parents are forced to choose between such liberal (usually public, though sometimes private) or traditional (usually narrowly parochial) schools for their children. Second, it must demonstrate the potential benefit of such a web of educational institutions to all who are faithful to particular traditions, and in this case specifically Christianity. Though perhaps neither necessary nor sufficient for the task, I hope that such an agenda will contribute to the development of a persuasive argument for transforming the current pattern of moral education. Toward that goal, I offer the following reflections.

The Inadequacy of Liberalism Located

The development of a compelling case against the prevailing liberal ethos pervading many public and some private schools requires first that the strengths of liberalism be recognized. Though it may strike some as paradoxical, only when it is viewed in the best light can the genuine weaknesses of liberalism be identified. Thus in this section of my essay I sweep away some misconceptions about liberalism and highlight some of the insights that undergird its moral framework. Such a focus will make the subsequent evaluation of liberalism more convincing.

Sweeping Away Decoys

Even though liberalism is one of the prevailing cultural frameworks for moral analysis, it certainly has its limits. However, in order to assess accurately its assets and its liabilities, it is necessary to examine liberalism at its best. All exaggerated accounts of liberalism must be dismissed as misconceptions and all degenerate versions recognized. Toward those ends let me identify three popular myths about liberalism that need to be corrected.

While it promotes political neutrality, authentically liberal thought does not seek to maximize individual freedom via such neutrality at the expense of *every* other moral consideration. Such an extreme commitment would (logically) result in a "neutral" response to repressive practices and in the dismantling of most, if not all, public institutions and practices because they promote one or another civic virtue. As Nancy L. Rosenblum has pointed out in her introduction to *Liberalism and the Moral Life,* liberal theorists are committed not only to noninterference and toleration but to a whole "bundle of virtues which they believe are compatible with a certain range of competing conceptions of human flourishing."[1]

Similarly the image of a liberal education as the value-free presentation of facts and the transmission of neutral skills requisite for subsequent value clarification and choice is partly denounced by liberal theorists themselves. Liberal theorists agree that a civic education in which one inculcates certain procedural virtues and habits is inevitable

1. Nancy L. Rosenblum, ed., *Liberalism and the Moral Life* (Cambridge, MA: Harvard University Press, 1989), p. 16.

and necessary. Indeed, they argue among themselves about just what virtues are most essential to the liberal state.[2]

In both of these instances, liberals recognize that it is not possible or desirable to serve freedom without advocating certain virtues. Personal liberty for substantive choices will not be available to individuals apart from certain procedural structures that require habitual and wide communal support. In order to obtain and sustain such broad political support for these "merely" procedural structures, liberal educators have gradually begun to remove from schools whatever proves to be offensive.

Once gutted of the inevitably offensive-to-some values that traditionally directed it, this "neutered" education appears to be merely a process whereby skills and information are transmitted. It is assumed that the broader substantive character formation that makes the liberal effort to ensure individual liberty partially intelligible occurs elsewhere — at home, in churches, etc.

Liberals have deceived themselves. Such public school instruction continues to be morally formative. Character is shaped by what is omitted from a curriculum as well as by what is blatantly endorsed within it. Thus a liberal education is far from substantively neutral. It actually favors secularism and cultural assimilation. It infringes upon — discriminates against, if you will — those who wish to withdraw from, live apart from, or transform the prevailing cultural ethos.

Even though strictly speaking political neutrality is commended only to a limited extent, liberals fail to recognize that their commitment to "merely procedural" virtues in fact reflects and reinforces the substantive value commitments that constitute the status quo. There is nothing "neutral" about either the commitment to make freedom one's center of value or about the political structures that support such a conservative commitment. Let us, however, return to the task at hand and clear the field of other false images of liberalism.

The advocacy of a significant degree of political neutrality is frequently misidentified as a reflection of personal indifference by some critics of liberalism. On the contrary, civic tolerance and governmental impartiality are virtues that liberals believe must be inculcated in citizens precisely because the passions behind their moral convictions require such discipline. Indeed, it is not apathy but a vivid sense of the

2. See the debate between Amy Gutmann and William Galston in ibid., pp. 71-101.

potential depth of moral conflict within society that motivates the liberal desire to minimize differences in the public order.

No Easy Target

Before we ask at what price such social harmony is bought, it is crucial that we identify the assets of liberalism, especially the insights underlying it. As just indicated, one cluster of insights frequently linked with liberalism stems from the modern appreciation of the extent and depth of moral pluralism. Agents experience moral values not only as diverse but also as in competition for their human allegiance. Some loyalties are found to be incompatible, if not incommensurate. Ultimately liberals err when they conclude that such moral pluralism necessitates political neutrality. As Joseph Raz argues in his book *The Morality of Freedom,* the recognition of the validity of many goods does not require that all efforts to eradicate some other values be forbidden.[3] One need not deny the soundness of this intuition about the conflictual, if not explosive, character of the moral life underlying liberalism in order to speak against the liberal response to it.

Likewise, behind liberalism's call for political neutrality is a profound respect both for the corrupting influence of concentrated — especially bureaucratic — forms of power and for the real limits of the best of human intentions and the wisest of human judgments. Beyond these intuitions is a real and important revulsion at the prospect of one person or a group of persons imposing their favored ideals or conception of the good life on other persons. Such a prospect offends our egalitarian sense of human dignity and integrity. These are legitimate concerns, but they do not self-evidently justify the exclusion of or neutrality between ideals that is liberalism. There are alternative responses to these intuitions. The liberal antiperfectionist platform needs careful argumentation and justification.

For example, respect for human dignity and personal integrity may be better expressed by restricting the choice of means — especially coerciveness — through which the government pursues such a favored goal. All the machinery of the state is not equally coercive. An ideal may be equally well or even better expressed by combining a nonviolent coercive mechanism with the opportunity and structures for conscientious objection to it.

3. Joseph Raz, *The Morality of Freedom* (Oxford: Clarendon Press, 1986).

Liberals do not err when they condemn moral indoctrination. People should be able to think and choose for themselves. After all, they are ultimately responsible for their moral beliefs and character. However, the liberal assumption that human beings *control* values is erroneous. It reflects an underestimation of the determinate side of humankind, and it assumes the possibility of objectivity rather than the necessity of recognizing the values already at play. It is distortive simply to equate moral indoctrination with all forms of moral training or orientation.

Enculturation is a person's formation by a tradition and induction into a corresponding social structure, whether that social structure is communal or atomistic and libertarian in nature. Clearly enculturation is not necessarily identical to indoctrination. While all catechesis aims to make people resistant to wholesale assimilation into other traditions and social arrangements, the degree to which it will foster or resist acculturation will vary. Though the line between (1) conversion to and (2) adaptation within another framework of meaning may be difficult to draw, the two options can be distinguished. Liberals err, not when they condemn moral indoctrination, but when they let their fear of it leave them rootless.

In this preliminary evaluation of liberalism we have highlighted its strengths and recognized the soundness of some of its insights. Nevertheless, even when it is properly described, liberalism remains indefensible except as a quite minimal account of and framework for the moral life.

A Critical Analysis of Liberalism

The search for a foundation for the moral life that would prove to be persuasive to all rational human beings has dead-ended. This project failed because it demanded of its participants that they deny their particularity — their traditions and communities — and adopt an abstract, ahistorical, impartial point of view. Such a request is ultimately impossible to fulfill. It rests on a misleading epistemology: no such nonperspectival position is attainable.

This project of the Enlightenment originated in the desire to disavow contingent provincial influences. Is it not wise to be suspicious of what is parochial? Do not such peculiar angles of vision inevitably skew and distort our perceptions? Ironically, foundationalist efforts like liberalism have proved to be quite imperialistic. In contrast, the forthright

119

advocacy of a tradition can amount to a commitment not to let the biases of what is received in that tradition as well as one's own interpretative biases remain hidden and unexamined. Because it does not recognize and acknowledge its embeddedness in particular and historical value commitments, liberalism has proven to be tyrannical and imperialistic.

It has both masked its own loyalties and eroded other communal loyalties. The isolated individual in the liberal state could do little more than establish contracts and address procedural issues. Within such a context schools can do little other than surrender their students to consumerist and externalizing values. To reduce morality to such arrangements is to distort the moral life. It also amounts to underwriting the perpetuation of whatever prevails. Liberals are deeply conservative agents of hegemony.

Liberalism, with its apparent neutrality regarding the content or substance of these contractual arrangements between consenting adults, actually undermines many moral traditions and many intermediary associations between the individual and society. Tolerance has turned out to be highly corrosive. For example, the promise of marital permanence requires many supports. Prenuptial agreements, both by making divorce less financially costly and by curtailing the extent of the conjugal union, erode rather than support this aspect of fidelity. Similarly, practices like monogamy cannot be sustained by individuals. The path of fidelity is impossible to travel alone. Liberalism can make little sense of parenthood. Without communal recognition and support such personal covenants are not viable. Indeed, I would argue that the survival of most virtues requires their embeddedness in a tradition and maintenance by a community based on that tradition. Liberalism undercuts these institutions and their traditions.

In a sense liberalism itself, or at least political neutrality, can be seen as a response to the claim that all of morality is tradition-bound. Are not liberals correct when they argue that such perspectivalism necessitates such even-handedness? I would argue that such a relativistic response is not necessary for two reasons. First, all traditions can be legitimately evaluated in terms of their own standards, via canons like consistency and internal coherence. Second, even when more than one such tradition fulfills its own criteria, relativism need not follow. The inability to establish objectively the truth of a particular moral tradition does not mean it is false.

In summary, liberalism is problematic because it is epistemologically impossible to be impartial. The illusion of such "neutrality" is not without effect: it corrodes many value commitments. For example, in those public schools that have been drained of all flavor by the liberal ethos, students, faculty, and staff alike find they are unable to give public witness to their deepest convictions. Furthermore, through the "vacuum" created in an effort not to impose any one viewpoint on all, a particular view is in fact imposed. Liberalism is especially pernicious because it has little sense of its own presumptions and of their formative power.

Traditional Alternatives

The acknowledgment of the canonical foundation of our moral convictions necessitates that we give up the project of seeking "objective" verification for them. It does not mean that we stop making claims about what is normatively human based on these particular traditions. Indeed, the ethical task is to mine these traditions for their riches — especially their comprehensiveness and fruitfulness. The task of moral education (which includes moral self-formation) is to nurture in oneself and in others an appreciation for and an understanding of the riches of one's traditions.

Such moral training can occur at home, in traditional and "reform" schools, in churches, and in other associations such as scouts, sports and clubs, etc. It is here that moral educators seek to inculcate dispositions toward, tastes for, and instincts about certain virtues and vices. A taste for steadfastness and a revulsion against infidelity, for example, can become axiomatic criteria against which other moral beliefs are tested. It is our consent to and adoption of these tradition-based convictions that enable us to evaluate the moral force of various categorical arguments at all.

Christian Traditions

Such traditions are of course particular, and the Christian tradition, like many others, is itself not singular in focus or uniform in design. There is more than one theme in the Christian story to be lived out and there may be some tension between them. For example, Christians must both

121

receive life gratefully as a gracious gift from God and embody the promise of liberation from oppression. Yet sometimes life itself can be oppressive.

Indeed, in my opinion many debates among Christians about moral education are rooted in this (problematic) complexity — that is, in the fact that there are potentially conflicting themes within the Christian story. Frequently debates among Christians about liberalism are misplaced. Often the issues that divide us are deeply theological, not political or philosophical.

Let me be more specific. A habit central to the liberal ethos is civility. Christians bring to this habit various presumptions. Some of us are suspicious of its vicious potential to disguise apathy and cowardice. Others of us are appreciative of its virtuous potential to model procedurally the value of every child of God. Who should carry the burden of proof regarding the complementarity of civility with Christianity? Attitudes vary among Christians about what constitutes proper public demeanor because Christians disagree about whether or not the faithful should assume there to be a fundamental tension or a fundamental continuity between the church and the world. In our case, they disagree about what should be the relationship between the Christian tradition and the liberal "tradition" (of being traditionless!).

Roman Catholic Insights

For theological reasons Catholics expect to find natural processes and cultural frameworks, including that of liberalism, "fertile with hints of God," to quote Timothy E. O'Connell's *Principles for a Catholic Morality*.[4] They do not view themselves as resident aliens or the world as essentially alien, though much of it may be so existentially. The doctrine of the incarnation reveals the world to be a fitting home for God's self-disclosure, not "enemy territory." Redemption reveals grace to be essential to the completion of creation. There can be no sharp dichotomy between a "supernatural" and a "natural" history, and no fundamental contradiction between the one God as Creator and Redeemer.

The implications of these theological convictions for the moral life are several. First, Christians can and do expect to find authentic

---

4. Timothy E. O'Connell, *Principles for a Catholic Morality* (New York: Seabury Press, 1978), pp. 30-41.

moral wisdom mediated in *any* normatively human structure or practice — even in one like civility whose traditional home is liberalism rather than Christianity. This reflects a theological conviction that God can operate throughout the traditions. Distinctively or traditionally Christian sources of moral wisdom cannot be viewed as exhaustive for or exclusive to Christians.[5]

There may be points of congruity, and even flashes of identity, between actual human practices and "grace-ful" (or normatively human) practices. The two are of course never simply convertible. But some measure of compatibility can be anticipated, and every instance of cultural adaptation and accommodation need not be feared. Christians need not be xenophobic. There may be points of complementarity between the liberal and Christian traditions, and for profound theological reasons Catholics hope to find them.

Concretely this means that a traditional school need not avoid all the procedural practices or concerns usually linked with liberalism, though the adoption of such practices must be selective and it must be recognized that such adoptions may erode other commitments. Thus the institutional preservation and transmission of other noncanonical sources of moral wisdom — that is, of other traditions — poses no inherent or necessary threat to Christians. Certainly some, even much, of what is so preserved will be proved to be antithetical and potentially corrosive to the faith, as has proven to be the case with regard to much of liberalism. Other aspects, however, will prove to be corroborative of it, if not crucial to its faithful reformation. (See my argument in the next section.)

Lest I be misunderstood, my point has not been to undermine the force of my own critique of liberalism. Nor do I intend to set up an exploration of the points of convergence or overlap, if any, between liberalism and Christianity. My purpose has been quite simply to explain something of why Christians vary in their approach to moral education.

It is not enough to declare that Christianity will inevitably be co-opted and corrupted by contact with liberalism. One must first demonstrate that it is unfaithful or theologically mistaken to anticipate some modest measure of congruity or complementarity between these traditions. Apart from such a theological analysis of the relationship between

5. See Patricia Beattie Jung, "A Roman Catholic Perspective on the Distinctiveness of Christian Ethics," *The Journal of Religious Ethics* 12, 1 (Spring 1984): 123-41.

Christ and culture, such predictions and accusations simply beg the question at hand.

All Christians know that their participation in society must be at times selective and that their way of life, if it is to remain authentic, may need to sign a stark alternative to what prevails. In this sense Christianity understands itself to be a distinctive tradition, potentially in tension with much of what prevails in society. Thus that web of institutions — families, schools, parishes, nursing homes, etc. — which constitutes the Church must be intentional about preserving its distinctive identity and immersing its neophytes in it. However, many Christians do not believe that their heritage is unique and altogether without parallel or close analogy in the wider world. Their particular canons do have a primacy in that they serve a criteriological function vis-à-vis other sources of moral wisdom. However, their traditional sources of moral wisdom are neither exclusive to or exhaustive for these Christians.

Reformed Insights

It would be too simplistic to suppose that a conscious effort to transmit a tradition or way of life removed those so nurtured from harm's way entirely. On the contrary, what makes the issue of moral education so thorny is that all traditions are biased and parochial by virtue of both human finitude and fault. All traditions, including Christianity, are in need of periodic, if not constant, reformation (however one understands such development).

A brief review of church history reveals not only that individual Christians were often unable to live in accord with their tradition, but also that the Christian tradition as it was transmitted and received was frequently distorted. To state the obvious, many deeply traditional Christian teachings about holy wars, slavery, women, Muslims, and Jews (to name a few) often needed — and in some cases continue to need — reformation.

However, not all traditionalists recognize this. Clearly if the status quo within a tradition is deemed unambiguously good, then *paideia* will consist simply of instilling the acceptance of a tradition, not inspiring its transformation. Some who hold to the irreformability of their tradition suffer from a kind of selective amnesia, especially regarding the deficiencies of that tradition. That ailment is ironically similar to the one that plagues their liberal, post-traditional antagonists. Often by virtue of their privileged position within a tradition, these adherents fail to bring to the interpretative process a hermeneutic of suspicion. Such a framework would enable them to assess critically their own tradition, retrieve voices historically silenced therein, and faithfully reconstruct it. Instead these non-reformists bolster all the procedural practices that stifle internal dissent and otherwise disguise the plurality of voices that constitutes their tradition. They also tend to be closed to sources of moral wisdom outside their unreconstructed tradition, even though important questions (if not answers) about holy wars, slavery, women, Muslims, Jews, etc., may be preserved in these extra-canonical traditions.[6]

Summary

Liberals deceive themselves when they believe that their idolization of individual freedom with its illusory claim to public neutrality is not itself a particular tradition, whose tenets cannot be verified apart from their presumptions. What is really dangerous about liberalism and other forms of post-traditionalism is that they have no critical awareness of their presumptions and no sense of the power — both formative and corrosive — of those presumptions.

Traditionalists deceive themselves when they claim too much for the particular historicity and distinctiveness of their own canon. They will in fact find therein some moral overlap with many other traditions. Moral education need be neither impartial toward nor xenophobic about the liberal ethos.

Finally, because post-traditional liberals and rigid traditionalists can be forgetful of their roots, they can both be oblivious to their inherently conservative bias. Neither point of view asks: ought children and neophytes to be uncritically socialized into either the status quo of my liberal society or the status quo of my alternative tradition?[7]

6. See, e.g., Karen J. Warren, "The Power and the Promise of Ecological Feminism," *Environmental Ethics* 12, 2 (Summer 1990): 125-46.

7. See Edmund L. Pincoffs, *Quandaries and Virtues: Against Reductivism in Ethics* (Lawrence, KS: University Press of Kansas, 1986).

Conclusion

To be a traditional conformist and/or a social conservative is not necessarily problematic. There is much of value to be received in many traditions, including liberalism and countercultural traditions. It is important, however, that all these virtues — whether they are procedural or substantive, liberal or traditional — be accepted only reflectively, and their reception can be tested in a pluralistic crucible only through public dialogue. Christians have no reason to be wary of such a public conversation, and the development and support of a web of traditional reform schools on the basis of Christian premises will play a large role in promoting such a conversation. Indeed, this is what it means to call the church a community of moral deliberation. Such a community is also — indeed, it must also be — a community of memory.

HIGHER EDUCATION

The Alienation of Christian Higher Education in America: Diagnosis and Prognosis

JAMES TUNSTEAD BURTCHAELL, C.S.C.

Every one shall consider the main End of his life and studies, to know God and Jesus Christ which is Eternal life. John xvii.3.

Laws, Liberties and Orders of Harvard College, circa 1646

As for the Universities, I believe it may be said, Their Light is now become Darkness, Darkness that may be felt. . . . Tutors neglect to pray with and examine the Hearts of the pupils. — Discipline is at too low an Ebb: Bad Books are become fashionable among them.

George Whitefield, 1744

All Scholars Shall Live Religious, Godly and Blameless Lives according to the Rules of Gods Word, diligently Reading the holy Scriptures the Fountain of Light and Truth; and constantly attend upon all the Duties of Religion both in Publick and Secret.

Yale Laws, 1745

A university cannot be built upon a sect.

Charles W. Eliot, 1876

An earlier version of this essay was published in *First Things* in 1990; it is included here by permission.

There are several major themes that command the attention of the historian of American higher education, but among these the oldest and the longest sustained is the drift toward secularism.

Richard Hofstadter, 1952

The history of American higher education is a sad story of loss of faith by religious institutions. The presence in so many parts of the country of secularized, non-religious, at times even antireligious institutions whose foundations were inspired by religious zeal and apostolic motives seems almost like empirical proof of the contention of positivists that faith and intelligence are incompatible.

Charles F. Donovan, S.J., 1963

We have disavowed a view of the relation between the colleges and the churches which would permit viewing them as agencies of the church in preference for a covenant relationship in which each is recognized to have its own function but a common commitment and point of view on crucial issues.

Edgar M. Carlson, 1967

The survival of recognizably Protestant colleges therefore seems to depend on the survival within the larger society of Protestant enclaves whose members believe passionately in a way of life radically different from that of the majority, and who are both willing and able to pay for a brand of higher education that embodies their vision. Such enclaves still exist, but they are few in number.

Christopher Jencks and David Riesman, 1968

*I have watched so many small colleges sucked down the drain by
specious appeals to "liberal values" and "top drawer scholarship,"
as though one cannot find excellent teachers who are also
Christians. It is no longer possible to believe that the great central
values of Christendom will so commend themselves to the wise
and just as to survive without special and even to some degree
coercive nurture. How do we meet that challenge without some
sort of new Inquisition?*

William Muehl, 1975

Legion are the universities and colleges in the United States founded
under the auspices of the churches. Princeton, Calvin, Hanover, Tulsa,
and Macalester were founded as Presbyterian or Reformed. Brown,
Baylor, Wake Forest, Spelman, and Vassar were Baptist. Haverford,
Swarthmore, Earlham, Whittier, and Guilford were Quaker. Williams,
Yale, Smith, Fisk, and Dartmouth were Congregationalist. Valparaiso,
Saint Olaf, Luther, Hartwick, and Wittenberg were Lutheran. Duke,
Emory, Northwestern, Southern California, and Syracuse were Methodist. Georgetown, Webster, Notre Dame, Manhattanville, and De Paul
were Catholic. The University of the South (Sewanee), Hobart, Bard,
William and Mary, and Kenyon were Episcopalian. Those were the
offspring of churches with numerous foundations: nearly one hundred
for the Methodists (surviving from some nine hundred foundations),
more than one hundred for Presbyterians and Reformed, and more than
two hundred and fifty for the Catholics (not including all those which
no longer exist). Then there is the scattering of other foundations:
Brigham Young, Bob Jones, Loma Linda, Eastern Nazarene, Bethel, and
so on.

The churches sponsored higher education before there were any
state-sponsored colleges or universities — indeed, before there were
states. For most of the history of the nation those Christian foundations set the patterns and carried most, then much, of the enrollment.
And now, out of that galaxy of institutions founded by believers so
that faith could house learning, there are few — very few — that in
any effective and outright way are confessional. There has been, from
earliest times, a tendency towards alienation. And that tendency has
been continually associated with a striving toward academic excellence
on the part of the educators, and a diffidence toward venturesome

131

thinking (or at least the expression of venturesome thinking) on the part of churchmen.

One is obliged to ask, however, whether the overall sense of this secularization enacted on behalf of progress may in some profound sense have involved regress as well. I say "overall" because at almost every step in the course of this journey there have been concrete and valuable purposes pursued and improvements attained. It is clear that those who were the chief engineers of secularization did not foresee or intend or wish the alienation of their institutions from their mother churches. But the secularization came. It is not yet complete. The Catholic colleges and universities were somehow the last great cohort to be drawn into the process, though having once put their feet to the path they are finding their way along it at unprecedented speed. Then there are the small and stubborn colleges with a campus ethos that is strongly enough at variance with the dogmas and dictates of modern scholarship to disdain and resist it thus far: one thinks of Wheaton, Liberty, Oral Roberts, Calvin, and Goshen.

Perhaps the trend is inexorable; perhaps there is some radical antagonism between a community of committed faith and a community of committed learning. Great academic leaders have been persuaded that the church is a counterproductive sponsor of ambitious higher education. The group that held this conviction most explicitly, and who acted on it in the largest sector of independent higher education — that which belonged to the Liberal Protestants — is well represented by William DeWitt Hyde, elected president of Bowdoin College in 1885 at the age of twenty-six:

> In its religious life the college should be as little as possible denominational. The narrowness of sectarianism and the breadth of the college outlook are utterly incompatible. Denominations may lay the egos of colleges; indeed, most of our colleges owe their inception to such denominational zeal. But as soon as the college develops strength, it passes inevitably beyond mere denominational control. Church schools are often conspicuous successes. Church colleges are usually conspicuous failures. A church university is a contradiction in terms.[1]

1. William DeWitt Hyde, "The College," *Educational Review* 28 (Dec. 1904):469-70. Hyde, a Congregational cleric at a Congregational college, succeeded in declaring Bowdoin nonsectarian in order to qualify for a Carnegie grant in 1907. Bowdoin was,

Hyde was a devoted follower of Charles W. Eliot, during whose early presidency he had been a student at Harvard. It was Eliot who had undone the last ties between that university and the Unitarian wing of the Congregationalists, their original church environment. He had pointed out the antipathy between religious authority and free inquiry in his inaugural address in 1869:

> The very word "education" is a standing protest against dogmatic teaching. The notion that education consists in the authoritative inculcation of what the teacher deems true may be logical and appropriate in a convent, or a seminary for priests, but it is intolerable in universities and public schools, from primary to professional. The worthy fruit of academic culture is an open mind, trained to careful thinking, instructed in the methods of philosophic investigation, acquainted in a general way with the accumulated thought of past generations, and penetrated with humility. It is thus that the university in our day serves Christ and the church.[2]

Whether or not emancipation from the church is the necessary condition or the inevitable result of intellectual excellence, it behooves us to understand the history and the elemental structure of this secularization. In order to do this we shall have to study primarily the colleges and universities affiliated originally with the "mainline" Protestant churches, for it is they who led the way. Our undertaking is to discern any features that recur regularly enough to be considered typical in the process of academic secularization. There are numerous theories about secularization in general; they would best be set aside here as we examine what may prove to be a process with distinctive lineaments of its own.

The process was usually unacknowledged, especially unacknowledged to themselves by those most responsible for its furtherance. Those who lived through the secularization of any institution would not easily know which events were marking its course. Secularization, like death, is one of those human events best understood in retrospect. I propose

---

he explained, replacing a formal legal relationship with one of sympathy and tradition. See Earl Hubert Brill, "Religion and the Rise of the University: A Study of the Secularization of American Higher Education, 1870-1910" (Ph.D. diss., American University, 1969), p. 568. This is an invaluable and thorough work, to which this essay is profoundly indebted.

2. Quoted in *American Higher Education: A Documentary History*, ed. Richard Hofstadter and Wilson Smith (Chicago: University of Chicago Press, 1961), 2:606.

to study first an archetypical case: a secularization that occurred swiftly, with little anticipation, then a rush of public events, then a formal severance between the parties, and lastly a slow, even protracted process whereby the spirit and loyalty and identity of the institution is drained of manifest faith. The story we shall examine is that of Vanderbilt University. If we can disengage a pattern from that story, we can then see whether its elements suggest enough comparisons with other secularization stories to allow us to venture a hypothetical model of the process. Lastly, if successful we might as well ask whether there are any points of wisdom to be drawn from what we discern.[3]

The Vanderbilt Story

Methodists in America were sundered in 1844 by their disagreement over slavery; the defenders of slavery formed themselves into the Methodist Episcopal Church, South. Ten years later their quadrennial General Conference created the Educational Institute, a working group of educators and ministers who resolved in 1857 that the church needed a university. Unlike their many colleges, it would offer mostly graduate studies, in medicine, law, and literature. It would be seated in Nashville, where the church's missionary center and publishing house were located. And it would be governed by the bishops. When they reported to the General Conference later that year, however, they were met with an almost hostile indifference. The existing colleges saw a new foundation as a rival, so their representatives persuaded the body to refuse the charter. And then the Civil War began.

After the war a campaign was mounted in the Methodist press on behalf of a central theological seminary. Most of the church's ministry was in the hands of coarsely educated rural evangelists. The next General Conference declined this proposal and said the money would be better spent subsidizing chairs in Bible studies at the church's existing colleges. At this point the two frustrated proposals — for a university and for a

---

3. The following account relies heavily on two histories of Vanderbilt: Edwin Mims, *History of Vanderbilt University* (Nashville: Vanderbilt University Press, 1946), and Paul K. Conkin, *Gone with the Ivy: A Biography of Vanderbilt University* (Knoxville: University of Tennessee Press, 1985). The first is affectionate and relatively uncritical; the second is better researched and in every sense critical.

seminary, both at an advanced level — were merged; this new proposal was sponsored by an articulate group that included several of the church's eight bishops and some of its most learned scholars. The Tennessee Conference hosted a convention in Memphis in 1872, and delegates from seven conferences attended. It is likely that the coalition formed there failed to notice that their merger was never perfected, for they separately envisioned two very different foundations: "one fully under the control of the bishops and . . . committed, above all else, to theological education . . . [and] a church-sponsored university but otherwise one without religious tests or even theological schools, one open to the latest science and scholarship."[4]

The conventions authorized the establishment of a "Central University," provided that no less than half the required million dollars were in hand, and named the members of its Board of Trust, who were to function under supervision of the bishops of the church. A new charter to that effect was quickly obtained through a Nashville judge in attendance. But only months later the Southern Methodist bishops declined to sponsor any such university or seminary, citing their commitments to existing colleges and universities.

The bishops, however, had other motives behind their reluctance that were perhaps expressed by one of their number, George F. Peirce: "Give me the evangelist and the revivalist rather than the erudite brother who goes into the pulpit to interpret modern science instead of preaching repentance and faith, or going so deep into geology as to show that Adam was not the first man and that the Deluge was a little local affair. . . . It is my opinion that every dollar invested in a theological school will be a danger to Methodism."[5]

In a church whose membership ranked lower than the older Protestant denominations in education and socioeconomic status, a bishop could well speak like that. The church-at-large was no more forthcoming: fund-raisers sent round the conferences took in less than their own expenses. The panic of 1873 appeared to make the entire scheme a fantasy . . . until Bishop McTyeire called upon Commodore Cornelius Vanderbilt at his home in New York. Vanderbilt had been stung, in his elder years, by public resentment of him as a crude and crooked profiteer, and he was anxious to offset this repugnant image with some

4. Conkin, pp. 9, 11.
5. Mims, p. 28.

philanthropy. The bishop came back to Nashville with $500,000 in his pocket and more to follow.

The Board of Trust quickly made him their president, as Vanderbilt had prescribed. McTyeire served in this position from 1875 until 1889, and in this time Vanderbilt University, on the strength of further benefactions from its namesake, followed a course of growth that was typical of the time, save that it was one of the best-financed universities in the post-bellum South.

In light of what was to follow, it should be noted that the small size of the young university, combined with the authority of Methodist bishops to control all assignments in the church, led President McTyeire to handle faculty appointments personally. He did not restrict them to Methodists; indeed, of his first ten faculty appointments two went to Presbyterians and two to Episcopalians.[6] He did refuse the appointment of one young scholar said to incline toward evolution (about whom one advisor had written: "He is not a Methodist, and is not even a religious man"). Another was terminated for Darwinian opinions, and a third was eased out after manifest problems with drink.[7]

The local newspaper thought well enough of all this: "Parents who have sons to educate prefer the safety of that atmosphere to genteel infidelity. Vanderbilt is safe. No other institution of learning in America, at the end of three years, ever stood so safe or so strong."[8] But among intellectuals it seemed otherwise: "Vanderbilt University, which ere this should have been a Cornell or an Ann Arbor, is now not much more than a theological seminary, where the free discussion of scientific truth will not be tolerated."[9] Commenting on one purge of a group of faculty who had objected openly to a salary cutback, Vanderbilt's very sympathetic chronicler construes McTyeire's later career as a season of retrenchment:

> Seemingly there was a growing tendency towards a less liberal policy, towards even ecclesiasticism and denominationalism that had not been apparent in the early years. As Senior Bishop he felt an increasing sense of responsibility to the Church. It was a striking fact that men

6. Ibid., p. 59. Vanderbilt himself, in a special message on the day of inauguration, expressed his desire that "your institution be ever blessed by the great Governor of all things." (Ibid., p. 66.)
7. Ibid., pp. 53, 99-101.
8. Ibid., p. 102.
9. Ibid., p. 104.

who went away had been either Episcopalians or Presbyterians, and that their places were supplied in every case, until 1886, by Methodists — three of them sons of Methodist preachers. There developed a feeling in the larger public that Vanderbilt was primarily a Methodist institution.[10]

That this was not the feeling pervading the faculty is shown by a public statement of physicist Landon Garland, the chancellor under McTyeire:

> I would not have you lay aside any denominational preference you may have brought with you here. We would have you cherish the religion of your fathers. This institution is indeed under the special patronage of the Southern Methodist Church, but in its ongoings it knows no denominational distinctions. The youth of all religious denominations have equal rights here. We require no religious tests.
>
> Bigotry can never find a lodgment in the truly Christian heart. A narrow and contracted piety in the conduct of this University would dishonor the name of Wesley and disregard the wishes of the founder. We stand for a broad and thorough education — fully abreast with the advancement of literature and science.[11]

McTyeire was succeeded after an interregnum by a layman, James Kirkland, who would serve with the title of chancellor for forty-four years. Paul Conkin depicts his ecclesiastical sense:

> Kirkland came to Vanderbilt a loyal Methodist. He joined actively in West End Church and for many years taught a Sunday school class, mostly to his own Vanderbilt boys. His opening lectures to students each fall were as much lay sermons as those of [former chancellor] Garland and not a whit less moralistic. Yet, his allegiance to Methodism never seemed so much doctrinal as a matter of family tradition and soothing familiarity. From his inauguration as chancellor on he always talked of Vanderbilt's "broad" or "liberal" religious identity. In effect, Kirkland reinterpreted Vanderbilt's church ties as a loose commitment to Protestant Christianity, and not at all to the distinguishing doctrines of the Methodist Episcopal Church, South. He defended only a loose Christian test in the recruitment of faculty.

10. Ibid., pp. 109-10.
11. Ibid., pp. 135-36.

Obviously, Kirkland had no reason to speak out on doctrinal controversies in the church, but his Sunday school classes and his private correspondence indicate his rather loose, conventional Protestant orthodoxy, and his openness to higher criticism and to Christianized versions of Darwinian evolution. Kirkland reflected the most tolerant and accommodating wing of southern Methodism without ever moving to an avowed "modernist" position. . . .

He always tended to translate "Methodist" into "Christian," and thus so broaden the religious ties of Vanderbilt as to include almost anyone in the South. He would not be sectarian or dogmatic, which is to say he would not be rigorous and thus exclusive on matters of religious belief.[12]

Kirkland's tenure marked a resolute climb of the university toward academic excellence. In his eighth year of office, however, one of the bishops, Warren Candler, stunned Kirkland by introducing a motion in the Board of Trust that, all things being equal, Methodists should be preferred for faculty appointments. The motion was accepted unanimously, and Kirkland let the occasion pass without turning it into a confrontation. In 1904, however, when he presented the name of a Baptist faculty member to be dean, Bishop Candler observed that now eleven of the nineteen faculty in that department were non-Methodists, as were all deans in the university but one. A motion to postpone the appointment failed by only one vote. Kirkland told the board shortly thereafter that he intended to resign. He stated his position in a long paper which Conkin summarizes:

Vanderbilt was Methodist in many ways, including the faith of board members. He even used the term "ownership" to express the church's claim. "I have felt that Vanderbilt University was Methodist, not in the sense that Methodists made it, but in the sense that it was a great trust committed to the Methodist Church to be carried out, not for selfish ends, but for the good of society and the upbuilding of Christ's kingdom." This could not mean that only Methodists had rights in the university. What about the Vanderbilt family? He had appointed suitable Methodists, which accounted for the higher percentage of Methodists than those of other denominations on the faculty. But to serve the trust given to Vanderbilt he sought those most suited to the task. Who, when ill, would choose a physician because

12. Conkin, p. 97.

he was a Methodist? Why was the teaching of young men different? Kirkland could not fill the Engineering or Medical faculties with Methodists. No one seemed to mind this. Why did they pick on the Academic [Arts and Sciences Division]? If Kirkland followed the policy suggested by Candler he would soon sabotage the university. Sectarian requirements would drive away all non-Methodists on the faculty and, even more critical, alienate major benefactors, for they endorsed a "liberal Christian policy."[13]

But it was when he spoke directly to this subject of financial support that Kirkland came closest to his fundamental purpose:

> I say to you candidly, as I have said before, I have never found a man, be he Methodist or be he non-Methodist, willing to contribute to our work here who has not endorsed a liberal Christian policy in the administration of affairs. . . . I have never denied our Methodist allegiance, I have never denied our Methodist history, but I have maintained that greater than Methodism was the cause of Christ and that the call for service in His name was greater than the call to the service of the Church.[14]

The board capitulated entirely and gave him a vote of confidence framed in terms as ambiguous as Kirkland's, though perhaps less wittingly so:

> *Resolved, by the Board of Trust of Vanderbilt University belonging to the Methodist Episcopal Church, South,* That in accepting and administering the great trust of a Christian University our chief concern is to promote the highest type of Christian scholarship and Christian character, and to this end we shall seek in the future, as we have in the past, to secure for its chairs the most competent scholars, of unquestioned loyalty to Christ and of the highest attainment in their several departments.[15]

Only four months later, however, Kirkland was striving to secure a substantial grant from a trust fund, and to its trustees he expressed himself in quite another way:

13. Ibid., p. 154; insert from Mims, p. 296.
14. Mims, p. 297.
15. Ibid., pp. 298-99.

Churchmen had conceived Vanderbilt but the Vanderbilt family had provided all the means. The church had contributed no funds except for limited donations to the "theological" department. The government of the university was "vested exclusively in its Trustees. No conference or other ecclesiastical body elects them, nor can any such body give them orders or directions. They elect their own successors and no law exists requiring that they be Methodist." The board made the bishops ex officio members of the board "in order to secure the support and patronage" of the church, and for the same reason submitted the names of other board members "*after election* to the General Education Board of the church for confirmation." In all likelihood, he said, the Vanderbilt board would soon change the role of bishops; some bishops desired a change. He insisted that Vanderbilt used no denominational test in appointing professors, save in the Biblical [department]. His purpose, he said, was to make Vanderbilt a "genuine university, broad and liberal and free. Outside its Theological Department we do not wish it to be the exponent of any sect or creed, save such as belongs to our common Christianity."[16]

Was this one man with a single policy, giving it appropriate inflections for different audiences? Or was this a man who was devious and equivocal, determined to alter the orientation of the university before anyone realized what he was doing? Kirkland's financial plans at the time make clear that he had spoken more candidly to the outsiders he was courting than to his own trustees.

A recent fund drive in the church, out of which Vanderbilt had been promised $300,000, had been oversubscribed, yet the allotment to the university amounted to less than one-tenth of that commitment. Kirkland clearly had to look in other directions for support. George Peabody College was a normal school in Nashville that would very likely come into a million dollars with the dissolution of the Peabody Trust, and Kirkland was working energetically to persuade its trustees to move their college across Nashville next to Vanderbilt, thereby making a well-funded school of education available to the university at no cost to itself. Andrew Carnegie was creating a ten-million-dollar foundation to finance pensions for retired faculty, but only for those at nonsectarian colleges. And the General Education Board, funded by John D. Rockefeller, Sr., was becoming a most promising source of funds for promising

16. Conkin, pp. 151-52.

universities. Kirkland was situating Vanderbilt for appeals to all three of these funding sources, and its ties to the Methodist Church were now a handicap; in the case of the Carnegie Foundation they were outright disqualifying.

Thus Kirkland had a plan quietly underway to change the charter of the school, removing from the bishops their right to ultimate control. In anticipation of this he had his board change the bylaws to restrict the number of bishops in their body. Since the school's founding, the church had increased its bench of bishops from eight to thirteen and was likely to add still more. Kirkland secured an arrangement that henceforth not all but only five of them would sit on the Vanderbilt Board of Trust — and not by right, but by the choice of the board. In addition, he was quietly working to acquire adequate financing for the biblical department to allow it to be separately though subordinately incorporated, with its own board. By segregating all that was unambiguously church-related from "Vanderbilt proper," he could hope to emerge with a university freed from denominational involvement and restraint. The dean, who thought of this as an upgrading of his department rather than as a quarantine of religion, became Kirkland's enthusiastic ally in the endeavor.

This ignited a man who was destined to become the university's bitter antagonist: Bishop Elijah E. Hoss, a former faculty member and editor of the leading Southern Methodist journal that McTyeire had once directed. Hoss had three chief grievances, besides his own disenfranchisement as a bishop from the Vanderbilt board. First, student behavior had become boorish and immoral (he had in mind intoxication and sex) due to lax discipline by the administration. Second, the theological teaching at Vanderbilt was becoming deviant, if not heretical. Third, the "whole inner drift and spirit of the University has been away from Methodism, and nothing short of a revolution can restore the original and true status."[17] Kirkland surely had the support of faculty, students, and alumni, but Hoss spoke to the convictions of many fellow bishops and of many in the church at large. He was strident and made few friends, but he raised the cry in a way that Vanderbilt could not stifle.

> He minded not that [Vanderbilt] remained poor if it remained holy. He rejected Kirkland's vision of a liberal university that joined the world in order to get worldly support [he spoke of Carnegie as a

17. Ibid., p. 159.

"thug"], that enlisted in behalf of all types of progress. He was not as narrow as he sounded. He wanted to keep the university close to the church, but this did not mean he wanted every professor to be a Methodist or that he advocated piety as the key qualification for a teacher. His real quarrel was with his fellow Methodists who compromised the older beliefs and practices or, worse, expressed contempt for them.[18]

Hoss was joined in his grievances by others in the church, and storm darkened the sky over Vanderbilt. The General Conference of 1906 appointed a commission of five Methodist civil judges to advise on the legal relationship between the church and the university. The judges found for the church. The Vanderbilt board received their report and ignored it. But as the bishops began to assert their supervisory powers through several vetoes, the Vanderbilt board, after various attempts to sidestep them, eventually rejected their authority. The College of Bishops went to court, and at the trial level they were thoroughly vindicated. But the Tennessee Supreme Court reversed this decision, resting its judgment heavily on the fact that the church had never validated its patronage by any significant financial subsidy,[19] and that during the first three decades of Vanderbilt's existence the bishops had never asserted their supervisory powers. A few months later an angry General Conference of 1914 shook the Vanderbilt dust from its sandals and walked away from even the limited participation in governance that the court had offered. The board's response was meticulously generic: "Dedicated in the beginning of its history to the union of education and religion, it proposes in the future, as it has done in the past, to make the upbuilding of character its chief task. Not learning alone, but learning transferred into life and dedicated to the highest service of God and man is to remain our ideal and standard."[20]

By this time Methodist students were a minority in all but the two weakest departments, the biblical and the academic. The faculty was three-fifths Methodist. The YMCA was brought in as the nondenominational campus ministry. What had already begun under Kirkland has

18. Ibid., pp. 158-59.
19. The university lawyers had pointed out to the court that the church had expended more on the lawsuit than it had contributed to the university before the controversy had arisen. (Ibid., p. 181.)
20. Mims, p. 317.

continued: the students' commitments have been more closely shaped by their being Southern and relatively affluent than by any imperatives offered by the church. The biblical department became a school of religion. "In their terms, they would not emphasize ethics over theology and reflect a 'serious scientific spirit.' They would emphasize convergent paths to religious truth and grant equality to students of all denominations."[21] Kirkland lived to garner nearly forty million dollars from Vanderbilt, Carnegie, and Rockefeller sources. On the occasion of his fortieth anniversary in the chancellorship he would be hailed by the presidents of all the colleges of the Southern Methodist Church as the unquestioned leader of education in the South.[22] His successor was a Presbyterian.

Elements in the Alienation Process

To situate the Vanderbilt transformation and ascertain to what degree it might be taken as typical, one must appreciate that there have been several distinct waves of secularization in higher education. The first occurred in the eighteenth century in continental Europe: the universities were secularized formally by being nationalized politically, after which they were secularized intellectually by the Enlightenment. That first wave of secularization had no discernible effect on either the British universities or the few young colleges in America, however.

The next wave of secularization, the second in the West and the first in the New World, the transition to which Vanderbilt belongs, affected liberal Protestant institutions — first the new universities, then the colleges — in the four decades after the Civil War, roughly 1870 to 1910. This change "consisted of gradual modifications called for by professing Christians rather than any sharp discontinuity achieved by militant secularists."[23]

A third wave of secularization then followed, affecting both state universities and colleges, as well as those church-related schools which had deactivated their church allegiance during the previous wave. This

21. Conkin, p. 263.
22. Mims, p. 318.
23. This is precisely the account given of the secularization in British universities during the same period by David Bebbington, "The Secularization of British Universities since the Mid-Nineteenth Century" (unpublished manuscript, 1990).

change, which replicated what the Enlightenment had done to most continental universities in the eighteenth century, discredited religious belief and practice as alien to valid scholarship and insisted that religious belief be allowed no status in higher education except as private and extracurricular. To the men who had led their universities and colleges into a churchless Christianity during the prior period this would, of course, have been viewed as a catastrophe, but it was they who had stripped their institutions of defenses that might have immunized them against this *Kulturkampf* of the secularists.

A fourth wave of secularization has been underway since World War II, affecting mostly the Catholic universities and colleges, and it seems to be following a dynamic very similar to the second, postbellum, wave. Those institutions that appear not yet to have been drawn into the undertow are the traditional black colleges, the Bible colleges, and the "enclaves" to which Jencks and Riesman referred in their epigraph at the beginning of this essay.

The first and third waves, which were the work of non-believers with overt ideological hostility to Christian belief, are matter for another study. What we are after here is the handiwork of professed believers who intended their actions to enhance rather than annul the Christian culture of their institutions — a process possibly common to the estrangement of the academy from the liberal Protestant churches following the Civil War and from the Catholic Church following World War II.

Let us now examine the basic elements of the Vanderbilt experience in order to suggest parallels that may be found in the wider Protestant experience.

(1) There had been a period of stagnation in higher education, which came to be blamed upon a depressive influence by the churches. This was followed by a period of great intellectual turbulence, when fresh findings and methods and disciplines raised fearful philosophical challenges to theology. Spokesmen for the church's concerns, by a compound of incapacity and animosity, exacerbated the apparent hostility between the church and rigorous scholarship.

At Vanderbilt, the Methodists had very few highly trained intellectuals who could help the faithful perceive that authentic scholarship might be an appropriate though astringent medication for their religion. In addition, Bishop Hoss, who was one of the few to intuit the destination for which Chancellor Kirkland was bound, happened to be a strident, impassioned, and unattractive antagonist, who defined the issues in so anti-intellectual a way that he strengthened Kirkland's credibility among those who sought an institution of rigorous learning. As often happens, the church was served by officers to whom advanced learning was an unknown. Hoss was the very incarnation of that to which an ambitious company of scholars would not wish to be accountable.

Just after the Civil War, bright young American *literati* exposed to the new surge of scholarship at continental universities came home only to be dismayed by the lethargy and intellectual squalor of their former alma maters. The mediocrity they now noticed had afflicted American campuses since the turn of the century: seven decades of torpor. The ancient, endowed colleges seemed hardly more serious or alert than the scores of younger antebellum foundations.

When the innovative publications of Darwin, Marx, Comte, Renan, James, and others raised theories that few American professors could cope with, the instinctive response of college faculty and administrators was either to shun them or to denounce them. In doing so they failed to notice that it was not the findings of Darwin, Marx, and company that threatened to bring the intellectual integrity of the Christian establishment tumbling down. It was the philosophical conclusions the innovators had so swiftly assembled, not their empirical findings or their first constructs, that put the Christians' feet to the fire. And since the liberal Protestant establishment had been left philosophically impoverished by their ancestors, their response was simple disdain for the entire challenge: facts, findings, and philosophy. In the eyes of the hotshot cadet generation, the impotent professorate and the authoritarian presidents and trustees only made manifest that it must have been the church's domination that had deadened their colleges.

There was a general impatience expressed by forward-looking educators about the ineptitude of the collegiate system. Francis Wayland had given it voice in his *Report to the Corporation of Brown University,* which anticipated in 1850 most of what would happen in 1870-1910:

> We have now in the United States . . . one hundred and twenty colleges. . . . All of them teach Greek and Latin, but where are our classical students? All teach mathematics, but where are our mathematicians? [Quoting George Ticknor:] "Who, in this country, by the means offered him, has been enabled to make himself a good Greek scholar? Who has been taught thoroughly to read, write, and speak

Latin? Nay, who has been taught any thing at our colleges with the thoroughness which will enable him to go safely and directly to distinction . . . ?"[24]

Wayland and the other reformers saw the church as a principal source of the conservative resistance that they met in their efforts to open higher education to intellectually capable students. It was not so much that the churchmen were convinced that the classical curriculum was the best; they were no longer capable of even discussing the issue in the breadth that it deserved. While claiming to follow a traditionally learned vocation, they had in fact ceased to be truly learned men.

Andrew White — who would become the founding president of Cornell University, one of the first institutions explicitly nonsectarian from its foundation — had been soured by his one year at a small Episcopal college. Dissipation among the students and history forcibly put to the church's service were the memories he carried away with him on his way to find serious love of learning at Yale and Michigan.[25] His Cornell inaugural address in 1869 declared: "I deny that any university fully worthy of that great name can ever be founded upon the platform of any one sect or combination of sects. . . . We will labor to make this a Christian institution; a sectarian institution may it never be."[26] He recounted a string of horror stories of sincere scholars being thwarted on church-run campuses. "Any institution under denominational control inevitably tends to make allegiance to its own form of belief a leading qualification. It may become a tolerably good denominational college, like the hundreds already keeping down the standards of American education, but it can become nothing more."[27]

24. Francis Wayland, *Report to the Corporation of Brown University, On Changes in the System of Collegiate Education, Read March 28, 1850* (Providence: George Whitney, 1850), pp. 18-19.

25. Brill, pp. 45-51.

26. Andrew D. White, "Inaugural Address," *Cornell University: Account of the Proceedings of the Inauguration, October 7, 1868* (Ithaca: Cornell University Press, 1869), p. 7. For the last sentence, see Waterman Thomas Hewett, *Cornell University: A History* (Ithaca: University Publishing Society, 1905), 1:269.

27. Hewett, *The Cornell University: What It Is and What It Is Not* (Ithaca: Cornell University Press, 1872), p. 18; reprinted in Brill, p. 152. This was an abiding conviction of White, who concluded his two-volume autobiography with this observation:

Both Religion and Science have suffered fearfully from unlimited clerical sway; but of the two, Religion has suffered most. When one considers the outcome of

As president of a university that drew to itself all of New York's land-grant income besides a founder's ample endowment, White's dislike for the church colleges, intensified by their resentment of Cornell's wealth, drew him to appreciate the animosity Henry Tappan had experienced at Michigan:

> The worst difficulty by far which [Tappan] had to meet was the steady opposition of the small sectarian colleges scattered throughout the State. Each, in its own petty interest, dreaded the growth of any institution better than itself; each stirred the members of the legislature from its locality to oppose all aid to the State university; each, in its religious assemblages, its synods, conferences, and the like, sought to stir prejudice against the State institution as "godless."[28]

Daniel Coit Gilman, founding president of the Johns Hopkins University, the other new nonsectarian institution of higher learning, grieved over a government report that as of 1876 there were 545 degree-granting institutions in the country. "Most of these colleges are inadequately endowed, and consequently the instruction which many of them offer is of a very secondary character. A very large part of them represent some sectarian or denominational opinion; some of them have little more than a name, a charter and a bias."[29] Years later he could "see all over the land feeble, ill-endowed, and poorly manned institutions, caring a little for sound learning but a great deal more for the defense of denominational tenets."[30]

---

national education entirely under the control of the church during over fifteen hundred years, — in France at the outbreak of the revolution in 1789, in Italy at the outbreak of the revolution of 1848, in the Spanish-American republics down to a very recent period, and in Spain, Poland, and elsewhere at this very hour, — one sees how delusive is the hope that a return to the ideas and methods of the "ages of faith" is likely to cure the evils that still linger among us. The best way of aiding in a healthful evolution would seem to consist in firmly but decisively resisting all ecclesiastical efforts to control or thwart the legitimate work of science and education; in letting the light of modern research and thought into the religious atmosphere . . ." (*Autobiography of Andrew Dickson White* [New York: Century, 1905], 2:573).

28. White, *Autobiography*, 1:279.
29. Daniel C. Gilman, "Education in America, 1776-1876," *North American Review* 122 (Jan. 1876): 216.
30. Gilman, "Present Aspects of College Training," *North American Review* 136 (June 1883): 538.

Charles W. Eliot, who with White and Gilman comprised the triad of influential educators who led the secularization movement in the late nineteenth century, has already been heard from. At the Johns Hopkins inaugural he joined in the critique, though somewhat more defensively: "A university whose officers and students are divided among many sects need no more be irreverent and irreligious than the community which in respect to diversity of creeds it resembles. . . . This University will not demand of its officers and students the creed or press upon them the doctrine of any particular religious organization; but none the less — I should better say, all the more — it can exert through high-minded teachers a strong moral and religious influence."[31]

This negative perception of church influence in higher education found explicit enactment in the removal of church officers from governing boards. At Harvard nearly half the seats on the Board of Overseers had been filled by clergy; by 1894 those fifteen had been reduced to one. The last Congregational minister had departed the board ten years earlier. This was the accomplishment of Eliot, the president who finally freed Harvard from clerical governance. Yale's board had from the foundation been composed exclusively of Congregational clergy from Connecticut. In 1905 the first layman was elected, and by 1920 there were only four clergy left among the eleven on the board. This was the accomplishment of Arthur T. Hadley, Yale's first lay president. At Princeton, where Presbyterian clergy had dominated the board, their representation was reduced by two-thirds by the end of the period we are studying. This was largely the accomplishment of Woodrow Wilson, Princeton's first lay president. And so it was, as well, at Amherst and Dartmouth and the rest of the Protestant colleges and universities. Clergy emerged from that period occupying only one seat out of every ten on their governing boards.[32] James Kirkland, Vanderbilt's first lay chancellor, was acting quite within the mainstream of his peer institutions when he drew his board away from the bishops in 1910.

It should also be noted that this only followed upon a severe reduction of clerical presence and dominance on campus. George

31. Eliot, cited in Brill, p. 161.
32. Earl McGrath, "The Control of Higher Education in America," *Educational Record* 17 (April 1936): 262-64; Brill, pp. 156-58, 430-34; Richard Hofstadter and Walter P. Metzger, *The Development of Academic Freedom in the United States* (New York: Columbia University Press, 1955), p. 352. See Thorstein Veblen, *The Higher Learning* (New York: B. W. Huebsch, 1918), pp. 63-64.

Schmidt has reported that 262 of 288 college presidents at the time of the Civil War were clergy.[33] A survey of campuses of the time suggests that somewhat more than a third of the faculty were ministers. The proportion of graduates entering the ministry from places like Harvard, Yale, and Princeton (at Harvard it had stood at 70 percent in the earliest days), which as late as 1830 amounted to about one-third, had plummeted by 1876 to one in thirteen.[34]

It was the explicit belief and claim of each of these presidents — as it had been of White and Gilman at Cornell and Johns Hopkins, and as it would be of Kirkland at Vanderbilt — that the absence of ecclesiastical governance rendered their universities and colleges nondenominational *but Christian* — indeed, they were freed to be more authentically (and surely more wisely) Christian than before. It would, they believed, be all gain and no loss.

The estrangement of Vanderbilt from the church began with an oppressively uncomprehending atmosphere among church officers, and an administrator decisive and deft enough to remove them. In this respect Vanderbilt seems to embody an experience that is typical of the other mainline Protestant foundations.

(2) There was a president determined to raise the institution to a higher cubit of excellence, who saw the ecclesiastical establishment as a real or potential adversary to his project and rival to his power.

Bishop McTyeire was himself both an intellectual and a bishop, and in his unique position as both president of the Board of Trust and chief executive officer he possessed unchecked power. Neither his fellow bishops nor the board nor the faculty could stand in his way. Nor were they likely to wish to do so, since his administration occurred at a time

33. George P. Schmidt, *The Old Time College President* (New York: Columbia University Press, 1930), p. 184.

34. Hofstadter and Metzger, pp. 297, 350; Richard Hofstadter and C. DeWitt Hardy, *The Development and Scope of Higher Education in the United States* (New York: Columbia University Press, 1952), p. 6. Bebbington reports significant parallels: "In 1850 at Oxford all heads of house except one were in the Anglican ministry; virtually all tutors were clergymen; and about 80% of undergraduates were intending to pursue a clerical career. . . . Of Oxford dons in residence between 1813 and 1830, 53% had a future career exclusively in the church and only 13% had one in a university; of those in residence between 1881 and 1900, 13% had a church career ahead of them and 57% a university career." Before the restriction was removed in 1877, most college fellowships were restricted to celibate Anglican clergy. By 1900 the 213 lay fellows outnumbered the 68 clerical fellows. (See Bebbington, pp. 1, 9.)

when the new university's initial affluence was large enough and the university-model still modest enough for the energies of growth to be well absorbed.

But President McTyeire held office at a time when Harvard, Johns Hopkins, Yale, Michigan, Brown, Princeton, and the other colleges that had just entered upon the ambition to become universities, were presenting a model which the Southern Methodist Church had no ambition to pursue, no resources to finance, and probably no readiness to permit. Kirkland, McTyeire's successor, took office with the conviction that Vanderbilt was called to follow the lead of those reforming universities. To do so would mean wresting the institution and all its constituencies out of their traditional norms and expectations, and this meant an exceptionally effective and decisive chief executive.

It was exactly in these years, the end of the nineteenth century and the beginning of the twentieth, that colleges such as those mentioned above made the break with their past and were transformed into universities, whereas others like Wesleyan, Union, Haverford, Randolph-Macon, and Kenyon, whose constituencies remained too regional, did not. A chief difference was that the former, unlike the latter, were led by chief executives of exceptionally sturdy ego who, in their campaigns to consolidate enough power to make a radical break with their collegiate past, used that power as well to sever any capacity of the church to obstruct their personal sovereignty.

What catalyzed the circumstances at Vanderbilt was the leading presence of a resourceful and ambitious administrator who saw clearly that the church was a hindrance, not a help, in the pursuit of all the academic goals he set before himself. To gain the university's freedom from the churchmen he forwent clarity in his public utterance in order to conceal as long as possible from his traditional constituency the full outcome of what he was doing. Inevitably the moment of crisis arrived when ambiguity could no longer blur the issue. Because of the inability of intellectually feeble church officials to engage him dialectically, the confrontation became a matter of sheer control. When Kirkland won, one might say that it was not the university that gained power but the chancellor himself, since in order to achieve his transformative program he had had to manage his own governing board to the point where they could present no real threat to his personal authority.

The Methodist bishops, as a group, were not really averse to the devout Methodist layman, Kirkland. Nor were their understated concerns to preserve the Methodist identity of the university designed to undermine his authority. It was their reserve power, usable in a last resort, that Kirkland saw as the only threat that could bring disaster upon his campaign to make Vanderbilt an institution of the highest rank.

The irony in all this, of course, was that the "full outcome" went quite beyond Kirkland's anticipation, affecting not merely the governance of the institution but its very character. His intention was that it be laicized, but it was secularized as well. His intention was that it no longer be sectarian, but the result was that it was no longer Christian or even religious.

Charles Eliot saw that the new universities were no longer educating only the clergy or the other traditionally learned professions, but the bankers, industrialists, engineers, statesmen, and scientists as well. For that new kind of education a new kind of leader was needed. It was not that the older presidents lacked great or even autocratic authority; it was that the present task was so formidable: the institutions had to be made over entirely and had to be made answerable to new constituencies. Stronger men were required, he wrote in the very year he assumed Harvard's presidency.

> The American colleges have taken, and still take, their presidents from the clerical profession almost exclusively. . . . It is gradually becoming apparent that even the colleges are suffering from this too clerical administration. Fortunately for the country, education is getting to be a profession by itself. For the discharge of the highest functions in this profession, the training of a divinity student, years of weekly preaching, and much practice in the discharge of pastoral duties, are no longer supposed to be the best, or at least the only preparation. Several other classes of men are now as cultivated as the clergy. As a class, ministers are as fit to be suddenly transferred to the bench at forty-five or fifty years of age, as they are to be put at the head of large educational establishments.[35]

Eliot somewhat overstates his case in omitting mention of numerous clerical executives who had come up through the academic ranks as scholars and teachers. What he meant in his put-down of parson-presidents was that the churches were not providing leadership for the

35. Eliot, "The New Education," *Atlantic Monthly* 23 (March 1869): 366.

new universities any more than they were providing financial subsidy. Instead, circumstance raised up a generation of exceptionally sturdy chief executives, each of whom led his institution away from the possible interference of a founding church: Wayland at Brown, Eliot at Harvard, Hadley at Yale, Wilson at Princeton, William Jewett Tucker at Dartmouth, Hyde at Bowdoin, William Rainey Harper at Chicago, G. Stanley Hall at Clark, David Starr Jordan at Stanford,[36] A. P. Barnard at Columbia, and James Kirkland at Vanderbilt.[37]

(3) The estrangement from the sponsoring church occurred at a time when the funding it may have provided was clearly inadequate for the new academic ambitions of the university and when new, secular sources were offering an infusion of funds.

The Vanderbilt crisis came at a time when the advancement of the university required massive financial help — help that the church was unable or unwilling to provide, but that was available elsewhere . . . on certain conditions. The Carnegie Foundation's program to fund professorial pension funds was, as we have seen, available only to institutions that were nondenominational. Only fifty-one institutions seemed, at first, to qualify. The Foundation then specified, however, that a college that was merely "in sympathy" with a church would not be excluded. There was an immediate wave of schools that renounced their denominational allegiance in favor of "sympathy" in order to qualify for the grants: colleges such as Dickinson, Goucher, and Bowdoin.

In many places, church control was an incubus which the college was attempting to throw off, or which it endured merely because the charter made remedial action difficult. In few institutions was it reck-

---

36. Leland Stanford, the founder, had stipulated that the campus church "is to be used regularly for the benefit of students. No creed or dogma will be permitted to be taught within its walls, but ministers of all denominations will be invited to deliver lectures on the fundamental principles of religion." In the Founding Grant of the university the trustees were charged "to prohibit sectarian instruction, but to have taught in the University the immortality of the soul, the existence of an all-wise and benevolent Creator, and that obedience to his laws is the highest duty of man." "To [the widowed] Mrs. Stanford the Church stood for high-mindedness, and for what are known as the Christian virtues, and it was as the teacher of these virtues that she wanted to pass it and its influence on to the members of this community living and yet to live." (Orrin Leslie Elliott, *Stanford University: The First Twenty-Five Years* [Stanford: Stanford University Press, 1937], p. 137.)

37. By way of contrast with these men, see Schmidt, *Old Time College President.* On Wayland, Eliot, Hadley, Wilson, Tucker, and Hyde, see Brill.

oned a positive, necessary good. When the Carnegie Foundation inquired as to "whether denominational connection or control ministers to the religious or intellectual life," the respondents in the denominational colleges declared "almost without exception that such connections played little, if any, part in the religious or intellectual life of the student body."[38]

The churches would almost surely have sustained their governance and influence over the universities and colleges if they had provided financial support for their schools, either as direct grants from the churches or as gifts from affluent church members. The churches, however, were mostly meager funders of their schools; what they gave amounted to only a token part of the budget that each college had to balance annually.

(4) There was a transfer of primary loyalty from the church to the "academic guild," especially on the part of the faculty.

Vanderbilt was founded at the very time that the German universities had introduced the doctorate as the appropriate preliminary for a more serious academic career. Yale, Michigan, and Cornell were often specifically mentioned as models to be followed, away from the liberal arts colleges and their more casual attitudes towards scholarship. Leading faculty were understood to be closely acquainted with their best peers at leading universities, and recruitment looked only to those research institutions. This quickly brought the Vanderbilt community to the point where it could criticize the church from the standpoint of the academy, yet it lacked any inclination to criticize the academy from the standpoint of the church. This proved to be a point of no return.

The shift from a clerical to a lay president, from a church executive to an academic, also drew Vanderbilt to appreciate the one professional guild more than the other. And in a season when churchmen were looking askance at the university for its libertine secularism, and intellectuals were looking askance at it from the opposite direction for its narrow sectarianism, Vanderbilt academics were at pains to deny both charges, but with this difference: while they denied both the norms and the accusation of their ecclesiastical critics, they embraced the norms and denied the accusation of their unbelieving critics. At a time when their colleagues who spoke for the church were conspicuously incapable

38. Hofstadter and Metzger, p. 362.

of giving the faith a good account in the eyes of the learned, the Vanderbilt academics preferred to dissociate themselves from their religious leaders rather than take up their cause as allies and persuade them that sound scholarship was God's good servant too. As a result, the university people had unwittingly transferred their primary sympathy and professional loyalty to the cultured despisers of their own church.

The Anglo-American model, set by the earliest foundations — Harvard, William and Mary, Yale, etc. — had been a college primarily for the education of future clergy. One of the motives for establishing new colleges was distrust between the churches, or between parties within the same church. Yet there was little that was specifically church- or faith-specific in those colleges. Academically, the colleges offered mostly Latin, Greek, and mathematics. The collegiate curriculum offered no theological courses; future ministers acquired that later, in apprenticeship to an older divine or in a divinity school. For undergraduates there was just the obligatory set of lectures on moral philosophy, often given by the president himself, typically to seniors. There was no pastoral system to speak of, save for obligatory chapel.

If the colleges were Christian it was due not to their program but to their immersion in the conventional piety of the surrounding church. The church was not so much *in* as it was *round about* a college. The Christian character of the early American Protestant colleges was nothing very reflective. It might never have been publicly asserted with much animus were it not for the invariable resistance of students to compulsory worship and punitive discipline, both of which had recurring need of justification by appeal to the godly character of the college.

The colleges were not only *for* the future clergy but were conducted *by* the clergy. Schoolteachers in colonial America and for years afterward were typically parsons in need of another sort of income. Indeed, until the 1890s the teaching faculties of the state universities continued to include sizeable proportions of clergy. But in a society perceived to be amiable to the Protestant conventions, there was little evangelical zeal or countercultural determination in these colleges. They were ecclesiastical because they were clerical, and they were clerical because learning at this level was traditional for scholar-parsons. They did not assert the church's faith; they presumed it.

It is ironic that the age when the colleges threw off the churches was really the first time, had they wished it so, when the churches could have sponsored an educational endeavor that might have been both intellectually and religiously vital, intentional, and integrative. This was a time when theology was beginning to mature to the point where it might have been strong enough to provide the unity and spunk in an institution of strenuous and innovative scholars. It was for want of any rigorously intellectual churchmen that the clergy were, both in their minds and in those of the reformers, content to be identified with the furtherance of mediocrity.

Those who might have spoken for the church — and many who did speak out — had the misfortune to range themselves in opposition to the movement to liberate the curriculum from "dead" languages and inapplicable mathematics, a reform led by men such as Francis Wayland of Brown, Charles Eliot of Harvard, and James McCosh of Princeton.[39] As Freeman Butts observed: "where the conception of a liberal education was firmly grounded upon religious and intellectual authority and discipline, the prescribed curriculum was more likely to be maintained longer against the inroads of the elective system with its attendant doctrines of freedom and flexibility."[40] Thus the interests of the church were identified with opposition to an enlarged curriculum, and were defended by men who appeared as nay-sayers to all that smacked of imagination in higher education.

American public culture was beginning to show itself skeptical and even covertly contemptuous toward Christian belief. The church officers were not learned or prophetic enough to read these signs of the times and had no imaginative sense or desire to be generous and eager patrons of a more purposeful (and costly) establishment. When the colleges and universities might — for the first time in America — have been purposively and competently engaged in formulating a higher culture within the churches, the churches lacked the competence and the determination to have it so.

All this came to a crisis in the years immediately preceding Vanderbilt's renunciation of church governance. The governance that the angry General Conference wanted to have — and sued to retain — would not have done the church any good in the days to follow, for it had narrowed its view of what it meant to be Methodist to things like a religious test

39. Although McCosh publicly debated Eliot on this very point and took the conservative side, their basic outlook was fairly much the same. (See Brill, pp. 252ff.)
40. R. Freeman Butts, *The College Charts Its Course* (New York: McGraw-Hill, 1939), p. 223.

for all faculty and disciplinary control over students. Without any larger vision of Christian education, this program was unrelievedly negative, and it assured the educational reformers that the church had no stomach for ambitious scholarship.

(5) Erosion of the will to consider active communion in the church as a requisite or even a qualification for admission to its several constituencies — governance, administration, faculty, and student body — extinguished the university's ability to consider itself a unit of the church.

The fact that without the biblical department Vanderbilt's student body included only a minority of Methodists could be construed in either of two contrary ways: either the university had failed to attract its native constituency, or it had been so academically successful that others were crowding in. Under either interpretation, an educational institution that enrolls less than half its students from within its sponsoring church begins to be an external activity of that church.

In the matter of faculty appointments, the critical issue was not simply the dwindling proportion of Methodists (and their fractional presence in the professional schools), but the growing conviction that it was impertinent even to consider someone's membership in a community of faith to be a professional credential qualification pertinent for a faculty position at Vanderbilt.

The fact that leadership positions (deanships) had been filled more rapidly than faculty positions by non-Methodists made it all the less likely that religious identity could be effectively favored in faculty recruitment.

Paradoxically, Methodist presence was strongest on the Board of Trust, yet this body had been so co-opted by the chancellor that they acquiesced in his view that overt deference to the church in any effective way would be adverse to Vanderbilt's academic ambitions. Thus, by unnoticed but inexorable depletion, Vanderbilt lost the ability to affirm in the first person plural that it was Methodist. The inertial force of custom prolonged the existence of religious observances: required chapel, behavioral discipline by church standards, pastoral activities such as YMCA centers. But the formal rupture with the church, in the belief that there could be a Christian house of learning bound by no communion to an actual church, made these activities inappropriate, and after a generation of increasingly awkward continuance they had to be eliminated.

This entire process illustrates well how formal, structural principles are followed, sometimes with considerable delay, by the actual social changes that they prescribe. For example, the charters of schools like Union, Columbia, Cornell, Princeton, Brown, and Michigan all provided that no religious test could be used in appointments. Yet for years there were religion-based norms that clearly limited what faculty could profess or how they could behave — including, in some instances, to what church they could belong — that excluded candidates from appointment at these institutions. Only later, when self-conscious identity shifted and the official rule was appealed to in dispute, did practice actually conform to the formal principle. Likewise, the structural disengagement of the universities from their churches preceded by at least a generation the functional sequestration of religion on campus to individual and private status.

It seems not to have been noted how powerful a change it was for the person presiding over the college or university no longer to be able (or, before long, willing) to preside over the educational community in prayer or worship. What Eliot called a "friendly but neutral" attitude toward religion simply did not have the stability he and his contemporaries imagined. Laicization need not entail secularization, but in this case they were inevitably linked.

(6) There was a progressive devolution of church-identifiers: from Methodist to generically Christian, then to generically religious, and finally to flatly secular.

Kirkland never considered that any formal bond between the university and the church was required to make Vanderbilt an effectively Christian university. In fact, it seems to have been his hope that by drawing back from the bishops' reach Vanderbilt could retain what was best in Methodism while protecting itself from the worst — which for higher education meant the streak of anti-intellectualism in the clergy. Kirkland eventually succeeded in renegotiating the church-campus relationship exactly as he wished, and he did not understand that he had destabilized it, that the formal break with the church began a process of alienation that would inevitably run its course to total secularization.

Kirkland's effort to finesse his program led to a purposeful blurring of nomenclature. At first he simply spoke of the university as "Methodist"; then he began to speak of the church's "ownership" of the school; soon he was using terms such as "sponsorship," "patronage," "support," and "affiliation," and finally merely "relationship." In an atmosphere where an effective bond to the Methodist church instinctively evoked references to bigotry, exclusion, narrowness, sectarianism, and selfishness, there was an effort to describe the relation to the church as inefficaciously as possible.

During the period when a college simply functioned as a gathering of the church, with its foibles and deficiencies as well as its advantages and virtues, its Christian identity seemed not to require affirmation or reflection. The church held quiet title. Only later, when many colleges, unmoored from their sponsoring communities of faith, began to drift out into ever swifter currents of learned disdain for faith, did school officers begin to assert volubly as never before that the schools were indeed Christian. They reached out for a vocabulary that was indistinct enough not to make them accountable to anyone, but with a familiar enough ring of piety to be reassuring. But the evidence shows beyond a doubt that such collegial Christianity as had existed began to lose vitality once there was no church link.

Then, when the severance was complete, the educators had no difficulty in interpreting their institutions' relation to the churches as no more than historical. We have already noted Eliot saying this at Harvard. The Princeton newspaper, on the occasion of the election of Woodrow Wilson as its first lay president, had claimed: "Princeton is and always will be religious." Wilson, a minister's son who led prayers as soon as he took office, promptly made it clear that Princeton was not religious by dint of any continuing bond with a church: "Princeton . . . is a Presbyterian college only because the Presbyterians of New Jersey were wise and progressive enough to found it."[41]

(7) In its anxiety to appeal to one constituency (the state, or the intellectual elite, or noncommunicant students, faculty, or donors) while at the same time not antagonizing another constituency (the church and its communicants on campus), the academy replaced its religious identity with reductionist equivalents.

The years of Vanderbilt's youth were a time when most Protestants had lost conviction about the particularities of their churches. Whatever had been the historical or doctrinal issues that had splintered the children of the Reformation and of Pietism into so many tribes and clans, those defining distinctions had a faint grip on the minds of bright

41. *Princeton Alumni Weekly* 2, 36 (14 June 1902): 628; *New York Tribune*, 2 Dec. 1902, p. 4.

Christians in postbellum America. The absence of an established church and of the antagonisms it would inevitably have aroused, plus the dominant nationalism that for many Americans was a sacred allegiance that exacted a loyalty higher than their churches could — together these influences made the specific differences between the Protestant churches seem to liberals not only insignificant but indecent. What is more, the post-Enlightenment knack of reducing Christianity itself to vague, generic qualities hardly distinguishable from gentle manners or sound citizenship yielded a foundational notion of Christianity — an "essence," it was often called — so insubstantial that it could hardly sustain any specificities or provoke any controversy at all. In the early Vanderbilt period all of this combined to leave a bright and ambitious scholar of liberal Protestant inclination wholly unaware of any particular advantage his church might offer to his college or university. At Vanderbilt, as elsewhere, *sectarianism* and *denominationalism* were invariably negative terms, suggestive of exclusive access, censorship, and obstructive ecclesiastical overlords.

During his struggle for independence Kirkland wrote: "I have never denied our Methodist allegiance, I have never denied our Methodist history, but I have maintained that, greater than Methodism was the cause of Christ and that the call for service in His name was greater than the call to the service of the Church."[42] The Board of Trust, in affirming him in the struggle, gave some sense of what "service in His name" would mean: "our chief concern is to promote the highest type of Christian scholarship and Christian character."[43] Nowhere in Kirkland's writings can we find that he acknowledged any intrinsic benefit for the mind in Methodism. And when he moved from this "sectarian" concern to regard Christianity transcendent, here too there is no exploration of the faith that would suggest that it was illuminative of the mind. Thus he was reduced to seeing Christianity as indistinguishable from the repertoire of cultivated America.

At Vanderbilt the constituencies found many reasons for reassurance that the university was persisting in its primal Christian commitment: high standards in academics, or a liberal or broad or thorough curriculum, or freedom from dogmatism, or the cultivation of moral character, or social conscience regarding racial integration and the relief

42. Mims, p. 297.
43. Ibid., p. 299.

159

of poverty, or decorum and discipline in fraternities and at football games.

The most appealing and frequent surrogate for religious faith was moral: the university would persist in its dedication to the cultivation of moral character. This was expressed in various ways. Hadley of Yale: "It is, I think, the distinguishing characteristic of a gentleman that he accepts self-imposed obligations . . . it is this that constitutes the fundamental character of a Christian."[44] Tucker of Dartmouth: Religion would culti-vate in the educator right-mindedness (clear thinking undistorted by prejudice, avarice, or vanity) and service (the capacity to give moral inspiration to students, especially those in the "distinctly commercial callings").[45] Compulsory chapel service, explained Yale chaplain Anson Phelps Stokes, is "a factor of social importance in making the college feel its unity by bringing together all its students daily, and of moral impor-tance in requiring that men must be up and dressed at an early hour, a serious deterrent to dissipation."[46] Wilson defended the chapel require-ment at Princeton, explaining that "it has been regarded of the essential tradition of the place to give this flavour to the day's appointments."[47]

Of course, this account of moral character saw it as a substitute for, rather than an outcome of, Christian faith and community. What is more, it did not relate moral character to the mind at all. Christianity

---

44. Arthur Twining Hadley, "The Christian Standard of Honor," *Baccalaureate Addresses* (New Haven: Yale University Press, 1907), pp. 24-25.

45. William J. Tucker, "The Religion of the Educator," *Personal Power: Counsels to College Men* (Boston: Houghton Mifflin, 1910), pp. 270-78. Tucker offers a typically indistinct account of what religion might mean:

> You naturally go farther and ask me for the content of the religious faith of an educator. I suppose that you do not mean to ask what are his theological holdings, for we do not express ourselves today in theological as much as in religious terms. This fact means that we have changed the emphasis from the content of faith to the tone of faith. The question in the popular mind in regard to any man in whom it is interested religiously is not, so much as formerly, what he believes, but much more than formerly, how he believes. Formerly the dis-tinction was, Is a man orthodox or heterodox? To-day the distinction is, — Is a man an optimist or a pessimist? (pp. 279-80)

46. Anson Phelps Stokes, "The Present Condition of Religious Life at Yale," in James B. Reynolds et al., *Two Centuries of Christian Activity at Yale* (New York: Putnam, 1901), p. 119.

47. Ray Stannard Baker, *Woodrow Wilson: Life and Letters,* vol. 2: *Princeton, 1890-1910* (Garden City: Doubleday, Page, 1927), p. 152.

was thus doomed to be extracurricular. Brill observes: "The major defect in the religious life at both Yale and Princeton was its lack of integration into the academic life itself. Religion was regarded as a kind of diffuse atmosphere. It was seldom subjected to rigorous analysis or evaluation."[48] It could not be otherwise, for generic Christianity must always be a diffuse atmosphere. The moral equivalencies that were imagined to be its goals and evidences functioned, in fact, as secular surrogates for sacred convictions and commitments.

(8) Theological studies and church ministry were set apart from the academic center, a strategy which they took to be an enhancement of their autonomy, but which in fact functioned as a banishment into marginality.

Kirkland strove to extract financial support from the Southern Methodist Church for the one element at Vanderbilt in which it could be supposed to have a direct interest, the biblical department. When that failed, the department was both an academic liability (as the least scholarly unit in the university) and a financial one (as unlikely to attract endowment from any other source, and a possible obstacle to the university's ability to receive funds from the state and certain foundations). The dean and faculty welcomed their redesignation as a nondenominational School of Religion, which then exposed them to almost total isolation when the church withdrew recognition of its right to prepare ordinands.

It might seem that in this respect Vanderbilt was atypical.[49] For

48. Brill, p. 464.
49. Hofstadter explains how, prior to this, freestanding divinity schools had been dissociated from the colleges:

> The colleges had never been theological seminaries, and theological training was a postgraduate affair conducted in a haphazard way and on an individual basis. By 1800 church leaders saw that a more precise vocational training was necessary in order to battle with deism and to win success in the renewed competition among the denominations. Finally, church control of the older colleges was too loose to satisfy the militant clergy, who wanted schools fully responsive to sectarian needs. A tendency to take the training of ministers out of the colleges began with the founding of three theological schools in the last two decades of the eighteenth century, and became very widespread in the first three decades of the nineteenth. Although the emergence of these schools, with their own specialized curricula, marked for many denominations an advance in the professional training of the ministry, they helped somewhat to free the ordinary college of those religious considerations that stemmed from the necessity of rearing clergymen, and then paradoxically established another minor landmark in the secularization of higher education. (Hofstadter and Hardy, pp. 8-9)

just as Vanderbilt was becoming secularized, some new universities and some colleges were looking to establish or reinforce their "religion" departments with newly serious biblical studies. These departments were generally acceptable to the other arts and sciences departments because they fostered studies that were philological, historical, and comparative and had dropped the older confessional courses that were expositions of or exhortations to the Christian faith. And in several institutions freestanding divinity schools were absorbed into the university.

Thus there were two distinct styles of religious instruction on the campuses: (a) disinterested, non-normative studies, conducted in a regular academic department, and (b) ministerial studies based on an assumption of shared commitment, conducted in marginal divinity schools. Yet despite minor structural differences at Vanderbilt and elsewhere there was an inflexible understanding at work: that a rigorous academy would not harbor learned discourse about religion in its central precincts unless conducted with the systematic detachment of nonbelievers. This was but a logical application of the principle of secularization itself, which wished neither to sponsor nor to countenance any overlap of the community of academic inquiry with the community of credal conviction. The divinity schools typically served as reservations or compounds where overt dealings with faith could be sequestered.

(9) Active Christians, not hostile secularists, have been most effective in alienating the colleges and universities from their communities of faith.

The transformation typically occurred in three stages. The first change, enacted by Christians without any intention of extinguishing or even compromising the Christian character of the college or university, consisted in muting all overt claims of the academic institution to be functioning as a limb of a particular church. Statements, decisions, and symbols that had been public, explicit, and unapologetic became private, silent, and bashful.

The period that followed, initiated by well-meaning and believing administrators of the first generation, was a time of high morale, because academic standards and aspirations were on the rise, funding and prestige were up, and the residual religious atmosphere was durable enough (and even somewhat more sophisticated) to reassure the reformers that the intellectual gain had been without religious loss. Faith was mute but present.

It was only later — usually about a generation later — that a new cadre of intellectuals, whose obedience was to a rational empiricism

162

with no hint of bashfulness in the exercise of its articles of faith, transformed an institution whose original identity could no longer be confessed or asserted into a secularized academy. This was the third stage. It is worthy of note that public faith, unlike an agnostic exclusion of faith, cannot survive without public profession.[50]

The reformers had unwittingly deprived their institutions of any capacity to retain their Christian identity when exposed to a secularist faculty in the third generation. Ambitious but improvident leaders had suppressed their schools' Christian immune systems, and since the virus of secularization would not seek out these now-defenseless institutions until the professional personnel could be replaced by scholars predominantly of no faith or a hostile faith or an intimidated faith, the reformers had no way of understanding how much farther their actions would carry beyond what they intended.

A Prognosis

If the Vanderbilt transition from Methodist to neuter exhibits a typical pattern of academic secularization, what we will find at the root of these events is a sponsoring church that was nonchalant about its burden: one that wished to be the patron of a college or university without being its benefactor. Usually the officers of the church included few persons who had benefited from advanced studies or were intellectuals. Deprived of native sympathy for academics and of a sense of ease in dealing with them — indeed, inclined to view them with misgiving — these ecclesiastics did not by instinct use their office to address themselves to their institutions as articulate exponents of their faith, nor as pastors, nor as prophets. They fell back upon the only role remaining: that of governors.

---

50. Robert H. Knapp and H. B. Goodrich noticed some time ago a three-phase process of secularization in the liberal Protestant colleges. During the primal period religious expression was naive and censorious, resources were limited, and intellectual disciplines undeveloped. In the second period there was a decline in religious observance and moral severity, a revision of curriculum favoring newly specialized disciplines, and a heightened interest in affluence exhibited by both educators and students: the former for new resources and the latter for more remunerative careers. This was a period of keen morale. In the third period the institution is wealthy and cosmopolitan, and religious discourse and expression is extinct. See Knapp and Goodrich, *Origins of American Scientists* (Chicago: University of Chicago Press; London: Cambridge University Press, 1952), pp. 272-84.

Facing these sponsors was usually an institution with the possibility and the determination to become more rigorous in its standards and more ambitious in its financial requirements. Because it lacked a sure sense of authentic advantage in being the undertaking of a community of faith, it tended to look uncritically to the best-financed institutions as its models, and these were invariably secular or secularized.

The alienation usually required, as well, an academic administrator whose determination to transfigure the institution and whose ego (if these are not synonymous) inclined him to neutralize all potential rivals to his leadership. Typically the board of trustees was reconfigured to follow administrative leadership without question or hindrance, the faculty was tamed with increased emoluments and funds for scholarship, and the donors and public were won over by a rhetoric of assurance. The only threat remaining resided within the church. Because the church membership, by and large, was not so impressed by higher education that they were surely ready to subsidize or even tolerate the school if it became too outspoken and critical, and because its officers sensed no competence in themselves to interact with academics save from a position of control, the administrator sensed rightly that these churchmen held the latent power to bring down everything he was striving to build up. They became, in a word, not worth the risk.

In the Vanderbilt story, the relationship between church and university during its first three decades of existence was commonly described as one of mutual goodwill and trust. The initiatives were meant to come from within the academy and the bishops were expected to use their veto power only as a last resort. This was exactly the position that Chancellor James Kirkland and his allies had publicly espoused all along. But events were pushed toward rupture — not really over matters of last resort, but because of an early and in a sense very premature outbreak of distrust. In other cases, where there was no outright or legal alienation, the impulse toward severance has likewise arisen to defend the college or university, not from an actually oppressive or seriously intrusive church, but from a church that could just possibly become so.

Whatever the drive for power on the part of the institution and its academic leadership, the desire to be free of the church was usually motivated by the belief that the Christian context and spiritual nourishment they regarded as a blessing could and would be continued after the removal of any authoritative link with the church. The widely shared church membership and piety of the campus population led them to suppose that faith has an inertial force that would carry them along after their relationship to the church became informal and inexplicit rather than legal. Or to put it another way, those who negotiated the withdrawal imagined the campus (or the culture) as a sort of auto-cephalous church.

The drawback in this is that precisely at the time they asserted their readiness to remove themselves from church oversight and still remain a community of faith, they proved unwilling to undertake any of the essential tasks a community of faith must perform in order to thrive or survive: the defining of authentic faith in seasons of dispute; the main-tenance of moral discipline on standards grounded in faith; the invitation to communion and its withdrawal; and concern for the entire personal welfare of its members, beyond professional performance. The secu-larized institutions could never make good on their claim. They asserted their independence while intending to preserve the Christian character of their community, but in fact they were forfeiting the principled nerve to function independently as a Christian community.

It should also be noted that although the liberal Protestant institu-tions were essentially secularized by about 1910, the capacity of religious identity to linger in confused and ambiguous observance and symbol allows strange and sometimes awkward outcroppings of "religion as heri-tage." Perhaps a few contemporary illustrations of this are permissible.

Ten years ago one originally Protestant university made the fol-lowing announcement:

> Those attending today's Opening Exercises in the University Chapel will notice several subtle but significant changes in the traditional ceremony marking the start of the academic year. Perhaps most ob-vious, the time of the program has moved from 11:00 a.m. to 2:00 p.m., so as not to conflict with the chapel's regular religious service.
>
> The substance of the program has also been modified to make it less ostensibly "religious" in a denominational sense while retaining its underlying spirituality. For example, such traditional parts of a religious service as doxology, Lord's Prayer, benediction, and offering have been eliminated. At the same time, the nondenominational prayer and responsive reading have been retained, and the musical program has been enhanced with inclusion of the University Glee Club and an instrumental ensemble in addition to the chapel choir. The changes, according to the associate university secretary, are con-sistent with the recent trustee report analyzing the role of the chapel

165

and of the dean of the chapel. In planning this year's opening exercises we have tried to emphasize the spiritual and intellectual diversity of A—— University. We think we have developed an imaginative program that embodies the important spiritual traditions of A——while recognizing its diversity.

An alumnus of another distinguished former Protestant institution wrote a letter recently to the alumni magazine:

> It appears from the photograph of V—— Chapel . . . that the chapel "restoration" has stripped the chancel of its specificity of religious symbolism. When I was first a student at the University, the Chapel represented a vision of Christian ecumenism. The Gothic architecture and the via media Protestant liturgy, the cross and altar beneath the reredos, expressed a generalized, yet specific, religious and cultural heritage, that of a reformed Western Christendom. Later, the liturgical movement of the Roman Catholic Church spilled over into the ecumenical Christian scene and the altar of V—— Chapel was reoriented. The most recent alteration no doubt represents an adjustment to a cultural setting that is on the one hand more religiously pluralistic and on the other more pervasively secularistic. . . .
>
> A worthy vision, symbolized by the V—— Chapel chancel of a past generation, has departed. I do not think it can, or should, be restored, nor even lamented. We require a new and wider ecumenism in religion and a new and wider humanism in education. I cherish a time when every University of B—— alumnus will have contemplated not only Greek philosophy and the Bible, but also the Gita and the Buddhist Sutras and the manifold issues of the hour. Secular, pluralistic civilization makes a fine setting for the spiritual search of serious-minded individuals in intellectual community.

At yet another formerly Protestant campus the recent appointment of a new dean of the chapel led one faculty member to write to another:

> Today word was received that
> a Jewish president
> has replaced an Episcopalian priest
> with a Congregationalist minister
> educated as a Nazarene,
> ordained in the United Church of Christ,
> married, this time, to a Unitarian-Universalist minister,

166

and "persuaded that the ultimate religious vision must be
    characterized by universality,"
to preside over Presbyterian worship at C———.
It was, truly, an opportunity missed.

By way of suggestive contrast, compare ambiguity problems of an
entirely different sort in the following:

> At D——— University, which negotiates the stressful task of being
> officially a secular university but unofficially Jewish, with a student
> body that is two-thirds Jewish, the equivocations run in the opposite
> direction. The calendar includes four unspecified holidays without
> admitting that they are the Jewish High Holy Days. Fearful that the
> university was appearing "parochial," the president attempted to
> make Asian students more comfortable by introducing "international
> cuisine," causing what the campus rabbi calls "the pig issue." While
> the rabbi thought the college might be growing shy about "its Jewish
> soul" a trustee explained they were "trying to be more hospitably
> open," and a professor of Jewish history and social ethics explained
> what Jewish concerns were: recognition of the value of learning and
> of ethics in scholarship and other areas of life, "challenges to the status
> quo issues," and concern for the elderly, sick, and needy through the
> school of social work.

On the main mall of a university that still claims ties to its founding
church, within sight of the campus chapel and almost within the ambit
of the founder's bronze statue, one may read on a handsome plaque the
words that expressed his founding vision and the university's mandate:

> The aims of E——— University are to assert a faith in the eternal union
> of knowledge and religion *set forth in the teachings and character of
> Jesus Christ, the Son of God;* to advance learning in all lines of truth;
> to defend scholarship against all false notions and ideals; to develop
> a Christian love of freedom and truth; to promote a sincere spirit of
> tolerance; to discourage all partisan and sectarian strife; and to render
> the largest permanent service to the individual, the state, the nation,
> and the church. Unto these ends shall the affairs of this university
> always be administered.

Perhaps not always. At the recent presidential inauguration, the chairman of the board of trustees read out this commitment — omitting,

however, the words italicized above. Tolerance is clearly putting an end to partisan strife.

Evangelical Protestant institutions partook to a much lesser degree in both the academic enhancement and the secularization of their mainstream cousins during the period between the Civil War and World War I. Some of them today (and they are mostly colleges, not universities) have succeeded, though at a more deliberate pace, in their ambition to maintain a Christian character while upgrading their scholarly performance. Indeed, some of the most impressive small colleges in the nation are in this group. Yet some evangelical institutions are now growing wary of what they consider the aggressively anti-intellectual leadership of their denominations and are moving to dissociate themselves from church-controlled governance.

On the campus of F—— University, where most trustees had always been selected collaboratively by the board and church representatives, the board withdrew itself from church involvement because it feared an imposition of fundamentalist tenets. The president explained that "We remain a Christian university with a W—— relationship. We have just redefined that relationship in a mutually supportive way." Those with a sense of history might wonder, however, whether a "relationship" of this sort might labor under some of the same ambivalences as "relationships" between some of the campus freshmen.

A college founded by another church has in the latter years of its nearly 170 years of existence redefined itself as "nondenominational." Chapel attendance has not been an integral part of campus life since the early sixties, but apparently prayers have continued at certain campus ceremonies. Faculty resistance has lately broken out since, as one professor put it, "prayer has become a symbol of division and exclusion for those who feel, some for secular and others for reasons of religious integrity, that prayer imposes a set of beliefs on them which they do not share and which are irrelevant to the academic mission of this college." The trustees responded by appointing a Committee on Religious Presence at G——, but the tenor of campus comment suggests that the dissociation from the church had signalled the end of religious presence anywhere but in the chapel.

Thus the initiative of Eliot, Kirkland, and the other Protestant educational reformers to free their institutions from church control continues to play itself out, and the alienation from particular churches seems to entail the delayed but inexorable estrangement from communal faith seeking understanding.

A Catholic Reprise?

The process whereby the liberal Protestant colleges and universities were separated from their sponsoring churches between 1870 and 1910 may have been repeating itself from 1950 on among the very large cohort of universities and colleges that were founded as Catholic. This assertion will require more by way of evidence than simply the high incidence of the familiar, irresolute "church-affiliated," "church-related," "tradition," "heritage," "background" nomenclature much in vogue in recent years. Yet we do not have available the abundance of historical literature on which the earlier part of this essay was able to rely. The Catholic alienation, if it is underway, is too recent to allow more than an impressionistic estimate. But if it is underway yet not complete, there is more at stake here than in appraising a transformation that occurred generations ago.

The question may not be whether Catholics have in fact completed the effective severance of their colleges and universities from the church. To the extent that this has already been accomplished, the question may be: How rapidly and pervasively have the profession of faith, its provocation to the mind's inquiry, the celebration of a community of belief, and the fostering of moral maturity withered, once their roots were severed?

Already in the 1950s a progressively emancipated atmosphere of public discourse allowed Catholic educators to raise critical doubts about the soundness of the enormous establishment of colleges and universities they had built and supported in this country. Best remembered, perhaps, is historian John Tracy Ellis's 1955 address in which he reproached his coreligionists for "the impoverishment of Catholic scholarship in this country, as well as the low state of Catholic leadership in most walks of national life." One reason for that, Ellis said, was "the absence of a love of scholarship for its own sake among American Catholics, and that even among too large a number of Catholics who are engaged in higher education. It might be described as the absence of a sense of dedication to an intellectual apostolate. This defect, in turn, tends to deprive many of those who spend their lives in the universities of the American Church of the admirable industry and unremitting labor in research and publication which characterize a far greater proportion of their colleagues on the faculties of the secular universities."[51] John Cavanaugh, Notre Dame's president emeritus, followed through with an oracle against Catholics' "inferior position where culture and intellectual achievement are concerned." "Where," he asked, "are the Catholic Salks, Oppenheimers, Einsteins? . . . Perhaps it is true that we are not yet generally conscious of our mediocrity and not sufficiently impatient about it."[52] Catholics who had in 1947 warmed to Boston Archbishop Richard Cushing's proud remark that there was not a single U.S. Catholic bishop born to a parent who held a college degree, now took it as a reminder that in neither head nor members were they a body academic.

Catholics began to hear scholars like Richard Hofstadter deplore their record:

> One might have expected Catholicism to add a distinctive leaven to the intellectual dialogue in America, bringing as it did a different sense of the past and of the world, a different awareness of the human condition and of the imperatives of institutions. In fact, it has done nothing of the kind, for it has failed to develop an intellectual tradition in America or to produce its own class of intellectuals capable either of exercising authority among Catholics or of mediating between the Catholic mind and the secular or Protestant mind.[53]

51. John Tracy Ellis, "American Catholics and the Intellectual Life," *Thought* 30 (Autumn 1955): 376-79.

52. John J. Cavanaugh, C.S.C., "American Catholics and Leadership," an address delivered to the John Carroll Society, Washington, DC, 15 December 1957 (manuscript from the University of Notre Dame Archives). Cavanaugh devoted most of his comments to educational institutions, but spoke as well to the domestic culture of the family:

> We need in the homes a renaissance of respect for culture and scholarship. Fathers and mothers have to recognize the terms upon which excellence is developed, that it comes only through habits of hard work, of serious reading developed very early in the child. Father LaFarge, in his charming book, *The Manner is Ordinary*, relates that before his sixteenth birthday, he was reading Herodotus and Plautus; Catullus and Theocritus; Dryden, Goldsmith, Michelet, Molière, Corneille and Victor Hugo. In too many homes today, boys are considered eccentric if they do not spend most of their time curled up before a television set, if they do not shrink in fear of mental hernia when they are required to study a few hours a day.

53. Richard Hofstadter, *Anti-intellectualism in American Life* (New York: Knopf,

In response to this humiliating appraisal, university presidents like Theodore M. Hesburgh of Notre Dame, Paul Reinert of St. Louis, Ann Ida Gannon of Mendelein, Jacqueline Grennan of Webster, and James Shannon of St. Thomas called their colleagues to a new level of academic excellence. Excellence also meant autonomy from control by church officials, and in 1967 a group of Catholic educators issued what was known as the Land O'Lakes Statement, which was as trenchant as anything Charles Eliot had said to his religious establishment:

> The Catholic university today must be a university in the full modern sense of the word, with a strong commitment to and concern for academic excellence. To perform its teaching and research functions effectively, the Catholic university must have a true autonomy and academic freedom in the face of authority of every kind, lay or clerical, external to the academic community itself. To say this is simply to assert that institutional autonomy and academic freedom are essential conditions of life and growth and indeed of survival for Catholic universities as for all universities.[54]

The motivation for this bold declaration was twofold: a recollection of the mediocrity and complacency that had handicapped Catholic learning in the past, and a fear of destructive intrusion by hierarchical authorities in the future.

Shortly after the statement, Notre Dame and St. Louis set an example that many Catholic institutions then followed; they removed the majorities of ecclesiastical persons — priests and members of religious orders — from their boards so as to leave the presidents effectively sovereign. This replicates the move led by Harvard, Yale, and Princeton to change over to lay boards of governance.

1963), p. 136. Robert Hutchins, president of the University of Chicago, who spoke of the Catholic Church as having "the longest intellectual tradition of any institution in the contemporary world," had his own accusation to make: "You have imitated the worst features of secular education and ignored most of the good ones. There are some good ones, relatively speaking — high academic standards, development of habits of work, and research." The bad ones are athleticism, collegiatism, vocationalism, and anti-intellectualism. (Ellis, pp. 374-75.)

54. Theodore M. Hesburgh, C.S.C., "The Catholic University and Freedom," *The Hesburgh Papers: Higher Values in Higher Education* (Kansas City: Andrews & McMeel, 1979), pp. 64-65. In excluding any relationship of accountability to authority (authority imagined in only one of its possible forms), the manifesto does not resolve how a university is to remain Catholic in any full, if not modern, sense of the word.

The president of one of these schools explains:

> At H——, we identify ourselves as an independent institution with a
> X—— [religious order] tradition; I mean X—— as being Catholic as
> well. We're independent of ecclesiastical control; we're independent of
> any attempt to indoctrinate, of denominationalism. Has that Catholic
> and X—— tradition disappeared completely? I would say no. The
> element of that tradition that I would hope would be subscribed to by
> people who are not coreligionists would be the idea that at this univer-
> sity, religious values, religious experience, are taken quite seriously, both
> as legitimate grounds for reflection, and also in terms of some kind of
> communal experience. In addition, while religious issues, religious ex-
> perience, should be taken seriously, it's also true that they need not
> preclude a wholehearted humanism: an enthusiasm for the arts, a rec-
> ognition of the ways of knowing, and all the rest.

Lest this statement be thought fuzzy, it is best appreciated by contrast
with a statement published almost fifty years earlier by one of his predecessors in the presidency, who was explaining why there was no room for
a graduate school, in the usual mode, on a Catholic campus. The immediate purpose of research is to increase the sum of human knowledge, to
find things never known before, he explains. For Catholics, however, the
most significant knowledge is already available, not through effort, but
through revelation. There are — literally — no big surprises left:

> Here we have the radically peculiar cast of the Catholic approach
> to learning and the objective without which its thinking is un-
> palatable, to itself vain and pointless. It is the simple assumption that
> wisdom has been achieved by man, and that the humane use of the
> mind, the function proper to him as man, is contemplation and not
> research. I do not deny that in others the marks of this cast of mind
> may be found. But in its plenitude and perfection, it is peculiar to the
> Catholic mind alone.

It would seem reasonable to infer that some process of a fairly
transformative dimension had been underway between the statement
of the earlier president and that of his successor, and to conclude that,
if typical, it suggests an upheaval comparable to that wrought by the
liberal Protestants in their educational establishment years ago.

The new ambitions of the Catholic educators carried heavy financial costs. The church had often been accused of providing little or no subsidy to its colleges and universities. This was not quite correct. Most Catholic colleges and universities were the foundations of religious orders who contributed their professional services for only token salaries. And the surge towards secularization arose only when diminishing numbers of vowed religious were rendering that contribution less significant in the total budget. Funds in abundance would eventually begin to flow from alumni and donors, but the most immediate sources were the foundations and the government. When government regulations appeared to require secularization as the condition of financial support, many Catholic institutions were prepared to conform. Shortly after the Land O'Lakes statement, the state of New York, which had many of its citizens enrolled in independent colleges and universities that were almost all laboring under severe annual deficits, made institutional grants available (known as "Bundy money"). The Blaine Amendment in the state constitution forbade tax moneys to go to any sectarian entities, so ninety percent of the Catholic universities and colleges in the state abruptly declared themselves nonsectarian. What Protestant colleges had done with surprising alacrity to qualify for the first Carnegie grants, Catholic colleges were now doing to qualify for state grants. One university rewrote its brochures to delete references to it as a Catholic university, took down the crucifixes from the classroom walls, and removed its entry from the annual *Catholic Directory*. Some years later it allowed the entry to be restored, but insisted that the ordinary diocesan heading "Colleges and Universities" be altered to "Universities and Colleges with religious in residence."

But even when outside financing comes unencumbered by the need to forswear an institution's religious identity, its very availability has tended to loosen its ties to the sponsoring but nonfunding church. Thus the G.I. Bill, the Public Facilities Act, the National Defense Education Act, and the various forms of student aid initiated in the 1960s — Work-Study grants, Pell grants, etc. — have subsidized the survival of many colleges and universities, but inexorably they have served to make the grantee institutions far more anxious to observe the laws and regulations of the state than the strictures of the church, whose sponsorship is, by comparison, so intangible.

In the new atmosphere questions were inevitably raised about whether preferential admission or appointment of Catholics was compatible with a dedication to academic excellence. One Catholic university, which had for years professed that it "does not discriminate on the basis of age, sex, race, handicap, color (or) religion" and "welcomes applications without distinction on the basis of race or religious beliefs," discovered that Catholics had thereby declined from 70 percent to 59 percent of its student body in only ten years. A decision to raise this to 62 percent was met with sharp condemnation on campus. Said the president of the student senate: "Of course, there's a strong Catholic tradition here, but I don't think the way to uphold it is to discriminate essentially against non-Catholics who may be qualified." The president of the faculty senate said he would hate to see the university lose its Catholic identity. "At the same time, though, the university is striving for excellence and it is trying to recruit the best possible students. You have to balance those two things." (Note that both statements assume that being Catholic is not one of the indices of an "excellent" student at a Catholic university.)

Catholics in this century have been as ready as Protestants in the last century to embrace, without any sense of contradiction, the belief that actions characteristic of faith could be guaranteed on their campuses without any unseemly insistence on guaranteeing that the personnel are from their church. The founding president of one large Catholic university told his first board of trustees that

> I—— is Catholic and "must ever remain Catholic" with regular instruction in Catholic doctrine being given to Catholic students. However, "true to the letter and spirit of the charter of the University, no religious test is applied to either students or teachers; no provision is made in the record forms for noting the religion of the students or professors."

A recent vice-president explained: "It didn't matter that a student was Catholic or not, any longer, it only mattered that people who were disadvantaged for one reason or another . . . had an opportunity." The second-ranking academic officer of the university states that "I think, by and large, this is not a Catholic institution. I think it is much more a Y—— [religious order] institution, and more people identify with the Y—— subset of Catholicism than with Catholicism per se." Yet there are presently only two members of the Y—— order teaching at this large university, and both of them were appointed within the past three years.

When the Vatican prescribed in 1990 that Catholic universities must maintain a majority of Catholics among their faculty, a number of university presidents responded that this was a requirement that would have to be adjusted to American practices. Yet if recruitment is intentionally blind to religious commitment and its attendant convictions, new faculty naturally bridle at any residual expectation that they might or ought to identify with the institution's traditional identity. One social scientist recently replied to a flyer on behalf of a political action committee advocating ethically consistent life commitments in political life (embracing protection for the unborn, welfare reform, and nuclear disarmament):

> Let me make it abundantly clear to you that I am unequivocally prochoice on the issue of abortion and that I would hate another tree to be felled sending out mass mailings to unsympathetic persons like myself. I am certain that you purchased, or worse, were given a mailing list of staff from the University of J———. I am angry that my employment there frequently results in false assumptions about my religious or political beliefs.

With the probable intent to avoid any institutional beliefs that would offend a dissident individual, the chairman of the religion department offered the following grace at an annual faculty dinner in one Catholic university:

> We gather here this evening as a community of many faiths and of many traditions. We are Christian and Jew, Catholic and Protestant, Anglican and Orthodox, Muslim, Buddhist, and Hindu, believer and nonbeliever alike.
>
> We gather to celebrate what we share in common: our humanity, our humane values, our commitment to this university and to its students, its faculty and its staff.
>
> We gather at the threshold of Christmas — a feast of peace and of goodwill to all — mindful of our call to be bearers and instruments of peace and goodwill, especially on behalf of those at the margins of society and those who suffer most keenly at this season of the year.
>
> We gather, finally, to eat — to sit at table one with another, and to grow in solidarity one with another.
>
> May our loving Creator bless this food, bless those of us who partake of it, bless those who prepared it, and bless those who do not have what we have. Amen.

The prayer invites into itself, not a congregation of faith, but an aggregation of individuals, and the invitation is for them to pray simultaneously, though not communally. No one can be offended because there is nothing to disavow.

The liberal Protestants had attempted being corporately Christian without any corporate link to a church. The Catholics have been drawn to a yet more difficult venture: remaining corporately Catholic without any public commitment to the church.

For Catholics during this period, the church seemed a more formidable adversary to intellectual prowess than local clergy of the Protestant churches — congregational, presbyterial, or episcopal — had seemed to their coreligionists a century earlier. The bishop of Rome, claiming immediate jurisdiction over every local congregation and individual, was served by administrative personnel whose readiness to require intellectual obedience was unsustained by any requisite theological or historical acumen or scholarship among the staff; nor did they have a habit of explaining their disciplinary actions. Thus Catholic educators faced threats of intervention by Rome which, while rare, were potentially quite devastating if erroneous. Rome's remembered obscurantism on such matters as biblical studies, natural science, and historical development made even potential threats seem intolerable to many educators of loyal but scholarly faith.

In order to achieve autonomy without appearing to violate continuity, the institutions have done what their pioneering precursors had done earlier: adopt ambiguous language that has quickly manifested a tendency to devolve. There is frequent talk of humanizing and of "values." For instance, one public relations brochure addresses the question: "What does it mean when you say you are a Catholic university?" It begins by mentioning that the institution was founded long ago by an order of priests, but then the language shifts to speak of "heritage," which is identified with "the Judeo-Christian tradition," which is about forming "lasting personal values." The remainder of the item assures incoming students that the half of the student body who are Catholic will openly discuss religion with them but "without pressure to conform to a particular religion." "Ours," it affirms, "is a community proud of its Christian heritage." Twenty years before, an earlier edition of the same university's brochure had spoken of Catholicism, of Pius XI's depiction of the Christian-Catholic character, and of endowment "with the redemptive merits of Christ which we call grace of supernatural life." From this to "lasting personal values" may have been a significant change.

The Catholic colleges, in a liberating ecumenical age one century after the Protestants did the same, have begun to welcome an increasingly diversified faculty in which the communicants of the sponsoring church are fewer, and often a minority. But there are several aspects of even greater significance. Increasingly, the noncommunicants are actually present, not in any ecumenical way, but by way of indifference. They are not explicitly welcomed as allies in a religious undertaking; they are recruited, evaluated, appointed, and welcomed without a frank word about religious commitment from the college or from the candidate — unless by way of apology. While the remaining believers of the sponsoring church may imagine that the newcomers are being incorporated into the traditional undertaking of the college, in fact the opposite seems to be happening. Instead of their even being asked to defer to the college's religious commitment, the college stands ready to defer to their many individual commitments or anticommitments out of what it calls hospitality but what may more frankly be called a failure of nerve. The ancient tokens of hallmark faith are withdrawn, evacuated, or desecrated so as not to make anyone feel estranged.

One college explained to its public:

> The first additions to the Z—— [religious order] faculty and staff were committed Catholic men and women. But it was apparent as the college grew to true university status that a pluralist society requires institutions which are effectively pluralist in outlook, and that education for life in this society has to be conceived as broadly as the full range of responsible opinion in the society is broad. A diversity of viewpoints contributes to the intellectual and spiritual health of the university, and it is inconceivable now that it be entirely or even mainly staffed by men who are members of one religious order or even by Catholics alone.

The brochure is headed by an epigram from Kierkegaard: "It is not worthwhile remembering that past which cannot become present."

In one Catholic college a student interviewed twenty-two members of the department of theology; fifteen were Catholics (five of them priests). He posed three questions: (1) "Should K——, a Catholic institution, try to cultivate an appreciation of prayer in its students?" The virtually unanimous answer was yes. (2) "What role, if any, do the theology faculty have in cultivating this appreciation?" The faculty suggested personal example, participation in retreats, or collaboration with campus ministry. (3) "Do you ever begin your classes with a prayer?" To this, eighteen answered no. (Throughout its history, until the last twenty years, all classes at this university had begun with a prayer led by the instructor.) The interviewer pressed for reasons, and they were forthcoming:

In the classroom, prayer must be looked at academically. It can be studied, but should not be practiced, at least not in any formal manner. Theology is an intellectual and academic discipline; "it is not religious education or catechism." Without the separation, the theological inquiry would be less rigorous. Beginning required classes with a prayer might confuse students and reinforce their previous simplistic ideas. Regular prayer in class might "shut the door to authentic prayer by identifying it with formality."

Another reason for not praying in class stems from a concern for the rights of the individual. Some might not be ready to pray; some may resent being subject to prayer. This reasoning sees prayer in class to be presumptuous, an imposition on individual freedom, and a practice that takes advantage of the students' required presence.

What of students in ministry courses? Here too there was reluctance. The class is not a faith community with a shared experience that would lead to prayer. Some said they would feel presumptuous to ask the class to pray because that simply is not their role. Their purpose is to teach, not to lead prayer.

The few faculty who did begin classes with prayer said they found the students uniformly sincere, even devout, and happy to join. And they found no conflict with prayer in any class at a Catholic university.

One president emeritus of a Catholic university wrote recently:

A peculiarity of the modern Catholic university is that it has taken to itself large numbers of faculty members who are neither Catholic nor, in many cases, Christian. On the other hand, all of them are fully aware of the kind of institution to which they have committed their lives and work, and in most instances they endorse both the university's preoccupations and the presence of the church within it.

Apart from the implausible claim that the university's Catholic character was a matter of explicit reflection and endorsement by the noncommunicants who had come to join it — without ever being asked for their

undertakings toward what he calls, not the university's "commitment," but its "preoccupations" — the statement seems to imply that there is some other effective way for a university to be Catholic if the faculty are not. What was first intended unreflectively as an act of denominational ecumenism devolves into interdenominational vagueness and then into nondenominational secularism. And just as it was a hundred years earlier, this is largely the work of clergy and religiously active lay educators, who find themselves opposed by church officials and some tendentious colleagues who give every sign of being intellectually cramped and authoritarian.

Religious faith comes forward nowadays in softer garments. Justice and peace, social service, awareness of and care for the environment, volunteer work; or liberal arts, discriminating inquiry, courses in professional ethics, gender studies — these are presented as the extracurricular surrogates for faith.

One study of Catholic values on Catholic university and college campuses disclosed that when administrators, faculty, students, and alumni were asked to identify core Catholic values in the culture of their institutions, "high academic standards," "academic freedom," and "respect for the individual" regularly ranked at or near the top, and "community of faith" trailed far behind.

The transformation of Vanderbilt's biblical department into a school of religion and then into a nondenominational divinity school had been a first phase in the typical marginalization of theology at the university. The second phase saw theology departments transformed into religious studies departments. Is this same secularization of faith-related scholarship occurring in Catholic universities and colleges? One recent study by sociologist Frank Schubert traced a shift in theological teaching at several Catholic universities. Course descriptions such as these had been typical of the decade 1955-65:

> *Learning Christ.* Palestinian Judaism at the time of Christ. Old Testament backgrounds. Apologetic questions connected with the written Gospel. Biblical inspiration, norms for fruitful reading of Scripture. A life of Christ in the gospels and Pauline letters. His teaching, testimony, redemptive Death and Resurrection.

> *Faith, Hope, Charity and Grace.* The nature, divisions, qualities, and necessity of the theological virtues, the eschatological doctrines of the Church, and the supernatural life and activity of elevated human nature.

179

The Sacramental Liturgy of the Church. The priestly quality of God's people; liturgy as communal, hierarchical, sacrificial, sacramental. History of eucharistic and other sacramental rites. The celebration of the Mystery of Christ.

Two decades later the institutional catalogs were offering such courses as these:

Global Ethics. Fifteen participation learning sessions aimed at sensitizing oneself to the global situation of political, social and economic imbalance — particularly in developing countries of the Third World. Emphasis is on both information and the clarification of attitudes and values. Some of the areas to be covered will include economic realities in the global village, capitalism and the distribution of wealth, an examination of the multi-national corporation, a case study of neocolonialism, power realities with a developing country, educational realities in the third world, a comparison of values — particularly East Africa and North America.

The Books of the Bible I-II. The Bible is, without rival, the most influential collection of writings in the history of western civilization. The ideas contained in this anthology, its languages, literary styles and lexicon are present in all the languages of the western world. One cannot assume to be educated without a knowledge of the Bible, its history and its concepts. This course will serve as an introduction to each of the books of the Bible, analyzing each in turn, studying its historical setting and comparing extra-biblical sources with the biblical text.

The Ritual Process. This course will be a laboratory workshop experience of the elements which constitute ritual expression, both as a historical and current phenomenon. Students will be expected to critique and, in some instances, perform established rituals. They will also be expected to adapt or create new forms of ritualized expression from existing or emerging patterns — e.g., ancient rites of initiation — the current rites of Baptism, Bar Mitzvah — a new or adapted rite based on these models.[55]

55. Frank D. Schubert, *A Sociological Study of Secularization Trends in the American Catholic University: Decatholicizing the Catholic Religious Curriculum* (Lewiston, NY: Edwin Mellen, 1990), pp. 53, 60, 66, 116, 120, 123.

The trend shown is an unresolved one. Catholic biblical departments are tending more and more to redesignate themselves by the intentionally neutral title of "religious studies." There is a strenuous determination to be acknowledged as Catholic while disclaiming accountability to church superintendency. And the secularized graduate programs that train new faculty have increasingly influenced Catholics to consider faith as a matter of private (and possibly emotional) preference inappropriate to academic interchange. So it may be that theological scholarship is on its way to the margin, if not there already.

This pastiche of contemporary anecdotes can be no more than suggestive, but the evidence does suggest that secularization is rapidly bleaching the Catholic character out of that church's universities and colleges, with all the elements we saw typified in the Vanderbilt story.

As with the Protestant alienation a century earlier, the severance of formal ties has been the achievement of enlightened and observant clergy, or members of religious orders, acting in order to shelter their upgrading institutions from church officers seen as anti-intellectual, intrusively authoritarian, and unable to offer any resources but their own unimpressive governance. Like a century earlier, the Catholic institutions enjoyed an immediate honeymoon period wherein autonomy actually enhanced the institution as both a faith community and a house of liberal learning. But soon the slow and inexorable pull of the secularism dominant in the academy begins to retard and then counteract the inertial momentum that has hitherto set the course of the Catholic college or university, until, after a period in which the forms and symbols of Christian identity are gradually emptied of their conviction, the institution finally emerges as a wraith of the Christian community it once was.

Morals to the Story

The only plausible way for a college or university to be significantly Christian is for it to function as a congregation in active communion within a church. If it is not a community that can worship together, on some church's terms, then it is or will inexorably become secular. In Christianity, communities that float free are not viable. There is neither faith nor ecumenism ungrounded in the church.

In every one of its component elements — governors, administrators, faculty, and students — the academy must have a predominance

181

of committed and articulate communicants of its mother church. This must be regarded not as an alien consideration but as a professional qualification. This means that every adjective whereby an institution wishes to qualify itself (including its Christian allegiance) must represent a quality that is openly and unapologetically appraised and solicited in every recruitment process. Various academic qualifications can be and often are traded off against one another, but when any one of them is systematically subordinated to the others, it will shortly disappear from the institution. Communal faith is in one sense, however, unique among professional credentials: commitment to Christ is apparently the only qualification that, if lost, is institutionally irrecoverable.

A Christian college or university must advise noncommunicant members openly and explicitly when welcoming them that the institution is constitutionally committed to its church in a way that must transcend and transfigure the commitments of individual members. Similarly, any institution will decline to let its foundational norms of scholarship yield to the private and personal standards of each individual scholar. Though the appropriate freedom of inquiry and advocacy will be protected procedurally for all, this cannot be done with prejudice to the school's filial bond to the church.

Granted the inveterate intellectual mediocrity within the churches and their officers, and the inveterate contempt for faith among intellectual elites, the Christian college or university must expect continual low-intensity distrust from either direction. It will have to be an active force in its church to assure that learning and scholarship are honored as professional qualifications for church office. And it will have to be an active force in the academic world to assure that Christian faith and commitment can introduce the mind to its most far-reaching insights and judgments. The polarization process typified at Vanderbilt, but associated with secularization generally, has considered veto power by church officers as the essential and unacceptable feature of affiliation. In an atmosphere of communal trust, it is still unclear whether there may be other arrangements, even untried thus far, that might service the affiliation.

And finally, whatever a university or college is committed to must be able to be professed out loud and honestly. When church-related colleges in America were in tranquil but lackadaisical union with their churches, little was said about their relationship because it was unreflective. It was only when a mutual antipathy began to pull the colleges and universities and the churches away from one another that the new religious rhetoric arose, largely in denial of what was happening. In retrospect it seems that most of the assurances and mission statements and vision statements were obituaries. That is because they were wistful or dishonest attempts to supply by talk what no longer existed in fact. The vacant talk came in as a counterfeit for the frank talk that was needed all along.

If our account of alienation as a repeating process is reliable, then the American Catholic institutions of higher education are nearing the end of a process of formal detachment from accountability to their church. Instead of exerting themselves to oblige that church to be a more credible patron of higher learning, they are qualifying for acceptance by and on the terms of the secular academic culture, and they are likely soon to hand over their institutions unencumbered by any compromising accountability to the church.

This past winter a graduate student grieved about his institution in the student newspaper:

> Although I am a Methodist, I cannot study philosophy in this country at a Methodist university. There are no longer any. My concern is that the process of secularization that removed the Methodist universities from the ranks of Christian academic institutions is now occurring here at L—— [a Catholic university].
>
> At the inaugural Mass of this University's 1954-55 academic year, President ——— contrasted the task of the coming year with the tasks facing non-Christian universities: "Here is an apostolate that no other secular university today can undertake — for they are largely cut off from the tradition of adequate knowledge which comes only through faith in the mind and faith in God, the highest wisdom of Christian philosophy and Catholic theology." Today, however, that task is to prevent L—— from becoming just one more secular university. Why would anyone believe that what the world needs is one more secular university?
>
> If our objective is to become an excellent Catholic university, and if we adopt as our criteria of excellence those by which the Ivy League schools are judged to be excellent, how can we become an excellent university without ceasing to be a Catholic (or even generically Christian) university? For what does it profit a university, if it gains worldwide recognition as an excellent research institution, and loses its own soul?

Looking Both Ways: A "Holy Experiment" in American Higher Education

MICHAEL G. CARTWRIGHT

I

At the most mundane level, looking both ways is a cautionary activity. With good reasons we teach our children to look both ways before crossing the street. Navigating traffic requires that pedestrians be alert to a variety of movements and signals. When the traffic is light, we may be tempted to be casual in the way we glance in either direction. But at other times, looking both ways can be disconcerting, especially if one finds oneself at a busy intersection in a strange city where different kinds of vehicles move toward one another in what appears to be a dangerous fashion despite the presence of traffic lights. In such a circumstance, one may be tempted to give up crossing the street and return to the

An earlier version of this essay was presented at the Symposium on Church-College Relations at Allegheny College on April 6, 1991, and was initially published as part of the *Proceedings of the Church-College Relations Conference*. The essay is included here by permission of Chaplain Donald Covill Skinner, convener and editor of the symposium essays.

   I wish to thank Ms. Margaret Moser, Head Librarian at Pelletier Library, Allegheny College, for providing several sets of historical documents and rare books from the Archives of Allegheny College and the Western Pennsylvania Annual Conference. My gratitude also goes to Mrs. Dawn Nelson, who retyped several of these documents for my use in preparing this essay. I am also grateful to Andrew T. Ford, Glenn Holland, James Sheridan, Dan Sullivan, Robert Rue Parsonage, Robert Conn, George Bashore, Brian Moran, Mary Wilder Cartwright, L. Gregory Jones, and Stanley Hauerwas for their comments and criticisms on earlier drafts of this essay.

safety of the sidewalk in the hope that some official will appear to usher you across the intersection.

I think this second image aptly depicts the uncertainty with which the Western Pennsylvania Conference of the United Methodist Church and Allegheny College have approached discussion of the possibility of reconstructing the relationship by which Allegheny College was constituted as a church-related college in 1833. Both bodies are not sure how best to enter this new intersection, and each has constituents who would argue that they would be better off if they could avoid the traffic problem entirely, in the absence of any official to direct the traffic.

Here, of course, we confront the limits of the image I have been using. For the mental picture I have tried to evoke is one of physical separation. But those of us who are Christians who teach and learn in church-related liberal arts institutions like Allegheny College find ourselves already in motion in the middle of this intersection where divergent streams of discourse flow. Thus, a more adequate image to use to describe our experience would be to leave aside images of spatial separation and think of the church-related liberal arts college as being situated in the intersection of two streams of traffic.

The shift in images is also important for another reason. For it is tempting to think that there is a way of "looking both ways" that does not require us to *move into* the flow of traffic. Christians in the academy are often tempted to adopt the Enlightenment perspective of neutrality, as if we are agents who do not act, but merely stand apart like spectators who shake their heads at the crazy people entering the intersection, but never step out into the flow of traffic themselves. In contrast, I would suggest that a better way to think of the church-college relationship is as the intersection of at least two overlapping but potentially conflicting traditions of discourse, the discourse of liberal arts education and of Christian discipleship.[1] As such, neither Christians in the academy nor college- and seminary-educated ministers can afford to deny the ways these overlapping traditions of discourse constitute us. Morally, theologically, and pedagogically, we have no choice but to perform our scholarly and ministerial tasks at the intersection of these traditions.

These initial observations about ambiguities experienced by those who live at the intersection of the church-college relation are important.

---

1. I am grateful to Prof. L. Gregory Jones of Loyola College in Maryland for suggesting this way of putting the matter.

Too often discussions of church-related colleges have failed to notice some of the more informal relationships that serve to anchor the formal ties that exist at the institutional levels. Following Wittgenstein's dictum — "Don't think, look!" — before we rush to judgment about what is right or wrong about the current state of United Methodist–affiliated colleges, we should take the time to scan those more subtle features of the relationship. Having done so, we may find ourselves more equipped to think about the many challenges that face church-related liberal arts institutions in the 1990s.

This admonition is offered for two reasons. First, too much of the discussion of church-college relations in recent years has been *mono-logical*. Those parties who are concerned about church-college relation-ships tend to conduct the discussion in a way that presumes that only the categories of one party in the relationship provide a solid basis for discussion. But arguably, the church-college relationship is best defined *dialogically*, taking into account the areas of mutual concern, allowing for honest disagreements and for the possibility of convergences that may emerge with respect to contingent concerns.[2]

Secondly, much of the discussion of church-related colleges has been *ahistorical*. In other words, we fall into the trap of assuming that the categories and classifications with which we are most comfortable de-scribe not only our contemporary situation but also that of the institution in earlier eras. This is a mistake that has been made by both the church and the academy in recent decades. As a result, our vision of the past is obscured and our vision of the future — including the possibility for the reconstruction of the church-college relationship — is myopic.

2. After reviewing the history of Allegheny College (and other church-related colleges like it), one can hardly avoid noticing the *accidental* (in Aristotle's sense of the word) character of the relationship between church and academy. By 1833, Madison College at Uniontown, Pennsylvania, had failed; in response, the Pittsburgh Conference of the Methodist Episcopal Church abandoned it and looked elsewhere. At about the same time, Allegheny College, which had closed its doors two years earlier, needed a sponsor; the Pittsburgh Conference was willing to oblige. The Board of Trustees of Allegheny College wanted to guarantee the future of the college by getting a leader who would bring in students, and according to all concerned, the man for the job was Martin Ruter. All of these events and relations were contingent; none of these events was necessary. Yet at the time that they occurred, they were not identified as such because of the postmillennial view of history that guided scholar-priests like Martin Ruter.

Of course virtually no one in the church or the academy likes to think that the programs and institutions within which we work have no necessary existence. We will do almost anything to avoid acknowledging it.

For these same reasons, I am grateful for the insightful analysis of Protestant efforts in higher education provided by George Marsden in his recent article "The Soul of the American University." Marsden offers a succinct sketch of the changes that have occurred in American higher education and mainstream American Protestant churches over the past century and a half:

> Until the Civil War era, the vast majority of American colleges were founded by churches, often with state or community tax support. Since higher education was usually thought of as a religious enterprise as well as a public service, it seemed natural for church and state to work hand in hand, even after the formal establishment of the churches. Protestant colleges were not only church colleges, but also public institutions.[3]

But over the course of the nineteenth century much changed, although in most cases the institutions involved had little sense of the changes that were occurring. As Marsden comments,

> Part of the reason why the religious dimensions of American higher education in the first half of the twentieth century have been so thoroughly forgotten is that even by then they had become peripheral, if not necessarily unimportant, to the main business of the universities. Then, under the heat of new cultural pressures in the 1960s and beyond, most of what was substantial in such religion quickly evaporated, often almost without a trace and seldom with so much as a protest.[4]

Marsden's narrative of the decline of Protestant involvement in American higher education is a narrative that many educators and churchpeople will recognize as generally accurate, even if some would differ about whether that decline was good or bad. Marsden's purpose is to inquire *why* it happened:

> So the puzzle is why a Protestant educational enterprise that was still formidable a century ago, and which until then had been a major component of the Protestant tradition, was not only largely aban-

3. George Marsden, "The Soul of the American University," *First Things* 1 (Jan. 1991): 34.
4. Ibid., p. 35.

doned, but abandoned voluntarily. Or in a larger sense, why has Christianity, which played a leading role in Western education until a century ago, now become not only entirely peripheral to higher education but in fact often come to be seen as absolutely alien to the educational enterprise?[5]

Marsden's historical narrative serves several purposes, not the least of which is to challenge mainline Protestant churches in American culture to reassert themselves in American higher education.

Marsden's agenda shall not be pursued for several reasons. First, we have to take seriously the fact that Protestants have been culturally disestablished from their preeminence in American higher education in a way that is roughly analogous to the earlier disestablishment of Christianity in American government. Just as we cannot return to the days when membership in a Protestant church was a precondition for running for public office in some states, we also cannot pretend that it is possible to return to the days when Protestant churches ran the majority of American liberal arts colleges.

Secondly, Marsden's diachronic (historical) analysis must be supplemented by a synchronic analysis of contemporary American Christianity and contemporary American higher education. We need to make sure we understand the wider array of church-related colleges in American culture if we are going to be able to make sense of the challenges before us.

Third, I believe we must candidly acknowledge the different pedagogical situation in which departments of religious studies in church-related colleges find themselves in the wake of the disestablishment of Protestantism. "Religious studies" is simply not the same today as it was in the days when colleges like Allegheny had a department of Bible and religion and a requirement that each student take a course in "religion" (i.e., Christianity). Not to accept this altered circumstance as the reality within which we teach and write is to distort the scholarly endeavor itself. Even worse, I would argue that such denial may also undermine the missionary endeavors of the contemporary Christian churches in American culture.

To accept this reality does not mean — and I would argue it must

5. Ibid. In the conclusion of his study, Marsden chastens American Protestants for having forsaken American higher education, and challenges Protestants to take up the challenge of Christian higher education that they once accepted with exuberance.

not mean — that we simply acquiesce in the celebration of secularism that has marked American higher education for at least the past three decades. With George Marsden, I would argue that secularism in the academy must be unmasked, challenged, and forced to argue its own case. But I disagree with Marsden insofar as his call for Protestants to reassert themselves in American higher education presumes that it might be possible to reestablish Protestantism in American higher education, thereby restoring the church-college relationship as it once was.

In the end, we must be candid with ourselves that the triumphalist vision of "Christian America" is dead. In its wake members of the church and the academy must reconstruct the significance of the church-college relationship in light of the multicultural reality of contemporary American culture. Given these circumstances, nostalgia for the good old days will not suffice. We can no more go back to the days when the Pittsburgh Conference of the Methodist Episcopal Church first assumed patronage of the recently closed Allegheny College than we can return to the era when "American" meant white Anglo-Saxon Protestant. For we now know that the *monocultural* representation of America common at that time was an illusion, albeit a powerful one. This illusion is even more dangerous now precisely because it denies the increasingly *multicultural* character of contemporary American life.

What we can do is to reevaluate the historical circumstances in which institutions like Allegheny College and the Methodist Episcopal Church joined forces, while we also reassess the significance of the church-college relationship in the present. Such reassessment might provide clues for possible areas for future mutual exploration between the church and the college.

I would also argue that we commit another kind of conceptual mistake if we presume that all colleges and churches face the same sets of issues. Here again, I think Marsden's narrative of "The Soul of the American University," while persuasive, is unnecessarily narrow. We need to assemble several more layers of (diachronic and synchronic) analysis if we are to come to grips with the manifold issues of the contemporary church-college relationship in a post-Christian culture. We would need to consider the different *kinds* of church-related colleges in American culture: Roman Catholic universities, mainline Protestant universities like Emory and the University of Chicago, evangelical "Bible colleges" and colleges in the evangelical Christian College Consortium such as Grove City College, and church-related liberal arts institutions like Allegheny. I would argue that each of these examples illustrates a *different* church-college relationship, and each deserves to be studied within its own historical and synchronic context.

For all of these reasons, I am not as confident as George Marsden is that we can give a global characterization of "the soul" of church-related liberal arts colleges, much less "the soul of the American university." The histories we must recount and interpret are much more particular and much less dramatic than the larger narrative.[6] But such histories are arguably much more useful for the task of reconstructing the relationship between the church and the college precisely because in telling such stories we are reminded of the contingency of the relationship.

II

The Beginning of a Church-College Relationship

The annual meeting of the Pittsburgh Conference of the Methodist Episcopal Church convened in Meadville, Pennsylvania, on July 17, 1833.[7] The stated reason for meeting in Meadville, "the furthest north the Conference had ever sat," was that the conference had agreed to take up two closely connected questions: (1) whether to abandon Madison College of Uniontown, and (2) whether to take charge of Allegheny College, an institution that had been founded by the Reverend Timothy Alden in 1815 but had closed in 1831 due to poor finances and too few students.

Unlike Madison College, Allegheny had resources that made it attractive for the Pittsburgh Conference to consider reviving. Bentley Hall, Allegheny's main building, not only had a commanding position on the hill overlooking the French Creek Valley, but also housed a library

---

6. For a good example of this kind of study of a particular church-related institution of higher education, see James Tunstead Burtchaell's study of Vanderbilt University, "The Alienation of Christian Higher Education in America: Diagnosis and Prognosis," pp. 129-83 in this volume.

7. In my narrative summary, I am following the account given in Ernest Ashton Smith, *Martin Ruter* (Cincinnati: Methodist Book Concern, 1915). For a similar account, see "The Church Patronage," chap. 3 of Ernest Ashton Smith, *Allegheny — A Century of Education* (Meadville, PA: The Allegheny College History Company, 1915), pp. 67-96.

that was envied by such people as Thomas Jefferson. At that time, its collection of nine thousand "well-selected volumes" made it the largest collegiate library west of the Allegheny Mountains. Allegheny's main problem had been its inability to obtain patronage. To his credit Timothy Alden, the founder and first president, had tried to obtain the support of the "Calvinist Christians" in Pennsylvania, but at the time the Presbyterians in western Pennsylvania had trouble enough dealing with the competing needs of Jefferson and Washington Colleges, south of Pittsburgh.

After two years of careful negotiations (1831-33), the Board of Trustees of Allegheny College and the Pittsburgh Conference of the Methodist Episcopal Church appeared to be on the verge of signing an agreement; the negotiations involved a series of compromises that would enable the Methodist Conference to ratify the agreement, making Allegheny a church-related college. The Methodist Conference would be allowed to nominate twelve trustees (lay and clergy) to the Board of Trustees of the College, and the Methodists, in turn, would send forth two hundred itinerant ministers into the fields and forests of western Pennsylvania to gather students, subscriptions, and cash for the college.

In keeping with the Pennsylvania State Charter, the new agreement specified that "no person would have any advantage or disadvantage because of religious beliefs."[8] Viewed in its historical context, this rule meant that no particular denomination or "sect" would be favored, but it was equally clear that everyone involved *presumed* that Christianity was the religious basis for the college's life and mission. At this point, the mutual goal of the church and the college was to gather enough students and financial resources "to make the institution permanent."[9]

Apparently the agreement between the Board of Trustees of Allegheny College and the Pittsburgh Conference hinged upon a key provision — namely, that the conference would agree to give its most celebrated and talented clergyman to be president of Allegheny College. From the pragmatic point of view of the trustees, this proviso signified the firm commitment the church was making to the college.[10] Ulti-

8. Article eight of the "Articles of Agreement between the Board of Trustees, All. Col. and the Pittsburgh Annual Conference of the Methodist Episcopal Church . . . ," as printed in *The Charter, Compacts and By-Laws of Allegheny College and Other Legal Documents* (Meadville, PA: Board of Trustees of Allegheny College, 1880), p. 13.

9. Smith, *Martin Ruter*, p. 84.

10. Smith, *Allegheny — A Century of Education*, p. 76.

mately, the Pittsburgh Conference did agree to this provision, and selected the Reverend Martin Ruter, S.T.D. (1785-1838), then pastor of one of the largest and fastest growing churches in the Pittsburgh area (Smithfield — Liberty Street), to serve as Allegheny's president.

By frontier standards, Ruter would appear to have been well qualified for the position of president at Allegheny College, having served from 1815 to 1820 as principal of the Academy at South Newmarket, New Hampshire (one of the predecessor institutions of present-day Wesleyan University), and from 1828 to 1832 as president of Augusta College, Kentucky, prior to coming to Allegheny. Also known as an eloquent preacher, Ruter served as pastor of one of the most prominent Pennsylvania churches, St. George's Methodist Episcopal Church, Philadelphia. In between stints as an itinerant preacher, Ruter served as editor of *The New England Missionary Magazine* and as the director of the Western Book Concern (Cincinnati) for the Methodist Episcopal Church (1820-28).

A visionary clergyman with an entrepreneurial spirit, Ruter was one of the earliest American Methodists to realize that "the Church needed seminaries of learning and could not conduct its important interests without them."[11] In an era in which ministerial training schools did not yet exist separate from liberal arts institutions, Ruter recognized that the Methodist Episcopal Church had no choice but to be active in founding colleges that could train leaders for the church as well as for the growing settlements on the American frontier.

Like other early American Methodists, Ruter was not inclined to support more established institutions such as Harvard, Yale, and Princeton because of their relationship with churches of "the standing order." After having had the experience of presiding over two struggling institutions in their infancy, Ruter realized that "these seminaries, unless carefully managed, would not accomplish the purpose intended."[12] Apparently Ruter's ministerial colleagues in the Pittsburgh Conference believed that Ruter was the one to carefully manage a revitalized Allegheny College.

The only problem with the agreement struck between the Allegheny trustees and the Pittsburgh Conference of the Methodist Episcopal Church was that the Reverend Dr. Martin Ruter did not want to

11. Smith, *Martin Ruter*, p. 52.
12. Ibid.

be president of Allegheny College. As Ruter recalled, his candid expression of disinterest provoked great concern among his ministerial colleagues in the Pittsburgh Conference:

> A new embarrassment arose in reference to what might be my duty. I had no desire to enter again upon college duties, but I earnestly desired, at least in reference to this college, to be excused from undertaking them. My brethren thought differently and urged upon me the importance to the church of improving the opportunity now offered, in securing the advantages of a good college for the benefit of our people and the community. I therefore consented to take charge of this college for a season.[13]

In the end, good Methodist itinerant that he was, Ruter accepted Bishop Roberts' appointment to serve as president of Allegheny College "for the sake of the Conference."[14]

From 1833 to 1837, Martin Ruter presided over the revived institution of Allegheny College. By all accounts, the college prospered during Ruter's tenure. Thanks largely to the diligent efforts of the itinerant ministers of the Pittsburgh Conference, students were recruited from eight states. In fact, within three years Ruter and the college could take pride in the fact that there were over one hundred students. However, tuition fees were fairly low, and despite the best efforts of the Pittsburgh Conference of the Methodist Episcopal Church, the subscriptions and other financial resources contributed to the college were not enough. Unfortunately, due to the financial stringency of the 1830s — which resulted in the famous panic of 1837 — Ruter was not able to succeed in his stated goal of "assuring" the college's permanent existence. That task would be left to Ruter's successors — in the college *and* the conference.

---

13. Ibid., p. 85. Smith cites Ruter's autobiography without giving the precise reference for this quotation.

14. This is not to say that Ruter did not use his position as a well-known minister to negotiate with the college about the circumstances of his appointment. In fact, Ruter succeeded in getting the college to grant several concessions, including a delay in the date he would report for duty. But in the end even these protective measures failed, as Ruter found himself forced by circumstances to plunge into the effort to get the college running again.

The Church-College Relationship

If there is anything that can be said to be constant about the church-college relationship, it is that the relationship is always incomplete, always in the process of being constructed — or rather, reconstructed — in light of changing circumstances.

In Martin Ruter's first baccalaureate address to the graduating class of 1834, he enunciated a vision of the complementary relationship of the church and the academy in language that clearly reflected early American millennialism:

> The arts and sciences are the handmaids of the Gospel, under whose glorious dispensation we now live. And while that is flying with the wings of the morning to every nation, diffusing its heavenly influence among men, they will follow it, and be in all places its ready attendants.[15]

But the same financial panic of 1837 that at the end of Ruter's tenure curtailed Allegheny College's dramatic turnaround also dealt a severe blow to the popular vision of the alliance between (Protestant) Christianity and the American nation, and thereby also altered the shape of the alliance between Christian denominations and institutions of higher education. Although the effect of this collapse would only gradually begin to be felt at institutions like Allegheny, the confident millennialist rhetoric of Ruter and company would be left behind.

Thus, eventually Ruter's successors at Allegheny would find themselves faced with another task: the necessity of redefining the church-college relationship in the wake of the collapse of the postmillennialist vision that had anchored the joint enterprise of missionary expansion and educational endeavor on the American frontier. But apparently Ruter's successors in the Pittsburgh Conference were slower to realize the implications of these changes for the Methodist Episcopal Church.

Early American Methodists thought of themselves as a "called-out people" raised up by God — as John Wesley put it — to "spread Scriptural holiness across the land and to reform the nation." This evangelical vision of peoplehood embodied in the practices of holy living and holy dying is largely foreign to contemporary United Methodists, many of

---

15. "President Ruter's Baccalaureate Address," *The Methodist Magazine and Quarterly Review* 17 (April 1835): 127.

whom no longer know what the "General Rules of the People Called Methodist" are, much less practice them. The United Methodist Church has clearly lost the kind of ecclesial identity that Martin Ruter and the Methodist Episcopal Church still largely retained in the first half of the nineteenth century.

This is but one indication of the pathos that marks the United Methodist Church's contemporary struggle for identity, a struggle marked by nostalgia for the past, uncertainty about the future, and a noticeable lack of substantive theological vision.[16] Certainly there are signs of promise in the United Methodist Church, but I fear that the majority of United Methodists are not really interested in the kind of renewal that would lead to a significant change in the church's relationship to American culture. However, without such change the United Methodist Church will not succeed in its historic mission as an evangelical order calling the ecumenical community of churches to reformation. And without such change, United Methodism's historic involvement in American higher education can hardly be maintained, much less changed for the better.

To be blunt, United Methodists cannot expect those in the academy to believe that we are a people who "unite the pair so long disjoined, knowledge and vital piety"[17] if our church continues to debase its own theological and moral discourse with the kind of pragmatic reasoning that mirrors — rather than challenges — the worst in American culture. Worse yet, I fear that many United Methodist laity and clergy do not even recognize the separations between thought and practice that exist in our church. Nor can we afford to deny the prevalence of anti-intellectualism among clergy and laity alike in the contemporary United Methodist Church. Obviously, these factors have a detrimental effect on the church-college relationship. Yet probably none of these problems betrays a more significant misunderstanding of the contemporary situation of church-related colleges than the desire — still heard in some quarters — to reassert control over denominationally affiliated colleges as in the days of "the Protestant Empire."

16. Elsewhere I have explored some aspects of the ecclesiological confusion of contemporary United Methodism. See my article "The Pathos and Promise of United Methodist Ecclesiology," *The Asbury Theological Journal*, Fall 1991.

17. These lyrics come from the third stanza of Charles Wesley's great hymn "Come Father, Son and Holy Ghost," *Methodist Hymnal* (Methodist Publishing House, 1964, 1966), 344.

Of course, not all American Christians are as driven by the objective of cultural establishment as American Methodists once were. Some churches, particularly the so-called "Historic Peace Churches" (Brethren, Quakers, Mennonites), are deliberately constituted as "free churches" — Christian churches that do not seek governmental sponsorship for their missionary activities. The distinctive witness of the Mennonite churches spills over into the way in which colleges related to these churches are constituted. In fact, not very long ago one could find the Board of Trustees of Goshen College (Goshen, Indiana) — an institution affiliated with the General Conference of the Mennonite Church — taking the time to clarify why it would want to continue its policy of *not* having an endowment.[18]

Now this may sound fairly odd to people schooled in the view that large endowments are necessary for those colleges that will survive into the twenty-first century. But in the Mennonite tradition, there has been more willingness to embrace the contingencies of life, albeit defined within a striking belief in God's providence. Therefore, church support of Mennonite-related colleges and seminaries is premised upon the belief that each generation of churchpeople should not try to make the challenge for the next generation any easier (or harder!) than they themselves find it to be. Instead, the challenges of the present are to be met with discerning selectivity, even or perhaps especially in times of economic well-being, trusting that God will sustain the church and those institutions related to it, as they continue to live out their witness in the present.

These Mennonites, you see, presumed some things that most of us do not presume. They regarded themselves as something like a colony of missionaries in a culture not their own. They took it for granted that hardship or suffering goes along with the task of Christian discipleship. For these reasons, the Mennonites at Goshen College decided that they

18. More recently Goshen College did begin an endowment, although at this point it has more pledges than deposits. Interestingly enough, the college initiated this at the point when its administration (led by Dr. Lawrence Burkholder) discovered that the Mennonite Church was no longer committed to living up to the standards that it wanted the college to embody. As Burkholder is reputed to have said when the endowment resolution was reconsidered by the college's administration: "The college is the church's mistress. When the church wants the college to be there, she is valued for her services. When the church does not like what the college does, she is regarded as a whore." I am grateful to Prof. Marlin Jeschke of Goshen College for clarifying recent changes at the college.

would deliberately *not* develop an endowment, acting upon the belief that they should not do anything that would deprive the next generation of Mennonites of the challenges of Christian discipleship.

The corollary is equally important: the Mennonites at Goshen College did not want to delude themselves — or their children — that it is ever possible to secure the future of the church in the present. Rather, they trusted that God's providential care will be adequate whatever challenges come their way, and they went about their fairly modest educational efforts in the confidence that they were meeting the challenges that God was presenting them. I suspect that the folks in Allegheny College's development office would find the decision of Goshen College nonsensical, yet it is a stance that is rooted in a profoundly Christian belief in God's providence, as well as the awareness that the way of discipleship involves corporate as well as individual suffering.

I have chosen the example of the Mennonites at Goshen College for another reason as well. In certain respects, Martin Ruter and other American Methodists associated with the reconstitution of Allegheny College in 1833-37 would have understood better than contemporary United Methodists do the moral significance of faith in God's providence. And although Martin Ruter would have been every bit as interested in creating endowments for Allegheny College as the current leadership of the college is, he would have shared the Mennonite sense of ecclesial vocation, missionary identity, and even the notion that suffering is an unavoidable part of the Christian life.[19]

In comparison with the Mennonite tradition, it is fair to say that American United Methodists have eagerly attempted to make it easier on the next generation, only to discover that many in the next generation do not see the point of perpetuating the institutions we have fostered and/or established. In the past, we United Methodists have presumed that we could build up a kind of "cultural capital" for ourselves and our children in (or through) church-related institutions. Now, in the waning years of the twentieth century, we discover that whatever "capital" we thought we had has been used up, and we, like other mainline Protestant denominations, are having to try to reclaim members of the

19. Ruter collated a martyrology that was published by the Methodist Book Concern in Cincinnati, Ohio, for use by Methodist clergy and laypeople: *The Martyrs or A History of Persecution from the Commencement of Christianity to the Present Time* (Cincinnati: E. Deming, 1830).

thirty-something and twenty-something generations in a context that is distinctly "post-Christian." As a result, we United Methodists are having to relearn what it means to be evangelists in a way that Martin Ruter would have found odd. Only this time we find ourselves confronting a culture that is no longer religiously homogenous, as it was thought to be in the days when Ruter came to Allegheny College, but is religiously pluralistic and increasingly multicultural.

In such a circumstance, we should not be surprised to discover that *as a church* we also find it difficult to articulate what we expect from the church-college relationship. In a very real sense, before we can talk about the "soul" of church-related higher education in America, we have to consider the state of the "soul" of the United Methodist Church.

The College-Church Relationship

Of course, the United Methodist Church is not the only organization in American culture that finds itself challenged by changes that have occurred during the past century. Liberal arts colleges like Allegheny also find the recent shifts in American culture disturbing because they call into question some of the slogans by which we have defined liberal arts education in the recent past, particularly the place of religion(s) on campus. In the process, members of the academy are also having to do some long overdue "soul"-searching of their own, and we are beginning to discover some of our own ahistorical tendencies.

As an example, I would like to call attention to a feature of the "Articles of Agreement" between the Trustees of Allegheny College and the predecessor bodies of the Western Pennsylvania Annual Conference of the United Methodist Church that I think has not been adequately understood. One of the conditions of the 1833 agreement between the Pittsburgh Conference of the Methodist Episcopal Church and the Trustees of Allegheny College was that the institution would be conducted in conformity with the rules of the Pennsylvania Charter,[20] "no

20. Section 13 of the Pennsylvania Charter concludes with the words, "but no one shall be refused admission as a pupil on account of his religious persuasion, he being of good repute." The following section focuses on the rules for replacing clergy members of the Board of Trustees: "But no particular religious denomination of Christians shall have any preference; provided, however, the place of a layman shall not be supplied by a clergyman." ("Charter of Allegheny College," as printed in *The Charter,*

person having any advantage or being subject to any disadvantage on account of his religious views."[21]

This article of agreement has its origins in the vision of religious freedom embodied in William Penn's "holy experiment" in the Pennsylvania colony (1682), the colony most noted for its hospitality to people of different cultures and religious backgrounds.[22] For nearly eighty years the Quakers were able to encourage religious expression while also permitting their own political power to be challenged by those they welcomed to "Penn's Woods."

Apparently "Article eight" has been subject to varying interpretations over the course of the college's history. Arguably, three different interpretations of this law can be discerned from the practice of Allegheny college administrations over the past 156 years.[23]

Compacts and By-Laws of Allegheny College . . . [Meadville, PA: Board of Trustees of Allegheny College, 1880].)

21. Article eight, as printed in *The Charter, Compacts and By-Laws of Allegheny College and Other Legal Documents,* p. 13. The full statement reads: "The Institution shall be conducted as the Charter requires, on liberal principles, no person having any advantage or disadvantage, or being subjected to any disadvantage, on account of his religious views." When the articles were revised at the time that Allegheny College was brought under the joint patronage of the Erie, Pittsburgh, and West Virginia Conferences (June 27, 1877), this statement was retained unchanged (see Article seven in *The Charter, Compacts and By-Laws of Allegheny College,* pp. 13, 19).

22. Of course, this statement should not be taken to imply that Pennsylvania is the only state with this kind of language written into its charters for academic institutions. It is not. Nevertheless, Pennsylvania does have a unique history with respect to religious freedom, and this history is reflected in many of the laws that have their origin in the earliest legislation of the "Holy Experiment" of the Pennsylvania Quakers.

For a good discussion of the vision and limits of Penn's "Holy Experiment" see chapter two of Peter Brock's impressive study, *Pioneers of the Peaceable Kingdom* (Princeton: Princeton University Press, 1968), pp. 65-114. Other scholars have also commented on the distinctively positive way in which religious freedom was interpreted in the Pennsylvania colony, in contrast to the more minimal conception of "toleration" in the other colonies (with the possible exception of Maryland).

Some scholars might wish to argue that this conception of religious freedom had been eroded by the time Allegheny College was chartered in 1817. But this secularist interpretation does not account for the fact that the representatives of the Pittsburgh Conference and the Board of Trustees of Allegheny College appear to have gone out of their way to make explicit the more positive conception of religious freedom, by integrating statements from Sections 13 and 14 of the Pennsylvania Charter.

23. In proposing this thesis, I do not presume that college administrators have necessarily acted consciously. Rather, I would argue that in all likelihood the only concern they may have manifested was the desire not to violate the letter of the law.

1. During the tenures of Martin Ruter (1833-37) and Homer J. Clark (1837-47), this article of agreement apparently was interpreted to mean that no one *denomination* of Christianity would have undue advantage.[24] Allegheny College, like much of American culture at the time, could be said to *prefer* Christianity even if it did not give any particular denomination undue advantage. Since most of American culture was Protestant at that time, anti-Catholicism went largely unacknowledged, although it was clearly present in a variety of forms. These presumptions are displayed in the fact that during Martin Ruter's tenure at Allegheny College, the president of the college conducted revival meetings in Meadville and officiated at chapel worship services. In this kind of atmosphere, evangelism and education could go hand in hand so long as it did not appear that the Methodists were seeking "undue advantage" for their denomination. I have no doubt that Methodists like Ruter exploited this circumstance, drawing on the traditional Wesleyan arguments for the "catholicity" of Methodism, in a circumstance still largely defined by the postmillennialist religious optimism of the Second Great Awakening.

2. Because Methodism was the most successful of the Protestant churches during the nineteenth century and well into the twentieth century, the Methodist Episcopal Church continued to benefit from what I call the "informal establishment" of Protestantism in American higher education. This enabled Allegheny officials to operate as if the Pennsylvania Charter permitted the preference of Protestantism, as long as the practice of Christianity on campus did not appear narrowly "sectarian." During this era, Christian rhetoric can still be found in official pronouncements of the college, but the millennialist language evident in the speeches and sermons of Ruter and Clark is not present. Such rhetoric was jettisoned because it was not necessary, having been replaced with the triumphalist spirit of Methodism as the "American" religion. Evangelistic emphases also waned during this period of time since most students who came to the college were already nominally Christian.

As time passed, Protestantism became more and more comfortable with what might be called the revival of humanist currents in American higher education. While the intensity of anti-Catholicism in American

24. Advocates of such a view might point to the language of Section 14 of the charter, where the same phrase occurs in another context. See note 20 above.

Protestantism waxed and waned, Methodists gradually left aside bigotry for ecumenism. At about the same time, denominations began to start seminaries, which in turn relieved church-related colleges of the responsibility to train ministers for the church. As a result, colleges like Allegheny began to emphasize the importance of the liberal arts tradition of higher education.

3. In the wake of the disestablishment of Protestant Christianity in American culture — and in particular in American higher education — a third interpretation of the Articles of Agreement can be discerned, a narrow construal that I call the "secularist" interpretation. Coinciding with currents in American culture, especially after World War II, colleges like Allegheny began to move away from the strongly Protestant character of their early history. In some cases, the veneer of Protestantism has been retained for pragmatic purposes, but underneath the substantial commitments of the college have been nonreligious.

Given the secularist rejection of the legitimacy of religious discourse, the college gradually began to distance itself from the appearance of favoring any religious point of view. The net effect has been that "Unitarian" theological discourse has been privileged — and Christian discourse has been marginalized — in the public ceremonies of the college. Now that a majority of Allegheny students come from Catholic families, the college provides for a Catholic campus chaplain[25] and a Catholic baccalaureate mass, yet such additions are conspicuously private, unofficial functions of the college. Thus the public stance as a nonsectarian college is in no way affected. The difference between this more recent era and that of the early-to-mid-twentieth century is that "nonsectarian" has now come to mean something much closer to "non-Christian."

Given the historical perspective I have narrated, many educators and possibly some churchpeople would claim that we have come to the end of a road; it is time to acknowledge that the church-college relationship is dead, they would say. Such people might not go so far as to claim that the Articles of Agreement between the Trustees of Allegheny College and the Pittsburgh Conference of the United Methodist Church are no longer relevant. However, they probably would argue that given the rules of the Pennsylvania charter, the college has no choice but to

25. The cost of this ministry is shared with the Erie diocese of the Roman Catholic Church.

continue with the "secularist" interpretation of the Pennsylvania Charter for Allegheny College if it wants to retain its integrity.

I would argue that it is a mistake to assume that this is the only option before us. Given the challenges before Allegheny College and the Western Pennsylvania Conference of the United Methodist Church, I do not believe that we can afford to succumb to the tunnel vision induced by the secularist mindset. In fact, I would argue that secularism is a fairly weak position, one that depends on narrow legalistic interpretations of such rules as the Pennsylvania Charter and the Articles of Agreement for its plausibility.[26] (And as I shall argue shortly, the Quaker "holy experiment" could even be seen to provide a model for church-related multicultural liberal arts colleges of the future.)

Ironically, many of those educators who are most militant about wanting to rid American higher education of the last vestiges of church-relatedness are the ones most resistant to admitting to the de facto "establishment" of secularism within the walls of the academy.[27] In this respect, these educators are more like late-nineteenth-century Protestants than they would want to admit. Like Protestants of the past, secularists have not wanted to have to argue for the merits of their position. Thus we discover one plausible explanation for appeals to the Pennsylvania Charter to describe Allegheny as a nonreligious college: in the absence of any substantive argument, the best strategy is to seek out a juridical rule.

The question remains: What alternatives are there to the three interpretations of the Articles of Agreement and/or the Pennsylvania Charter that I have discussed? I would argue for a *revisionist* interpretation of these statements, one that is hopefully in keeping with the vision of religious freedom espoused by Penn at the founding of the Pennsylvania colony in 1682, vestiges of which are present in the Pennsylvania Charter as well as in the Articles of Agreement. In order to present my case effectively, it is necessary to review the 1833 Articles of Agreement one last time.

26. Here I would note that the 1831 agreement between representatives of the Pittsburgh Conference and the Board of Trustees of Allegheny College reflects a much richer construal of the Pennsylvania Charter, one that retains the substance of William Penn's vision of religious freedom as something more than *toleration* (negatively defined as permitting religious expression), as a positive vision that *encouraged* religious expression.

27. George Marsden offers a brief discussion of how this circumstance came about in "The Soul of the American University," pp. 39-40.

Recall that Article eight reads: "no person having any advantage *or being subject to any disadvantage* on account of his religious views." As I have already described, the problem with the secularist interpretation is that it presumes that religious discourse is illegitimate. Indirectly, this interpretation effectively places Methodists, Black Muslims, Hindus, and practitioners of Krishna Consciousness at an equal *disadvantage* within the college. According to the secularist interpretation, this may be the best we can do in a liberal arts college; all religions are to be tolerated, no religions are to be encouraged. In comparison, the article of agreement based on the Pennsylvania Charter seems to me to be both more subtle and more positive, thereby reflecting a more positive view of religious freedom in the academy, one that bears more similarity to the vision of the Quakers than it does to the secularists.

Under the revisionist construal of the "liberal principle" of the Pennsylvania Charter that I am suggesting, Christians would be free to make their case within the college, just as Buddhists and Moslems would also be free to present their arguments. At the same time, the college would continue to encourage all members of its faculty and its student body to aspire to the highest standards of scholarship. Thus, those who would aspire to profess Christian theology — or Jewish or feminist theologies — would be expected to argue their case without expecting that their viewpoint would automatically be validated by other students and faculty. Similarly, those students and faculty who are nonreligious would also be encouraged to make their case without expecting that anyone on campus would simply assent to that perspective. As a result, academic integrity would be enhanced to everyone's advantage.[28] Allegheny College would pride itself in being a college where religious traditions would not only be permitted to flourish, but would also be *encouraged* to do so.

28. Here I am conscious of the fact that the description I have offered of what Allegheny College might become has striking parallels to William Penn's image of what the Pennsylvania Colony was to be. Granted that the ethos that Penn wanted to cultivate did not specifically include the kind of academic enterprise that Allegheny seeks to embody, I see no reason why the image of Penn's colony cannot serve as a suggestive image for the kind of religious and multicultural flourishing that could take place at Allegheny.

III

This proposal may or may not be found acceptable by members of the Western Pennsylvania Conference of the United Methodist Church and Allegheny College, but pragmatists in both bodies will almost certainly call attention to the fact that thus far I have not offered an answer to a very important question — namely, given the changes I have identified, is there any reason for Allegheny College and the Western Pennsylvania Conference of the United Methodist Church to reconstruct their relationship? I would argue that there are several important reasons why both parties *should* be interested in reconstructing the relationship, each of which stems from taking seriously the circumstance of the church-related college as situated at the intersection of these overlapping discourses of liberal arts education and Christian discipleship training. Ironically, the reasons I would identify also apply to two contemporary conflicts in American higher education: the rise of the so-called Christian colleges and the conflict posed by advocates of the "politically correct" on college campuses. Each of these movements poses certain challenges to church-related liberal arts education, and each challenge also points to the importance of reconstructing the church-college relationship.

"Christian" Colleges?

One of the competing voices that would define the future of church-related liberal arts education is the growing phenomenon of "Christian colleges." Interpreting the post–World War II shifts in American culture as producing an epic struggle between evangelicals, liberals, and secularists, some conservative evangelicals hope to win "the struggle for America's soul"[29] by establishing colleges to inculcate "traditional values" in American youth. So-called Christian colleges are conceived as a weapon in the battle with secularism and its alleged accomplice, liberalism. The scene in which the battle is to be fought is American higher education. In such institutions, Christianity is taught not only in religious studies courses, but also in other disciplines ("Christian physics"?), and campus life is strongly marked by what is claimed to be a Christian ethos.

---

29. Robert Wuthnow, *The Struggle for America's Soul: Evangelicalism, Liberalism, and Secularism* (Grand Rapids: Eerdmans, 1989).

Although these institutions can lay claim to the virtue of being forthright in making their religious convictions central to the academic enterprise, they are also more vulnerable than they realize to the moral problem of self-deception. At their best, Christian colleges appear to deny the reality that American culture is "post-Christian" (under the illusion that it remains possible to resurrect the nineteenth-century vision of "Christian America"). Christian colleges also mask an intellectual laziness that has often characterized twentieth-century American Protestantism. Protestants have not wanted to be faced with the challenge of having to argue their case before the world, expecting that church-related institutions would defend their case for them. Still worse, by trying to create the equivalent of a "one-way street" in American higher education, Christian colleges leave themselves open to the possibility of unwittingly supporting ideological distortions of the Christian faith — often cast in the guise of nationalistic sentiments — in their efforts to secure the belief of the next generation.

Recently I received a mailing from a nearby college in western Pennsylvania, a "Christian college" that has access to so much financial support that it can do without the financial aid for students provided by the federal government (a rarity in contemporary American higher education). As I perused this newsletter, I noticed an article by the chairman of the economics department, who was extolling the virtues of education at this particular "Christian college." Among other things, this professor noted that instructors in the social sciences "expound that Christianity is the basis of republican government and the foundation of the private property economic order."[30]

As I read this article, I tried to imagine one of my colleagues in the departments of economics, political science, or philosophy and religious studies at Allegheny College making such a statement without substantial qualification. In the end, I could not think of a single person who would make that statement. The reason is not that there is no relationship between Christianity and Western political institutions and traditions, but rather that the relationship is much more complex and requires more nuance and conceptual argument than this baldly stated assertion allows.

---

30. Hanns Sennholz, "Choosing the Right College," *Grove City College Update* 6 (Jan. 1991): 3. Sennholz is referring to Grove City College. He goes on to offer a brief, if inadequate, rationale for his comment: "Both are possible only because the moral laws of the Gospel give dignity and assign responsibility to every individual."

This is a good example of what happens when church-related higher education is constituted as the equivalent of a "one-way street" where non-Christian questions or perspectives are not welcome, whether they arise out of the exchange between disciplines of the liberal arts or out of the exchange of views between different cultures. Indeed, it is difficult to know how the professor of economics at this Christian college would be able to identify the difference between Christianity and Western civilization, given the monological approach to education displayed in his article.

And precisely for this reason, United Methodists in the Western Pennsylvania Conference have reason to be concerned, for it is very possible that United Methodist students attending this college are being taught a monocultural version of Christianity that is corrupted by its totalizing identification with Western political and economic traditions. In this circumstance, the discourse of discipleship has become captive to an enculturated vision of "Christian America" that is foreign to the earliest vision of what it meant to be "the people called Methodist." The United Methodist Council of Bishops has recently called upon the membership of our church to renounce its nostalgia for the past.[31] This situation offers the Western Pennsylvania Conference an excellent opportunity for putting that resolve into action.

"Politically Correct" Colleges?

Of course, "Christian colleges" are not the only kind of "one-way streets" that have been proposed for the transformation of church-related higher education in America. During the past decade *multiculturalism* has become a buzzword on American college campuses. With the advent of multicultural emphases, the "new orthodoxy" of the "politically correct" has also emerged, thereby obscuring some of the most promising multicultural proposals. As a result, what multiculturalism means is not immediately clear, since its advocates differ among themselves as well as with advocates of the politically correct about the limits of this new approach to higher education. In general, however, there is broad agreement that the "canon" of literary and philosophical works identified with Western civilization must be "opened" in order

---

31. The Council of Bishops of the United Methodist Church, *Vital Congregations — Faithful Disciples: Vision for the Church* (Nashville: Abingdon, 1990), p. 39.

to encourage students to study perspectives that are representative of non-Western cultures.

To take a multicultural approach to higher education, then, poses particular challenges for the typical liberal arts college with its tripartite division into the faculties of the natural sciences, social sciences, and humanities. For it is not adequate simply to study "Oriental" cultures; one must also consider the ways in which the "Orient" has been constructed within categories that presume Western imperial power structures that have imposed national identities on Islamic and Asian peoples, which also may be related to scientific claims of the past.[32] Multicultural education requires the willingness to attend to the ways in which Western culture is understood in the Orient, and therefore to reassess one's own epistemological assumptions.[33]

Beyond such curricular reform, many advocates of the politically correct appear to bring a definite ideological agenda to the pedagogical task that stems from their opposition to racism, classism, and sexism, and the ways in which these biases are reflected in American culture. This approach to multiculturalism can also be said to be *monological* insofar as it has its own kind of "doctrine" to communicate in the classroom. Thus, what is valued is not the particularities of Guatemalan culture or the worldview of Xhosa tribesmen, but rather the use to which these non-Western cultural narratives can be put in the course of underwriting particular conceptions of political liberalism.[34]

One of the areas where advocates of the politically correct are particularly inconsistent, or at least unclear, is the rationale by which religious topics are to be included within a multicultural approach to education. In general, non-Western religions (tribal religions, etc.) are

32. For a good example of this kind of reassessment of a traditional Western discipline of study, see Edward W. Said, *Orientalism* (New York: Random House, 1979).

33. The account of the tensions between advocates of the politically correct and others interested in multicultural curricular reform reflects the author's ongoing participation in conversations with faculty colleagues at Allegheny College. As such, the author assumes that the conversation at Allegheny College is but a microcosm of the wider discussion currently being conducted on campuses around the United States.

34. See Dinesh D'Souza, *Illiberal Education: The Politics of Race and Sex on Campus* (New York: Free Press, 1991). While D'Souza's study also clearly reflects a definite ideological agenda, many of the examples of political advocacy in the classroom that he has collated do not reflect an interest in different cultural visions of truth so much as the way in which these alternative visions can serve the agenda of advocates of the politically correct.

included, if for no other reason than that they are *not* Judeo-Christian. But where Christian religions are included for study, it is because of other factors, such as race, sex, or class. Thus, given the widespread interest in African-American culture in multicultural education, the spirituals of the black church are the subject of intense study, but not always for their religious content.

To offer another example, advocates of the politically correct are not so sure whether it would be appropriate to study the Amish in a multicultural curriculum. Insofar as they know anything about the Amish, multiculturalists find them intriguing as an example of a reaction to modern culture. The problem, of course, is that the Amish, much like the Xhosa tribespeople of South Africa or the Hmong people of Laos, do not separate the life of the spirit (religiosity) from culture. That kind of separation is itself a product of Western Enlightenment culture, and to the extent that the advocates of the politically correct rely on it, they are as narrowly "Western" as the traditionalists they oppose so vigorously.

At this point, multiculturalists have a problem because they do not have an adequate rationale to explain why they would want to exclude the Amish but include the tribal religion of the Xhosa people, except that they are concerned about right-wing religiosity (an admission that betrays their ignorance of the more important features of Amish faith and practice). At research universities such as Penn State, the absence of such a rationale may not be an issue given the diverse programs of study within the university, but at a liberal arts college like Allegheny, such arbitrariness cannot be overlooked. Indeed, the vision of liberal arts education itself seems to require that multicultural perspectives (including religious perspectives) be integrated into the curriculum without succumbing to the ideological warfare of the politically correct.

Curiously, advocates of the politically correct are often deeply suspicious of something that they know relatively little about — namely, Christianity. Students who wear T-shirts that say "Christianity is stupid!"[35] as a protest against right-wing religiosity simply advertise their inability to discriminate between fundamentalist Christianity and the Amish or between Fundamentalism and the Roman Catholic Church. Such problems as these suggest that any substantial attempt to

35. This incident occurred at Allegheny College in May 1991.

encourage the integration of multicultural perspectives in a liberal arts curriculum will need to take seriously the fact that religious views cannot simply be jettisoned when cultural perspectives are brought into the classroom.

At their worst, proposals for multicultural liberal arts education provide a thin veneer for what is essentially the "commodification of diversity";[36] instead of challenging American cultural dispositions, they simply reinforce our students' sense that they can pick and choose what they want to know without having to contend with the real intellectual (moral, scientific) challenges posed by other cultures. At their best, proposals for multicultural liberal arts education challenge those aspects of Western culture that are most parochial, challenging students and faculty alike to grasp the rich complexity of the culture — or people-hood — of those who are radically different from us (Iraqis, Black Muslims, the Amish).

Clearly, in order to pursue such curricular reform, colleges like Allegheny will need to consider such problems. At present, however, Allegheny College does not have an adequate rationale for meeting the challenge of multicultural liberal arts education. The question still to be answered is: Can the fact that it is a *church-related* liberal arts college help Allegheny to negotiate this kind of challenge?

A Church-Related Multicultural Liberal Arts College?

Earlier I evoked the image of church-related liberal arts education as situated at the intersection of two overlapping yet potentially conflicting discourses. Now I have called attention to two competing paradigms of education, which at their worst proffer a conception of education that is more like a "one-way street" than any kind of intersection. Neither conception seems to have room for the other; both are totalizing and therefore ideologically distorted visions of liberal arts education. Oddly enough, it is exactly at this point that authentically church-related liberal arts education can be reconstructed.

Whatever else we may want to say about fundamentalist "Christian colleges," they are one of the groups that have exposed the self-deceptive

36. I borrow this phrase from Fredric Jameson, the literary critic who has argued against consumer-oriented conceptions of pluralism and universality precisely because they serve as a thin veneer for the more egregious forms of capitalism.

character of *normative pluralism* in American culture.[37] Indeed, members of the academy have little choice but to accept the fact that normative pluralism is no longer viable as a paradigm for American higher education. Normative pluralism discredits itself by eliminating the struggle for truth, claiming in effect that there is no truth except the "truth" that there are a plurality of claimants. While there is no question that we live in a diverse world, we are now more self-conscious about the fact that in a culture in which no one group's viewpoint is (or should be) established — including that of the secularists! — all groups must argue for the merits of their case.

Whatever else we may want to say about the advocates of the politically correct, in calling attention to the lingering vestiges of monocultural views of liberal arts education they have raised the question of truth in the context of the competing views of history, peoplehood, and morality in different cultures. This challenge points to the need for *contested pluralism*. This modified approach to dealing with the reality of pluralism is superior to what I have characterized as "normative" pluralism because it does not presume that pluralism is an end-in-itself. It is not simply that we all have fourteen different viewpoints and that all are equally valid, resulting in a vicious relativism; rather, contested pluralism assumes that all participants in the debate have the responsibility to offer well-reasoned arguments about their truth-claims in the various forums that exist for such argumentation.

It is exactly at this point that I think colleges like Allegheny have something to gain from the fact that they are related to a church. For at its best Christianity seeks to proclaim the gospel of Jesus Christ in the awareness that its message must be lived — performed — if it is to be believed by others. Therefore, Christians must take it for granted that they offer their witness in the context of competing claims about God,

---

37. The normative pluralism of the secularists is being challenged by those same groups who often found themselves excluded from the discussion in the name of "pluralism." As a result, secularists in the academy are being forced to offer intelligible responses to those groups which find their arguments inadequate in the increasingly multicultural world in which we live.

Thus it is not uncommon to discover Islamic peoples challenging Western or Anglo-European notions of universality on the grounds that these ostensibly inclusive frameworks actually serve very different ends, including the subjugation of minorities in the name of some larger vision of unity. Similarly, the Black Muslims have criticized the conception of inclusivity supported by political liberalism because it does not stop white Americans from publicly stating that the world would be a better place if black women would stop having babies.

the history of the world, and morality. As in the case of the "holy experiment" of the Pennsylvania Quakers, the truth Christians profess is most faithfully performed when that witness is offered nonviolently. Not only should no one be coerced into becoming a Christian, but also Christians have a stake in assuring other religious and cultural groups the freedom to offer their witness in academic contexts in the same way that Christians want to be free to make their claims.

In particular, the tradition to which the United Methodist Church is the heir could also be drawn upon to support multicultural curricular experiments. I would hope that the United Methodist Church's strong conception of the "catholicity" or universality of the church, including its awareness of its own provisionality as a claimant to be part of the church catholic, provides the kind of warrant for multicultural education that is so noticeably lacking in most Western secularized notions of universality and diversity. Moreover, the church's "apostolic" charge has urged it to be willing to accept the challenge — and risk! — of translating the gospel into the language of other cultures. At its best, the church has been able to meet this challenge without succumbing to the temptation of clothing its message in the all-too-comfortable garb of Western culture.

Therefore, there are important theological and ethical as well as politically pragmatic reasons why Christians should support liberal arts colleges like Allegheny that would offer courses on "Islamic Politics" or "Chinese History" or "Black Religion and Black Radicalism." Such courses would seek to explore the claims for truth made by non-American or non-Christian peoples of the world precisely for the purpose of understanding their truth-claims. Thus, a church-related multicultural liberal arts college will deliberately avoid the "one-way streets" in favor of the dialogical model described here as "contested" pluralism.

In contrast to a "Christian college," a church-related multicultural liberal arts college will take it for granted that the discourse of Christian discipleship has its *primary* locus in the life of Christian churches. This does not mean that Christians on campus cannot gather for prayer, worship, and ongoing discussion of their discipleship, but it does mean that such gatherings will be useful or legitimate only to the extent that the participants (faculty, students, staff) are — or become — part of congregations in which their discipleship is anchored in practices such as baptism, the eucharist, and mutual admonition.

In contrast to a "politically correct" college, a church-related multicultural liberal arts college will not exclude the discussion of Christian

211

discipleship from the campus or classroom, for it understands that part of what it would mean to be an authentically multicultural college would be to encourage the exchange between different peoples, including those people who are Christian. It will do so despite the fact that such inter-religious and intercultural dialogue entails the risk of religious conversion. In fact, a church-related multicultural liberal arts college will acknowledge the fact that to do otherwise would be to retreat to a secularist posture, or to enter into one of the other "one-way streets" discussed above.

In this sense, then, a church-related college offers the opportunity for critical reflection on Christianity (or any other religion), without ruling out *either* the possibility of Christian discipleship (as the advocates of the politically correct tend to do) *or* external challenges to the adequacy of Christian practice in particular cultures (as Christian colleges tend to do).[38] There is no question that this approach to liberal arts education requires an *experimental* pedagogy. Accordingly, I have been using the image of the church-related college as the intersection of two intellectual discourses, each of which supports the other while also raising questions about the adequacy of the other.

Finally, without claiming to be "objective" in the sterile sense of the secularists, a church-related multicultural liberal arts college will also provide programs of study that explore such "one-way streets" as the Christian college and politically correct movements. In so doing, students and faculty alike will learn about and participate in the "struggle for America's soul." And they will do so in the knowledge that the institution in which they study and learn is committed to the pursuit of truth conducted at the intersection of overlapping discourses. That an institution like Allegheny College would do this in the face of contemporary movements that isolate the discourses of liberal arts and Christian discipleship would also be a testimony to the uniqueness of church-related multicultural liberal arts education in contemporary American culture.

38. Nor does it mean that the discourse of Christian discipleship cannot be explored elsewhere, such as in classrooms. Certainly courses on "Christian ethics" in liberal arts colleges such as Allegheny College also provide contexts for the exploration of discipleship. The difference between what goes on in the classroom of a church-related liberal arts college like Allegheny and the kind of "indoctrination" that one finds in an economics class at a "Christian college" can be located in the kinds of questions that are introduced and encouraged by faculty. In the former, the topic of economics as practiced in late-modern capitalist nations such as the United States may be discussed critically. In the latter, Christian ethics has already been distorted by its captivity to the ideology of capitalism.

Conclusion: Toward Another "Holy Experiment"

At present very few institutions of higher education in American culture could be named that have been able to maintain the art (dare I identify it as one of the "liberal arts"?) of "looking both ways" without succumbing to the temptation of secularism, the pitfalls of the politically correct, or the intellectual retreat of the Christian colleges. Moreover, as Page Smith has persuasively argued, in recent decades American research universities have the dubious distinction of having "killed the spirit" of many undergraduates by excluding religious discourse from the classroom.[39] Ironically, many of the same institutions that were supposed to be the models for liberal arts colleges to emulate have been doing a far inferior job of providing opportunities for discussing religious issues.[40]

Could it be that church-related liberal arts colleges could provide the model not only for multicultural education but also for academic exploration of religious issues in American higher education in the twenty-first century? Could it be that Allegheny College would be one of the multicultural pioneers in this very different frontier situation in American culture? Would the Western Pennsylvania Conference of the United Methodist Church be willing to support this kind of reconstruction of the church-college relationship? These questions can only be answered as the church and the academy continue their dialogue.

I would hope that the Western Pennsylvania Conference and Allegheny College could agree that these are goals to which they both could aspire. If, in the process, both the church and the college learn that they have reason to be grateful for the existence of article eight of the Articles of Agreement (reflecting the Pennsylvania state charter), I cannot think of a more appropriate vindication of the practical wisdom displayed by the Quakers in founding their "Holy Experiment," the Pennsylvania colony. In fact, what better image could there be to reflect the kind of relationship that would foster such a venture in church-related multicultural liberal arts education than that of a "holy experiment"?

39. Page Smith, *Killing the Spirit: Higher Education in America* (New York: Penguin Books, 1990), pp. 172-73.

40. The irony is even more telling; Smith argues that over time the small church-related liberal arts colleges have provided the research universities with some of their best graduate students (ibid., p. 85).

On Witnessing Our Story:
Christian Education in Liberal Societies

STANLEY HAUERWAS

I. On the "Tonto" Principle

The story goes that one time the Lone Ranger and his faithful Indian sidekick, Tonto, found themselves surrounded by twenty thousand Sioux. The Lone Ranger turned to Tonto and asked, "What do you think we ought to do, Tonto?" Tonto responded, "What do you mean by 'we,' white man?" An amusing story, but one whose implications are not easy for those of us schooled by Enlightenment presumptions to understand, much less act on. For the "Tonto" principle means that we cannot avoid asking Alasdair MacIntyre's questions, "Whose justice? Which rationality?"

For example, as representatives of cultures formed by the cosmopolitan outlook of modernity we simply assume that it is always possible to communicate with another linguistic community.[1] What-

1. Indeed, as MacIntyre makes clear, both in *Whose Justice? Which Rationality?* (Notre Dame: University of Notre Dame Press, 1988) and in *Three Rival Versions of Moral Inquiry: Encyclopedia, Genealogy and Tradition* (Notre Dame: University of Notre Dame Press, 1990), perhaps the most determinative characteristic of modernity is its presumption that there is no "otherness" that is not capable of being understood if we just work hard enough at it. I suspect this accounts for the stress on otherness associated with such extraordinary thinkers as Adorno, but one of the difficulties with the abstract category of otherness is how it tends to domesticate that which we fear. However, there can be no question of the significance of the category of the other as a challenge to the presumptions of Enlightenment rationality.

For an attack on the very language of pluralism, see John Milbank, "The End of Dialogue," in *Christian Uniqueness Reconsidered: The Myth of a Pluralistic Theology of*

ever difficulties such communications may involve can be overcome by thorough education. Thus it is assumed that one language is always, in principle, translatable into another. There is no doubt about the possibility of translation of some sayings; but this account of translation assumes that there is something like English as such or Hebrew as such or Latin as such, and that each can be translated into another. But as MacIntyre argues, there are no such languages but only "Latin-as-written-and-spoken-in-the-Rome-of-Cicero and Irish-as-written-and-spoken-in-sixteenth-century-Ulster. The boundaries of a language are the boundaries of some linguistic community which is also a social community."[2] Thus the Irish "Doire Columcille" can never be translated into the English "Londonderry" once it is recognized that even names for persons and places are used *as* identification *for* those who share the same beliefs and presumptions about legitimate authority.[3] In fact, Doire Columcille resides in a different narrative tradition than Londonderry.

MacIntyre reminds us that arguments concerning commensurability and incommensurability have failed to attend to the difference

---

Religions, ed. Gavin D'Costa (Maryknoll, NY: Orbis Books, 1990), pp. 174-91. Milbank contends that the

> terms of discourse which provide both the favored categories for encounter with other religions — *dialogue, pluralism* and the like — together with the criteria for the acceptable limits of the pluralist embrace — social justice, liberation, and so forth — are themselves embedded in a wider Western discourse become globally dominant. And the implication of this paradox is evident: The moment of contemporary recognition of other cultures and religions optimistically celebrated by this volume, is itself — as the rhetoric of its celebration makes apparent — none other than the moment of total obliteration of other cultures by Western norms and categories, with their freight of Christian influence. . . . [Y]oking the good causes of socialism, feminism, anti-racism and ecologism to the concerns of pluralism, actually tends to curb and confine them, because the discourse of pluralism exerts a rhetorical drag in a so-called liberal direction, which assumes the propriety of the West-inspired nation-state and the West-inspired capitalist economy. (p. 175)

As Milbank asks later, "How can a consensus about social justice, which is relatively independent of religion, possibly help to mediate the differences between religions?" (p. 182). For an equally compelling challenge see Ken Surin, "A 'Politics of Speech': Religious Pluralism in the Age of the McDonald's Hamburger," in D'Costa, pp. 192-212.

2. MacIntyre, *Whose Justice? Which Rationality?* p. 373.
3. Ibid., p. 378.

between language as such and language in use.[4] To know the latter is to be part of practices and habits that allow one to know how to go on in a manner that is poetic. According to MacIntyre, that is why the young are initiated into such languages through poetic expression. "It is in hearing and learning and later in reading spoken and written poetic texts that the young in the type of society with which we are concerned learn the paradigmatic uses of key expressions at the same time and

4. Stephen Fowl argues that MacIntyre has overstated his case concerning translation by confusing translatability with acceptability. He follows Jeffrey Stout's arguments, drawing on Donald Davidson, to argue "that for any group of expressions to which we ascribe the term language, there must be sufficient overlap with our own expressions to allow analogies to be drawn and translation to begin. If there were absolutely no parallels between another group's expressions and our own, we would lack sufficient reason for ascribing the term language to their expressions." ("Could Horace Talk with the Hebrews? Translatability and Moral Disagreement in MacIntyre and Stout," *Journal of Religious Ethics* 19, 1 (Spring 1991). Fowl's point is not, however, to undermine MacIntyre's general position in favor of Stout's in *Ethics After Babel* (Boston: Beacon Press, 1988), but rather to indicate that total disagreement on any issue is impossible. I am not as convinced, however, as Fowl and Stout are by Davidson's general arguments concerning incommensurability. As Michael Quirk points out, Davidson tends to think of language fundamentally as a locus of belief. He thus fails to note that languages depend on what Wittgenstein calls "agreements and judgments." That is only made possible against a background of skills and practices. That, I take it, is the heart of MacIntyre's position on these matters. Quirk's views are expressed in his paper "Stout on Relativism, Liberalism and Communitarianism" (unpublished manuscript).

John Milbank, in *Theology and Social Theory: Beyond Secular Reason* (Cambridge: Basil Blackwell, 1990), agrees with Fowl that it is certainly the case that there must be some background of agreements for a radical disagreement to be even possible, yet he asserts that

> MacIntyre is surely right to deny that an outsider's knowledge is just equivalent to that of the insider; the difference is small, but vital. For the outsider can know all the rules, even the rules for modifying the rules, and in many circumstances will be able to predict the behaviour of the cultural aliens. However, he will be unlikely to have the ability for "poetic" innovation, nor to be able to predict this, precisely because the sense of a continuity-in-difference involves an imprescribable judgement which necessitates a belief that the condition in question "is going somewhere," pressing towards a *telos* that it can never adequately express in words. The outsider, being by definition a non-believer in this immanent/transcendent directionality, will only be able to make innovations which he finds "attractive" in a playful spirit, but is bound to see these as essentially arbitrary departures, not further specifications of an elusive *telos*. . . . So, for an alien tongue to be comprehensible to us need not mean that we have found some linguistic equivalents, merely that we have begun to be ourselves alien to our former selves through the process of the encounter. (pp. 341-42)

inseparably from their learning the model exemplifications of the virtues, the legitimating genealogies of their community, and its key prescription. Learning its language and being initiated into their community's tradition or traditions is one and the same initiation."[5]

Yet modernity is characterized by the development of late twentieth-century English, an internationalized language that has been developed so that it can become potentially available to anyone and everyone, whatever their membership in any or no community.[6] This reinforces one of the defining beliefs of modernity — namely, that we are able to understand everything from human culture and history, no matter how alien. That we might not be able to reach a common understanding with another is unthinkable. It is merely a problem of communication that will surely be solved by their learning our language.

The institution we use to achieve this kind of communication is the school. Of course, education involves much more than just what happens in our schools. Indeed, I suspect that the most determinative education most people receive in modern societies is received outside schools, whether the schools are public or private, secular or church-related. Yet schools are the places where we legitimate the assumption that we basically share the same language that makes communication possible between diverse and different peoples. This, we believe, is what makes a pluralist society possible.

Yet the Sioux just will not go away. And the battle is being waged in the schools from the elementary grades through the university. Blacks, Native Americans, and women have challenged the alleged bias of the curriculum of our schools, both public and private. The depth of the challenge can be judged by the very terms used to describe the challengers — *blacks, Indians,* and *women.* Blacks do not wish to be known exclusively for their color; Native Americans remind us that there is no people called "Indian," but rather that they are Sioux, Blackfoot, or Iroquois; and women often do not want to underwrite gender assumptions that go with the very designation "woman."

Moreover, they are quite right to be concerned about such designa-

5. MacIntyre, *Whose Justice? Which Rationality?* p. 382. By introducing the poetic, MacIntyre does not mean that innovation in a language can only be accomplished by poets, since knowing how to go on and how to go further in the language is potentially an ability that every language user is capable of acquiring. The poet is simply one who has that ability to a peculiar degree.

6. Ibid., p. 373.

217

tions, because much more is at stake than how a group is named. But putting the matter in those terms is still not strong enough, for what could be more important than one's name? For, if MacIntyre is right, a name is shorthand for a story of who you are and what you care about. A name is power to determine memory for how the story continues to be told. Moreover, a name can suggest who has the authority to tell the story. "Blacks," "Indians," and "women" too often sound like stories told by others rather than like stories those people would tell about themselves.

I am aware that such claims often appear exaggerated, but I think it would be a mistake to dismiss them. For example, I think the most determinative moral training we provide in schools is the history told and/or presupposed, not only in history courses specifically, but throughout the curriculum. Through that history we often inscribe or reinforce ourselves and our students in traditions that are corrupt. Yet all this is done in the name of objectivity and rationality.

For example, no story grips the imagination of our educative practices more determinatively than "Columbus discovered America." Of course there can be disputes about whether Columbus was the first discoverer of the "new world," or whether he really discovered what we now call "America," but the main outline of that story is not questioned. It is the story that forms our educational system, privileging as it does the necessary background we call Europe, the Holy Roman Empire, the Roman Empire, Greece, the role of science, the great philosophers, and so on.

Yet Michael Shapiro, drawing on Tzvetan Todorov's book *The Conquest of America,* observes that this story enshrined now in the language of objectivity effectively silences other voices. From Columbus we proceed to tell the story of the Spanish conquest by making the Spanish necessary actors in "our" narrative. Yet "in locating the Spanish rhetorically as discoverers of the 'New World' (and as 'conquerors,' which implies a different role in a narrative than 'slaughterers'), we reproduce the original Indians, not the Spanish, as the Others inasmuch as we trace our origins to that which we have called the European 'discovery' of the 'New World.' As Todorov remarks, 'We are all the direct descendants of Columbus, it is with him that our genealogy begins, insofar as the word *beginning* has a meaning.'"[7]

7. Michael J. Shapiro, *The Politics of Representation* (Madison: University of Wisconsin Press, 1988), p. 107. He is quoting Tzvetan Todorov, *The Conquest of America,* trans. Richard Howard (New York: Harper Torchbooks, 1987), p. 5.

Shapiro, I think, is right to draw our attention to the importance of accounts such as Todorov's because they illumine how "objective" accounts of "our" history can conceal the voice of the other. The Spanish in discovering the "Indian" in fact discovered themselves — just as whites "discover" blacks and "Indians," and men "discover" women. Yet those very "discoveries" can mask a history of violence and terror that never ceases to be present in the ongoing descriptions — descriptions we need for our present understanding and action.

For example, Shapiro notes that from the time of the Spanish "discoverers," the Native American voice has not been able to challenge the practices that the nation of the new world entered into, producing what we call the "international system." He notes that the first scripting of Guatemala into international speech was by Pedro de Alvarado, Cortez's infamous captain, who described his subjugation of Guatemala in the following terms: "After having sent my messengers to this country, informing them of how I was to come to conquer and pacify the provinces that might not be willing to place themselves under the dominions of His Majesty, I asked them as his vassals (for as such they had offered themselves to your Grace) the favor and assistance of passage through their country; that by so doing, they would act as good and loyal vassals of His Majesty and that they would be greatly favored and supported in all justice by me and the Spaniards in my company; and if not, I threatened to make war on them as on traitors rising in rebellion against the service of our Lord the Emperor and that as such they would be treated, and that in addition to this, I would make slaves of all those who should be taken alive in the war."[8]

We — that is, those of us who inherit the "civilized social orders" made possible by Pedro de Alvarado and others like him — recoil in horror at such brutality used against the Native Americans. Yet we must remember that Pedro de Alvarado and the rest did not understand themselves to be brutal; rather, they represented the drive toward the universal victory of Christianity. As Shapiro notes,

> Christianity implanted in Spanish culture a social self-centeredness that equated everything connected with Spain and its Catholicism as natural, true, and right. Without getting into an extended analysis of

8. Shapiro, p. 108.

this relationship between Christianity and ethnocentrism, it should suffice to cite as an example the Spanish *Requerimiento*, which was the injunction required by Spanish law to be read to the Indians whenever Spaniards would first step on appropriated soil. The text gives a history of humanity centered on the appearance of Jesus Christ. Christ was the "master of the human lineage" who bestowed his power on Saint Peter, and in turn the pope, who, it seems, authorized the Spanish to take possession of the American continent. In addition to being informed, the Indians are given a choice: become Christians and vassals or "we shall forcibly enter your country . . . make war against you in all ways and manners that we can, and shall subject you to the yoke and obedience of the church." In this text, then, spiritual expansion and sovereign power are combined. More important, the universalistic notions of Christianity are incorporated into Spanish colonialist pretensions, producing a cultural intolerance toward things constituted as alien.[9]

Shapiro notes that the use of the *Requerimiento* certainly had its critics among the Spanish. For example, Bartolomé de Las Casas strongly criticized Alvarado for "killing, ravaging, burning, robbing and destroying all the country wherever he came, under the above mentioned pretext *(Requerimiento)*, that the Indians should subject themselves to such inhuman, unjust, and cruel men, in the name of the unknown King of Spain, of whom they had never heard and whom they considered to be much more unjust and cruel than his representatives."[10] Certainly Las Casas's position is more humane than Alvarado's, but Todorov argues that even this constitution of the Indian other has a subjugating effect. As Todorov points out, "Las Casos loves the Indians. And is a Christian. For him these two traits are linked: he loves the Indians precisely *because* he is a Christian, and his love *illustrates* his faith." Yet as Todorov further observes, Las Casas's perception of the Indians was poor exactly because he was a Christian. Las Casas rejects violence but for him there is only one true religion, "And this 'truth' is not only personal (Las Casos does not consider religion true *for him*), but universal; it is valid for everyone, which is why he himself does not renounce the evangelizing project. Yet is there not already a violence in the conviction that one possesses the truth oneself, whereas this is not

9. Ibid., pp. 109-10.
10. Ibid., p. 109.

220

the case for others, and that one must furthermore impose that truth on those others?"[11]

We recoil at this suggestion. If it is true, it seems we are simply silenced. Moreover, we fear its implications. For it seems to imply that the very histories that we teach our children as Christians, the narratives acknowledged and unacknowledged that we inhabit and pass on, are narratives that continue to legitimate the coercive imposition of the Christian story. It is no wonder that we seek to silence those whose very description — as "blacks," "Indians," or "women" — challenges our claims to objectivity. The "Tonto" principle, once acknowledged, is hard indeed to domesticate.

II. The "Tonto" Principle and Education

As I have already suggested, nowhere are these issues more acute and troubling than in our institutions of education. Of course the stories that form us, that we inhabit, are much more determinative in the practices of our culture than in education per se. Yet it is in our educational institutions that we reify those stories as "objective" and true. They become what anyone would believe if they just thought about it or were better "educated."

For example, think how the very idea of the "United States" is reified in the histories we teach in our schools. We assume they are innocent sets of objects that require no justification. They are simply part of the story. Yet as Michael Shapiro observes, in evoking the idea of the "United States," for example,

> we could refer not to an administrative unit controlled by the federal government but rather to the process by which white Europeans have been consolidating control over the continental domain (now recognized as the United States) in a war with several indigenous ("Indian") nations. This grammar, within which we could have the "United States" in a different way — as violent process rather than as a static, naturalized reality — would lead us to note that while the armed hostilities have all but ceased, there remains a system of economic exclusion, which has the effect of maintaining a steady attrition rate

11. Todorov, pp. 168-69.

among native Americans. The war goes on by other means, and the one-sidedness of the battle is still in evidence. For example, in the state of Utah, the life expectancy of the native American is only half that of the European descendent.[12]

Yet in our schools, especially in our public schools, we tell the story of the United States as the story of unity. As "history" this story may not be told as a moral exercise, but it becomes all the more morally powerful exactly because of its assumed "objectivity." The extent of its power is nowhere better exhibited than in the inability of people such as Native Americans to tell their story in any way except as it fits into the larger story of the United States. To fail to make their story so "fit" means they risk being called uneducated. It sometimes seems the only option you have to resist domination is by being a drunken Indian, a lazy black, or an angry woman.

As Shapiro points out, however, there is little attempt to resist the story we call the "United States" because it is the language necessary for us to do business. If you employed the alternative understanding of "United States" — as a violent process — you could not negotiate everyday life. Instead, dominant discourses about the United States are accepted so that those of us who seek to be good citizens, political actors, and/or socially concerned will be able to be concerned about "foreign policy" problems. For example, Shapiro calls our attention to *Time* magazine's article on the death of thousands of workers at the Union Carbide plant in Bhopal, India. The article was accompanied by a photograph of the victims, with a large caption reading "Environment." The obvious implication is that we should understand Bhopal as a pollution accident.

That it was so treated may have to do with interdepartmental rivalries at *Time;* the environmental department may not have had a cover story for a while. Yet the depiction of Bhopal as an environmental problem goes deeper than the internal politics of *Time.* As Shapiro observes, there is

12. Shapiro, p. 95. Of course it may be objected that Shapiro's evidence in this respect is weighted since Utah residents generally live longer than most Americans. The majority of Utah residents are Mormons who for religious reasons do not engage in practices that are so disastrous for the health of the general population. Yet Shapiro's point remains valid because it is hard to see how anyone could fail to acknowledge that Native Americans are at a decided disadvantage in this country just to the extent that they determine to remain Native Americans.

a kind of ideological scripting of the allocation of danger around the globe. Within their scripting, controlled by the dominant modes of representing problems of foreign and international politics, events involving the use of weapons against foreign nationals on their own soil yet recruited into the foreign-policy discursive space, while killing them with pesticide chemicals does not. Business interests in powerful nations with sophisticated health and safety conscious populations find themselves, with the complicity of their governments, exporting their more dangerous forms of working. Taken as a whole, this can be thought of as a general pattern of policy making. Those nations with strength and thus disproportionate shares of well-being and safety for their populations tend to increase this kind of international inequality by exporting dangers. And those groups (collaborating classes) in the host nation who, because of domestic inequalities, are protected from the dangers while benefiting from the activities, contribute by encouraging their importation. In this context, the effect of *Time's* Bhopal coverage is to help maintain the kind of discursive space that exonerates the foreign-policy making of powerful nations and collaborating weaker ones from one of the more deadly effects of international politics, the allocation of danger. Within the discursive space of "environment," we are more prone to invoke the concept of accident or, at least, to limit responsible agents to the occupational safety and health practices of the corporation invoked instead of politicizing the event by locating it within the discursive space of policy-making in the international system.[13]

It is interesting how these presumptions are even carried over into the maps we use in our schools. In America the United States is always on the top half of the globe because we are sure that north is up. We are equally sure that Australia is down and that it is much smaller than

13. Ibid., p. 97. The issue that Shapiro raises through this example is one of the most pressing in contemporary ethical theory. For ethics as conceived on the liberal model presumes that the descriptions are already in. The only question then is what one ought to do or what principles justify the various alternatives that are thought to be available. What is missing in such accounts of ethics is where the descriptions come from and whose interests they are serving. This is the fundamental question involved in discussions of whether the Gulf War did or did not correspond to just war. For a wonderful account of these difficult issues, see John Howard Yoder's "Just War Tradition: Is It Credible?" *The Christian Century* 108, 9 (13 March 1991): 295-98. Also of interest is Richard John Neuhaus's "Just War and This War" and my response, "An Open Letter to Richard Neuhaus," both in *First Things* (May 1991).

North America. The very nature of our maps, moreover, denotes our presumptions toward objectivity as they are meant to give us a complete picture of the "world" — thus they are meant to impress by their close attention to detail. Our maps, those innocent objects in every first-grade classroom, underwrite the Enlightenment story that we — that is, we Americans — are rightly in control of the world because we can produce the "best" maps.[14]

Christians ironically have entered into this grand educational project in the name of objectivity, the quest for the universal, and most of all societal peace. For education, whether it is public or religious, in most liberal societies has had as its purpose the suppression of minority voices, ironically in the interest of fostering communication. It is, of course, true that in the past explicit Christian social orders suppressed dissenting voices, but it is even more the case today that the alleged pluralistic states of the present that profess to be guided by no visions of human nature or destiny are in fact, as Lesslie Newbigin argues, guided by a very specific ideology of the Enlightenment.[15]

In the name of objectivity that serves the politics of the liberal state, we have accepted the notion that the state can be neutral in religious matters. But as Newbigin observes, there is no way that students passing through schools and universities sponsored by the Enlightenment can avoid being shaped in certain directions. The very omission of religion from the curriculum of schools in the name of a fictional neutrality speaks loudly about what a society believes and wants its children to believe. Indeed, Newbigin notes that for Muslims, who now constitute six percent

14. Michel De Certeau notes in *The Practice of Everyday Life* (Berkeley: University of California Press, 1984) how maps, particularly in the Middle Ages, are structured on the travel story: "stories of journeys and actions are marked out by the 'citation' of the places that result from them or authorize them. From this angle, we can compare the combination of 'tours' and 'maps' in everyday stories with the manner in which, over the past five centuries, they have been interlaced and then slowly disassociated in literary and scientific representations of space. In particular, if one takes the 'map' in its current geographical form, we can see that in the course of the period marked by the birth of modern scientific discourse (i.e., from the 15th-17th century) the map has slowly disengaged itself from the itineraries that were the conditions of its possibility" (p. 120). De Certeau's reflections on the relationship between stories and space, as well as time and place, provide a fascinating way to rethink the strong distinctions between history and nature so prevalent in our modern discourse. I am indebted to Phil Kenneson for calling my attention to this extraordinary book.

15. Lesslie Newbigin, *Foolishness to the Greeks: The Gospel and Western Culture* (Grand Rapids: Eerdmans, 1986), p. 140.

of the English population and over eighty percent in some inner-city schools, the very idea of treating religion as a subject that can be put into a list alongside physics, history, and literature is itself an assault on the foundations of their belief.[16] Our neutrality about religion has been an attempt to suppress conflict in the name of peace, but the result is the creation of people who think that all substantive convictions are a matter of opinion. They are violent only against those, like Muslims, who refuse to relegate matters that matter to opinion.

The strategy of Christian education to supplement the secular subjects with courses in theology or to identify the religious dimension with concern for the "total student" have clearly failed. Nor is it sufficient to identify the religious with the "value" dimensions of knowledge, since that will only privilege the "factual."[17] Again, as Newbigin suggests, most modern accounts of the world exclude purpose as a factor in the ultimate constitution of things. "That the development of the individual person is governed by the program encoded in the DNA molecule is a fact every educated person is expected to know and accept. It will be part of the curriculum in the public school system. That every human being is made to glorify God and enjoy him forever is an opinion held by some people but not part of public truth. Yet, if it is true, it is at least as important as anything else in the preparation of young people for their journey through life."[18] Moreover, I might add, it cannot be excluded; in fact, any knowledge, including the knowledge of DNA, must manifest the glory of God if it is to be truthful.

16. Ibid.

17. MacIntyre notes, "The commonest candidate, in modern versions of what is all too often taken to be *the* correspondence theory of truth, for that which corresponds to a judgment in this way is a fact. But facts, like telescopes and wigs for gentlemen, were a seventeenth-century invention. In the sixteenth century and earlier 'fact' in English was usually a rendering of the Latin 'factum,' a deed, an action, and sometimes in Scholastic Latin an event or an occasion. It was only in the seventeenth century that 'fact' was first used in the way in which later philosophers such as Russell, Wittgenstein, and Ramsey were to use it. It is of course and always was harmless, philosophically and otherwise, to use the word 'fact' of what a judgment states. What is and was not harmless, but highly misleading, was to conceive of a realm of facts independent of judgment or of any other form of linguistic expression, so that judgments or statements or sentences could be paired off with facts, truth or falsity being the alleged relationship between such paired items" (*Whose Justice? Which Rationality?* pp. 357-58). To continue to use value language, therefore, only underwrites this sense of the factual which seems so clearly wrong.

18. Newbigin, *Foolishness to the Greeks,* p. 38.

So we must ask why it has been blacks, Native Americans, and women — and not Christians — who have been challenging the curriculum of the so-called "public schools." Why have we left it to fundamentalists to challenge the reigning assumption that our world makes sense even though all acknowledgment of the universe's created status is excluded?[19] I suspect the answer is that non-fundamentalist Christians have feared appearing foolish in the eyes of the world — or, to put it less charitably, the eyes of non-fundamentalist Christians have in fact become the eyes of the world. As a result, we have failed to challenge those stories that legitimate the powers that rule us.

I suspect that we have been tempted in this direction because we have assumed that the universality of the Kingdom is now carried by the forms of knowledge sponsored by the Enlightenment. We think we are different from the Spanish, such as Alvarado, because we are not killing but only educating. After all, objectivity is the necessary standard for all right-thinking people. Of course it is important to hear the voices of blacks, women, and perhaps even third-world authors by introducing some works into our established canons, but such works must meet the standards of recognizable academic merit. In short, to be part of the conversation we have to agree to abide by the Enlightenment's *Requerimiento*.

Such a *Requerimiento* was nicely embodied in a recent advertisement that ran in the *New York Review of Books,* sponsored by an organization called the National Association of Scholars. The ad was titled, "Is the Curriculum Biased?" It began by summarizing the charge that the curricula of higher education are "Eurocentric" and patriarchal and the demand for the addition of more works by blacks, women, and other minorities. The National Association of Scholars disputed these claims and demands by arguing:

> First, any work, whether formerly neglected or widely known, should be added, retained, or removed from the curriculum on the basis of its conformance to generally applicable intellectual and aesthetic stan-

---

19. These questions are obviously too complex to be treated adequately here. It is my own view, however, that part of the difficulty is our acceptance of the term *nature* as having more descriptive power than the Christian affirmation of creation. Things go decisively wrong when nature is understood primarily as a contrast to human beings rather than to God. *Creation* rightly reminds us that all being has a created status and is in service.

dards. A sound curriculum cannot be built by replacing those standards with the principle of proportional representation of authors, classified ethnically, biologically, or geographically.

Second, the idea that students will be discouraged by not encountering more works by members of their own race, sex, or ethnic group, even were it substantiated, would not justify adding inferior works. Such paternalism conveys a message opposite to the one desired.

Third, other cultures, minority subcultures, and social problems have long been studied in the liberal arts curriculum in such established disciplines as history, literature, comparative religion, economics, political science, anthropology, and sociology. But more important, mere acquaintance with differences does not guarantee tolerance, an ideal Western in origin and fostered by knowledge of what is common to us all.

Fourth, the idea that the traditional curriculum "excludes" the contributions of all but males of European descent is patently false. From their beginnings, Western art and science have drawn upon the achievements of non-Western societies and since have been absorbed and further enriched by peoples around the globe. That the liberal arts oppress minorities and women is yet more ludicrous. Even if the curriculum were confined to thought strictly European in origin, it would still present a rich variety of conflicting ideas, including the very concepts of equality and freedom from oppression invoked by those who would reorient the curriculum.

Fifth, while diversity of background is valuable to the discussion of issues to which those differences are germane, objectivity is in general not enhanced but subverted by the idea that people of different sexes, races, or ethnic backgrounds necessarily see things differently. The assertion that cognition is determined by group membership is itself an example of stereotypic thinking which undermines the possibility of a true community of discourse.

Sixth, the study of the traditions and achievements of other nations and of ethnic subcultures is important and should be encouraged. But this must proceed in a manner that is intellectually honest and does not serve as a pretext for inserting polemics into the curriculum. Furthermore, "multicultural education" should not take place at the

227

expense of studies that transcend cultural differences: the truths of mathematics, the sciences, history, and so on, are not different for people of different races, sexes, or cultures, and for that reason alone their study is liberating. Nor should we further attenuate the study of the traditions of the West. Not only is knowledge of those traditions essential for any evaluation of our own institutions, it is increasingly relevant to our understanding of other nations, which, in striking testament to the universality of the values they embody, are rapidly adapting Western practices to their own situations.

The National Association of Scholars is in favor of ethnic studies, the study of non-Western cultures, and the study of the special problems of women and minorities in our society, but it opposes subordinating entire humanities and social science curricula to such studies and it views with alarm their growing politicization. Efforts purportedly made to introduce "other points of view" and "pluralism" often seem in fact designed to restrict attention to a narrow set of issues, tendentiously defined. An examination of many women's studies and minority studies courses and programs discloses little study of other cultures and much excoriation of our society for its alleged oppression of women, blacks, and others. The banner of "cultural diversity" is apparently being raised by some whose paramount interest actually lies in attacking the West and its institutions.[20]

I must admit that when I first read this I thought someone had meant it as a satire. I simply did not think that anyone could possibly believe that tolerance is an "ideal Western in origin" that is justified by knowledge "common to us all." I assumed that "Western in origin" might give an indication that "common to us all" might be problematic. The statement does acknowledge the importance of conflicting ideas, but it fails to see that the very concepts of equality and freedom might be contested — in fact, might not and should not be acknowledged as goods. Moreover, the claim that there are studies that transcend cultural differences cannot help but underwrite the story that underneath all our differences we all share the same story, and that through increasing

20. *The New York Review of Books*, 1 March 1990, p. 17. I have subsequently learned that this is the National Association of Scholars' statement of purpose. It has been widely distributed across universities. For an extraordinary alternative to the kind of position represented by the NAS, see Edward Said, *The World, the Text, and the Critic* (Cambridge: Harvard University Press, 1983).

enlightenment by way of education we will discover that we all want the same thing.[21]

Christians have on the whole underwritten this story as our own. We have allowed this story to become the "history" of our time. We have stood for allowing more voices to be part of the "history," but we have not conceived that the history itself might need to be challenged in the interests of the gospel. If we have to choose between those who represent the Enlightenment (MacIntyre calls them the encyclopedi-asts), and those who deny rationality and morality altogether (MacIn-tyre calls them the genealogists), most Christians think we must stand with those who still care about "truth" and morality and against those who "reduce" all conflicts to power struggles, who embrace "relativism" and threaten anarchy.[22]

21. The first drafts of this chapter were written in May of 1990. When I selected the NAS statement of purpose I assumed it was just a random example of widely held presuppositions. I was quite surprised, therefore, to receive the statement in an envelope mailed by a colleague at Duke, who was asking me to become a charter member of the National Association of Scholars at Duke. Of course I wrote to decline the honor, explaining that I could not join such an organization since it embodied presuppositions about "objectivity" that have resulted in Christian theology no longer being recognized as a legitimate academic enterprise. I find it equally problematic to think there is a set of "classics" that could be known separate from a tradition. MacIntyre's analysis in *Three Rival Versions of Moral Inquiry* seems completely confirmed by this debate.

One of the oddest sets of claims I find associated with those who fear a lessening of academic rigor in the loss of something called "the canon" is their presumption that the so-called "multiculturalists," "deconstructionists," and/or "anti-foundationalists" represent a politicization of the curriculum. Such a claim presumes that the curriculum is not already politicized. That people could assume that "Columbus discovered Amer-ica" is objective history is but an indication that the curriculum is already political. Such descriptions are made to appear apolitical by hegemonic power. Indeed, one of the oddities of the debate is the assumption that there is something called a canon of Western literature to be preserved. Jews and Christians rightly believe they have a canonical scripture, but I find it hard to understand how those who do not share our theological presuppositions can even use the word *canon*.

22. MacIntyre identifies the encyclopediast with Adam Gifford, Thomas Spencer Baynes, William Robertson Smith, Henry Sidgwick, D'Alembert, Diderot, and, of course, Kant, among others. The great genealogist was Nietzsche, and more recently, Foucault. In many ways MacIntyre is obviously closer to the latter than to the former. I think MacIntyre is well aware of this, but yet he does not encourage comparison with the anti-foundationalists because he regards that position as directly correlate to the ency-clopediast project. He is trying to provide a different way of reading the current debate by demonstrating that the epistemological term of philosophy in modernity was a mistake. That is, it was a mistake to attempt to meet the skeptic's challenge by vindicating

What we must ask, however, is how we Christians ever got our-selves in the position of believing we must make such a choice. The crucial question is how we can make the story that we believe to be true, not just for us, but for the world, compelling in a world caught between such unhappy alternative stories. In short, the challenge to us as Christians is to find a way to witness to the God of Abraham, Isaac, Jacob, and Jesus, without allowing that witness to become an ideology for the powers that would subvert our witness. I think we can do that if we take seriously the very character required of us by the story that we believe to be the truth about our existence — that is, that we be witnesses.

III. On Witness and Education; or Telling the Old, Old Story

I grew up with a gospel hymn called "I Love to Tell the Story":

---

something called rationality in general. The only way to answer the kind of skeptics created by the encyclopediast project is by showing that there is an alternative narrative. Of course that does not prohibit MacIntyre from trying to show that the genealogists may lack sufficient resources to account for themselves. That is, they cannot, given their position, show why the moral presuppositions in writing as well as in reading texts can be sustained. See, for example, his arguments in *Three Rival Versions of Moral Inquiry,* pp. 52-57, 196-215. MacIntyre, however, is quite aware that he cannot finally provide any knock-down arguments against the genealogical project, since trying to provide such an argument would only confirm their position. John Milbank follows a very similar strategy in his *Theology and Social Theory,* pp. 278-325.

The oft-made charge against the genealogists as being either nihilist and/or rel-ativist seems to me to be misplaced. Though some may be one or both, such charges in fact presuppose exactly the issues at stake. For example, the oft-made claim that anti-foundationalists assume that you can make anything you want from a text is simply not true. Consider, for example, Stanley Fish's account in *Doing What Comes Naturally* (Durham: Duke University Press, 1989): "Interpretive communities are no more than sets of institutional practices; and while those practices are continually being trans-formed by the very work that they do, the transformed practice identifies itself and tells its story in relation to general purposes and goals that have survived and form the basis of a continuity. . . . The fact that the objects we have are all objects that appear to us in the context of some practice, of work done by some interpretive community, doesn't mean that they are not objects or that we don't have them or that they exert no pressure on us. All it means is that they are interpreted objects and that since interpretations can change, the perceived shape of objects can change too" (p. 153). For an extremely interesting comparison of Fish and MacIntyre, see Allen Jacobs, "The Unnatural Prac-tices of Stanley Fish: A Review Essay," *South Atlantic Review* 55 (1990): 87-97.

I love to the tell the story
Of unseen things above,
Of Jesus and His glory,
Of Jesus and His love.

I love to tell the story,
Because I know 'tis true;
It satisfies my longings
As nothing else can do.

I love to tell the story,
'Twill be my theme in glory.
To tell the old, old story
Of Jesus and His love.

In spite of the lack of all theological, poetic, and musical merit, I am sure this old hymn has got the matter right. For it is because we are "storied" as God's creatures that we must be witnesses. Moreover, the only way we can educate is through witness.

What we must understand is that witness is necessary because we are so storied. If the gospel were a truth that could be known in general, then there would be no necessity to witness. All that would be necessary would be to confirm people in what they already know. If the gospel were about general, unavoidable human experience, then it would not be necessary to be confronted by anyone as odd as a Christian. But because the story we tell of God is the story of the life and death of Jesus of Nazareth, the only way to know that story is through witness.

The trick, of course, is how the necessity of witness, the oddness of witness can be recovered in a world that thinks it already knows what that story is about. The problem, as Lesslie Newbigin has stressed, is how Christians can learn to think of themselves as missionaries in a world that we have at least in part been responsible for making.[23] The problem is how we can critically appropriate those aspects of the societies in which we find ourselves, without remaining blinded to the destructive practices that are all the more powerful because they so often promise to serve good ends.

Such destructive practices, as Jim McClendon has reminded us,

23. Lesslie Newbigin, *The Gospel in a Pluralist Society* (Grand Rapids: Eerdmans, 1989).

are called powers in the New Testament. For the salvation wrought in Christ is about the conflict with and the conquest of these powers.

> This point is so crucial for us that it must be expanded: In the Epistles the narrative of Christ's conflict with and conquest of the powers is typically represented in summary, proclamatory form, as for example, in Colossians 2:15 RSV: "He disarmed the principalities and powers . . . and made a public example of them, triumphing over them in him." In the Gospels, however, these conflicts take the form of a story, indeed, they are *the* story, and the opponents are no longer called "the principalities and powers"; rather, they are the human overlords of state and temple, the Herods and Caiaphases and Pilates, or they are the demonic forces that sponsor illness, madness, and temptation, namely the demons and Satan. These can be cast as actors in the drama — while abstractions such as "headship," "authority," and "power" cannot. Note further that the contra-power that Jesus (and through him, God's Spirit) mounts against these is nothing less than the whole course of his obedient life, with its successive moments of proclamation, healing, instruction, the gathering of a redemptive community, and costly submission to the way of the cross and its death and resurrection. Therefore it is at a decisive moment in *that* story that the Lucan Jesus says, "I saw Satan fall like lightning from heaven" (10:18 RSV).[24]

If we are to educate as Christians we cannot fail to introduce our children and one another to the gospel in a manner that helps us name those powers that would determine our lives. The only way to do that is by telling a counter-story to that called the United States and/or its correlative presumptions that underwrite the necessity of what we call the nation-state system. The moral and intellectual courage required for the task is great. Indeed, we cannot pretend to possess such courage on our own; we can only hope to fulfill that mission, as we would anticipate from the story itself, by being part of a community that can help sustain such witness.

As Christians this means that we cannot avoid coming into conflict in school or state. Again, as Newbigin reminds us,

> Christians can never seek refuge in a ghetto where their faith is not proclaimed as public truth for all. They can never agree that there is

24. James Wm. McClendon, Jr., *Ethics: Systematic Theology* (Nashville: Abingdon Press, 1986), p. 174.

one law for themselves and another for the world. They can never admit that there are areas of human life where the writ of Christ does not run. They can never accept that there are orders of creation or powers or dominions that exist otherwise than to serve Christ. Whatever the institutional relationship between the church and the state — and there are many possible relationships, no one of which is necessarily the right one for all times and places — the church can never cease to remind governments that they are under the rule of Christ and that he alone is the judge of all they do. The church can never accept the thesis that the central shrine of public life is empty, in other words, that there has been no public revelation before the eyes of all the world of the purpose for which all things and all peoples have been created and which all governments must serve. It can never accept an ultimate pluralism as a creed even if it must — as of course it must — acknowledge plurality as a fact. In fact, it cannot accept the idea, so popular twenty years ago, of a secular society in which, on principle, there are no commonly acknowledged norms. We know now, I think, that the only possible product of that ideal is a pagan society.[25]

So what are we to do as Christians? Must we build separate schools? Perhaps. But such schools will be of no use if we continue to teach subjects as though what we taught is from anyone's point of view. Until our teaching reflects the witness we are called to make to the story of Christ, we will simply be wasting our effort. Such a witness can happen as easily at "secular" schools as at religious ones. What is important is our willingness to take our story seriously for determining what we are to know as well as what and how we teach.

But are we not left, then, with the problem of Bartolemé de Las Casas, the priest who criticized the use of the *Requerimiento* by Pedro de Alvarado, but who nonetheless was willing to see the "Indians" as potential Christians? How can we be witnesses, how can we be educators, how can we communicate the gospel without explicitly or implicitly underwriting patterns of domination and violence antithetical to the Kingdom brought by Christ? If I have been even partly right, we can begin by acknowledging the gospel to be just what it is — a story, the story of Jesus. We believe the power of God for our salvation is in the telling — or better, the embodiment — of that story in worship. As

25. Newbigin, *Foolishness to the Greeks,* p. 115.

Christians, therefore, we tell the story not because we lack respect for those different from us; rather, as Newbigin says, the Christian tells the story

> simply as one who has been chosen and called by God to be part of the company which is entrusted with the story. It is not her business to convert the others. She will indeed — out of love for them — long that they may come to share the joy that she knows and pray that they may indeed do so. But it is only the Holy Spirit of God who can so touch the hearts and consciences of the others that they are brought to accept the story as true and to put their trust in Jesus. This will always be a mysterious work of the Spirit, often in ways which no third party will ever understand. The Christian will pray that it may be so, and she will seek faithfully both to tell the story and — as part of a Christian congregation — so conduct her life as to embody the truth of the story. But she will not imagine that it is her responsibility to insure that the other is persuaded. That is in God's hands.[26]

---

26. Newbigin, *The Gospel in a Pluralist Society*, p. 182.

THE SCHOOL OF THE CHURCH

Imitating Jesus in a Time of Imitation

MICHAEL WARREN

In this essay I wish to examine the problem contemporary culture has for religious groups, especially local Christian communities. While trying to avoid alarmist categories, I admit to being more alarmed the more I study the situation. Orwell's prediction in *1984* that society would come under total control has come true, but not in the way he envisaged it. In his imagined world, control comes about through surveillance. In our world, massive amounts of surveillance notwithstanding, it has come about through the orchestration of desire and the production of consumption.[1] Control what people long for, and the precise monitoring of consumption becomes the most effective form of surveillance. The sacralization of demographics found in the near-worship awarded to opinion polls is one indication of the importance of such surveillance. Busy monitoring desire, such polls ignore social awareness and moral judgment. Since religiousness is about a particular quality of human longing and desire, religious people will be concerned when human desire is socially produced without attention to ultimate questions of value.

In this first part of my presentation I ask about a single characteristic of contemporary life in the United States as it has been described by four recent writers working from differing backgrounds. As they

---

1. This reflection was prompted by the interview "Truth and Power," chap. 6 of Michel Foucault's *Power/Knowledge* (New York: Pantheon Books, 1980), pp. 109-33. Foucault explores the evolution of subtle social controls over the past two centuries.

sketch it, this feature of life in the United States affects all people, including churchgoers and the smaller group among them actively seeking discipleship. In the second section, I examine the problem culture poses for religious people and offer a way of thinking about culture's connection with religion. In a concluding section I reflect on communities seeking to be disciples of Jesus.

Style as the Embracing of Impressions

The characteristic of contemporary American life I wish to describe has to do with the preference of many people for appearances rather than substance, for impressions instead of thoughtfulness, for semblance over reality. Commentators use varied terminology to describe the same basic phenomenon. The name Stuart Ewen gives it is "style."[2] His use of the term differs from that of art historians, to whom "style" means the ornamental tastes elites succeed in having registered as the unified spirit of an age. Though it is a preoccupation of all sectors of society, style today is different from the unified spirit of an age. It draws its inspiration from any and all social sectors. In our culture, style is all about surfaces, "mouthwatering" objects promising to free life from the daily humdrum, allowing it to float beyond the terms of the real world. "Without ever saying so explicitly, the media of style offer to lift the viewer out of his or her life and place him or her in a utopian netherworld where there are no conflicts, no needs unmet; where the ordinary is — by its very nature — extraordinary."[3] Like a fancy hat, style offers to all a kind of surface prestige.

Ewen describes how these attitudes are communicated by ordinary televiewing, where the uninterrupted message is that style makes up a way of life, a utopian way marked by boundless wealth. The characters depicted most often dwell in a world of bounty, their living space sumptuously appointed, following their whims and fantasies effortlessly. Whatever the cost, paying it is depicted as painless, effortless. Affordability is not an issue. Such illusions are essential to the enchantment of style, with its promise to swoop us out of the dreariness of necessity.

2. Stuart Ewen, *All-Consuming Images: The Politics of Style in Contemporary Culture* (New York: Basic Books, 1988).
3. Ibid., p. 14.

At the other end of this tunnel of television, Ewen finds the viewer harassed by the actual conditions of life, where desire is hemmed in by the constraints of circumstance. Exactly within such specific conditions is the viewer engaged in a relationship with style. It is a quasi-religious relationship marked by promises of transcendence. Through the sorcery of style, the right consumer goods will transport one beyond the every-day to a dreamworld of perfection.

Ewen notes that while style makes statements, it has no convictions. Citing a specific ad for jeans, he shows how the supposed "egalitarianism" of the product is underscored by information given about the blond, blue-eyed model: "Waitress, Bartender, Non-professional AIDS Educator, Cyclist, Art Restoration Student, Anglophile, Neo-Feminist." Ewen comments: "In the world of style, ideas, activities, and commitments become ornaments, adding connotation and value to the garment while they are, simultaneously, eviscerated of meaning."[4] Instead, "Modern style speaks to a world where change is the rule of the day, where one's place in the social order is a matter of perception, the product of diligently assembled illusions." Ewen cautions us against seeing style as only a matter of subjectivity. We must understand how it is created to support the centers of power in social, political, and economic life.

Most helpful in Ewen's account of style is his survey of the historical roots of contemporary attitudes toward it. That history goes back to the rise of the profit economy in medieval towns. As capital became a mobile form of wealth, merchants came to mimic the consumption practices of the nobility, which at first included elaborate clothing. The new merchant-class wealth looked to a variety of objects and products that might signal the status their wealth deserved. As style became something one could purchase, a new commerce in appearances emerged. Entrepreneurs devised ways of reproducing desirable books, such as lavishly illustrated Books of Hours, so as to make them more widely accessible to those who craved the status of owning them. As those with capital chose portraits as a way of signifying their status, art moved beyond the monasteries, churches, and castles. Various kinds of images and artwork became a form of social currency, something that advanced in the following centuries down to our own day. However, a key difference to emerge today is the ready access to the trappings of

4. Ibid., pp. 19-20.

style, which Ewen calls the "iconography of prestige," due in large part to the capacity for the cheap reproduction of this iconography.[5]

As signs of status became cheaply available, a new kind of democracy developed — a consumer democracy — wherein most people had access to the styles once reserved for the elites. If not actual wealth, then "the coded look of wealth" came within the means of many. Now machine-cut bric-a-brac glass could give the illusion of fine hand-cut glass. Factories developed processes of embossing and applying veneer that gave their products the look of quality. One commentator called these developments "delight in the unreal." Eventually even architecture adopted the separation of surface and substance in the way buildings were designed. The development of photography gave everyone except the very poorest accessibility to cheap images. According to Ewen, of all the nineteenth-century developments, photography augmented the power of image over substance as a hallmark of modern style. "Photography became — almost immediately — a prime medium of pretention."[6] Photo studios could invest near-paupers with the accoutrements of wealth and status, which they could then proudly display to others.

From this account one can understand why Ewen might emphasize the illusory or fake aspect of this culture of style:

> Style today is an incongruous cacophony of images, strewn across the social landscape. Style can be borrowed from any source and turn up in a place where it is least expected. The stylish person may look like a duchess one week, a murder victim the next. Style can hijack the visual idiom of astronauts or poach from the ancient pageantry of Guatemalan peasant costumes.[7]

And in another place, highlighting style's illusory kind of change that domesticates the human yearning for transformation, he writes:

> If the style market constitutes a presentation of a way of life, it is a way of life that is unattainable for most, nearly all, people. Yet this doesn't mean that style isn't relevant to most people. It is very relevant. It is the most common realm of our society in which the need for a

---

5. Ibid., pp. 26-30. Additional background for Ewen's historical survey might include the first two chapters of Lester Little's *Religious Poverty and the Profit Economy in Medieval Europe* (New York: Cornell University Press, 1978).

6. Ewen, p. 39.

7. Ibid., p. 14.

better, or different way of life is acknowledged, and expressed on a material level, if not met. It constitutes a politics of change, albeit a "change" that resides wholly on the surface of things. The surfaces, themselves, are lifted from an infinite number of sources.[8]

Ewen is describing quasi-religious promises about what is salvific in life and what can transform it to a new plane.

Behind everything Ewen writes is the idea that people today have a penchant to copy in their own persons the images presented to them. Though he never uses this precise terminology, he is pointing out the centrality of mimesis, of imitative behavior in our day. I had always known that young children are busy copying behavior as their major life work at that age. It took me some while to realize that young people between the ages of 12 and 22 are also very busy copying behavior or searching frantically for models to copy. Finally I came to see the drive for imitation as a central but underestimated character of all human life. In religious traditions such as the Jewish and Christian traditions, imitation is a prime value, with the imitation being of God and God's ways. The kind of imitative "style" Ewen describes reduces imitation to what might be its least form. This theme of imitating a world of "seeming" reality is given close study by the French thinker Jean Baudrillard.[9]

Baudrillard's World of Simulation

As a social philosopher, Baudrillard has given special attention to the character of contemporary culture. Most recently he has been struggling with the structure of communications in a world dominated by electronic media. In his effort to name what many people are actually living, his analysis correlates with Ewen's.[10] For Baudrillard, a key aspect of our former industrial society was production, whereas in today's post-industrial society it is simulation. Industrial production was able to crank out in series products that were exact replicas of one another, first

8. Ibid., p. 16.
9. I cite the work of a French thinker here for two reasons: Baudrillard himself cites many examples from the United States; and the culture of simulation he describes is international because of the proliferation of images in postindustrial countries.
10. Although Ewen does not mention any of Baudrillard's writings, his historical survey supports Baudrillard's overview of the phases of simulation. See Jean Baudrillard, *Selected Writings*, ed. Mark Poster (Stanford: Stanford University Press, 1988), pp. 166-84.

through, human-labor assembly lines and later through automation. These replicas were in a sense simulations, but in a qualitatively different degree than today's simulations. In the current world of simulations, all reference to the real has been replaced. Now models create a "real" that has no true reference to reality or to origins.

Baudrillard uses an allegory from a Juan Luis Borges tale to ground his idea. In this story, the map-makers of the Empire draw a map exactly detailing its territory. As the Empire deteriorates so does the map, and in the end only shreds of it are found rotting in the deserts, actually returning to the very earth the map had represented. Unlike Borges' map, representation today no longer follows on and represents a reality such as the Empire's territory. Instead, today the map precedes and creates the Empire. Indeed, to make the fable applicable to today, the territory itself — the reality — would have to rot in shreds, not the map; for today it is the real that one finds here and there in bits and vestiges.

When I first read this essay of Baudrillard, I was sitting quietly trying to get behind his somewhat obscure point. My phone rang and I answered it. There was a voice, but no person, on the line. A reproduction of a voice exhorted me to buy something. Music and a cheering crowd in the background had also been simulated to add a certain character to the voice of the person on the phone who was not really there. This phone message helped me understand Baudrillard's claim that

> present-day simulators try to make the real, all the real, coincide with their simulation models. . . . Something has disappeared: the sovereign difference between them that was the abstraction's charm. . . . [Today] the real is produced from miniaturized units, from matrices, memory banks and command models — and with these it can be reproduced an indefinite number of times. . . . It is a hyperreal.[11]

Baudrillard would surely have understood the former New York City police inspector's claim that many officers are having their job imagined for them by film and TV renditions of police, and are performing more in that mode than in the way they were initially trained.

The significance of the new kind of simulation can be seen in the difference between dissimulation and simulation. To dissimulate is to make believe one does not have what one actually does have or does not

11. Ibid., pp. 166-67.

know what one in fact does know. The act of dissimulation implies a presence: what one really has or really knows is present but not admitted. To simulate, however, is to make believe one has or knows what in fact one does not. Thus it implies an absence: what one pretends to have or know is really not there. Yet the matter is complicated by the fact that to simulate can involve a step beyond feigning or make-believe, as the case of feigning illness makes clear. To simulate an illness one must *produce some of the symptoms* of illness, a pretense that threatens the difference between "true" and "false," between "real" and "imaginary." In contemporary society simulation endangers the reality principle itself, a point Antonioni underscored almost thirty years ago in his film *Blow-Up*.

I presume that for a philosopher like Baudrillard, this possibility of masking the difference between true and false has chilling consequences. Indeed, his alarm at the erosion of meaning appears to me to underlie all his writings I have seen, but it is hinted at in the following passage:

> Since the simulator produces "true" symptoms, is he or she ill or not? The simulator cannot be treated objectively either as ill, or as not ill. Psychology and medicine stop at this point, before a thereafter undiscoverable truth of the illness. For if any symptom can be "produced," and can no longer be accepted as a fact of nature, then every illness may be considered as simulatable and simulated, and medicine loses its meaning since it only knows how to treat "true" illnesses by their objective causes.[12]

The example he uses to illustrate the character of simulation today is Disneyland in southern California. Here he finds a quasi-religious celebration of "real" America. Though the park is a world of fantasy, it lays out in miniature an objective profile or map of the United States. Both the map and the "reality" it supposedly stands for are illusions. Here in miniature and comic-strip form, the nation's values are exalted, but in an infantilized mode. According to Baudrillard, Disneyland is a double kind of simulation since it aims

> to make us believe that the rest is real, when in fact all of Los Angeles and the America surrounding it are no longer real, but of the order of the hyperreal and of simulation. It is no longer a question of a false representation of reality (ideology), but of concealing the fact that

12. Ibid., pp. 167-68.

the real is no longer real, and thus of saving the reality principle. . . . [Disneyland] is meant to be an infantile world, in order to make us believe that the adults are elsewhere, in the "real" world, and to conceal the fact that real childishness is everywhere, particularly among those adults who go there to act the child in order to foster illusions [regarding] their real childishness.[13]

He goes on to name the various "imaginary stations" surrounding Los Angeles: Enchanted Village, Magic Mountain, Marine World, and film studios.

In other places in his writings, Baudrillard applies this same "chain of illusions" analysis, where one illusion fosters a sequence of further illusions. The Watergate scandal, for example, had the effect of allowing the law to seem to triumph, thus disguising the fact that capital truly runs the country. Immoral and unscrupulous, capital needs a moral superstructure behind which to hide. And so, when the *Washington Post* journalists help regenerate public morality and the rule of law, they prop up the very illusions that allow capital to run free once more. From this sort of analysis there seems no escape. All are trapped in a system that cannot be contested.[14]

Baudrillard would seem to deny all real agency in his description of the way people are coded into a simulated order. For Baudrillard, as one commentator puts it,

responses [of citizens] are structured into a binary system of affirmation or negation: every ad, fashion, commodity, television program, political candidate and poll presents a test to which one is to respond: Is one for or against? Do we want it or not? Are we for X or Y? In this way, one is mobilized in a coded system of similarities and dissimilarities, of identities and programmed differences. . . . The political upshot of his analysis seems to be that everything in the system is subject to cybernetic control and that what appears to be oppositional, outside of, or threatening to the system are really functional parts of a society of simulations.[15]

13. Ibid., p. 172.

14. See ibid., pp. 172-74, where he seems to ridicule his compatriot Pierre Bourdieu's efforts to expose how force works in society. Baudrillard's position seems to be that we can only distort and understate our condition of being socially manipulated.

15. Doug Kellner, "Postmodernism as Social Theory," *Theory, Culture, and Society* 5 (1988): 245. I have found Kellner's summary of Baudrillard's positions very helpful.

If followed to their logical conclusion, these ideas seem to say that persons in society, in whatever combination of group effort, are incapable of social action. Only conformity is possible because the masses are satisfied with spectacle. Baudrillard repeats this idea in many places. •

In an essay on the relation of the masses to media, he finds in these masses "a radical antimetaphysics": a radical lack of will, by which they choose not to will, not to decide about themselves or their world, not to wish, not to desire. They hand over the responsibility for all these activities to someone else — not a special surrogate but anyone — who will wish, desire, and decide for them. They prefer to rely on publicity-type information to offer them a choice or on the political class to order things for them.[16]

Baudrillard's analyses are insightful but discouraging, describing an almost hopeless situation. My suspicion, in the end, is that his essays are meant as kinds of philosophical morality plays, mirrors held up to us to help us see and judge the absence of moral judgment and action in our time. If what Baudrillard says is true, then religious people must take note, for what he describes afflicts many affiliated with religious groups. The issue of what is real and worth suffering for is at the heart of true religious consciousness, and religion's sacred writings are dialogues about reality claims. Religious sensibility has a robust regard for the reality principle, found in its scathing denunciation of false gods.

The Culture of Surface: Corroboration of Baudrillard's Position

If Baudrillard's and Ewen's critiques have significant differences, they still correlate so well that Baudrillard could have written Ewen's reflection that

> modern style speaks to a world where change is the rule of the day, where one's place in the social order is a matter of perception, the product of diligently assembled illusions. . . . Style speaks for a society in which coherent meaning has fled to the hills, and in which drift has provided a context of continual discontent. . . . The production of sumptuous images, for the very few, was once limited to the sacred

16. Baudrillard, "The Masses: The Implosion of the Social in the Media," *Selected Writings*, pp. 207-19. At the end of this essay, Baudrillard does offer the hypothesis that hidden in the abdication of the masses is a kind of resistance, but I find his argument cryptic.

workshops of the medieval monasteries; now, the production and marketing of style is global, touching the lives and imaginations of nearly everyone.[17]

These convictions are borne out by two journalists working independently of one another in the United States. Barbara Goldsmith reports on a Manhattan dinner party whose celebrity guests included a U.S. senator, an embezzler, a woman said to spend $60,000 a year on flowers, the host of a talk show, the chief executive officer of one of the nation's largest corporations, a writer who had settled a plagiarism suit, and a Nobel laureate. Goldsmith points out that such an assemblage blurs the distinction between fame and notoriety, between talent and its lack, between accomplishment and merely being well known, between heroes and villains. What these persons had in common was celebrity status. They all gave an "image" or impression of some quality: wealth, success, heroism, glamour, leadership, danger. When such synthetic personalities become heroes and heroines, it is a sign that a society is absenting itself from the ethical judgment needed for social health. Echoing Ewen and Baudrillard, Goldsmith writes, "We no longer demand reality, only that which is real seeming."[18]

Since the characteristics of a society are found in those it celebrates, an increasing lack of concern about the qualifications of these celebrities has ominous portent. Beyond the preference it shows for synthetic persons vicariously acting out a society's noblest and basest desires, it portends a preference for illusion over reality. In a vein again similar to Baudrillard, Goldsmith says,

> In today's highly technological world, reality has become a pallid substitute for the image reality we fabricate for ourselves, which in turn intensifies our addiction to the artificial. Anyone who has attended a political convention or a major sporting event knows that watching the proceedings on television, where cameras highlight the most riveting moments, then replay and relate them in similar situations, provides us with more stimulating and complex perceptions than being there does.
>
> Next year's visitors to the Grand Canyon need not see it. One mile

17. Ewen, p. 23.
18. Barbara Goldsmith, "The Meaning of Celebrity," *New York Times Magazine*, 4 Dec. 1983, p. 75.

from the boundary will be a $5 million complex where they will be able to view a film of the way the Canyon looks during all four seasons and take a simulated raft ride through artificial rapids.[19]

And so the mechanically recorded and technically altered reality has greater value than the actuality. Kennedy Fraser, a journalist specializing in fashion, picks up the same theme from her own perspective — but only after stepping out of her usual role of commenting about the fashion industry and turning to critique fashion itself.

Fraser finds that in its deepest sense fashion is about something more significant than couture or frivolities of taste. Neither named or noted, it is rather "the lens through which our society perceives itself and the mold to which it increasingly shapes itself." Hidden and unacknowledged, this mental kind of fashion needs to be brought into the light and evaluated. Mental fashion or the search for the fashionable idea has much in common with the old frivolous, pirouetting kind of fashion — that of dress: both hold appearances to be of greater significance than substance. "Among [their] shared limitations are fickleness, a preoccupation with descrying the will of the majority in order to manipulate it or pander to it, and a concern with the accumulation or protection of power and profit." Though often passing itself off as rebellious, fashion actually works to support power: "to think or act for reasons of fashion in any given field is to support that field's established centers of power."[20]

Fraser is describing the nose for trend in the search for "the right stuff" — not in the sense of the correct clothing styles but rather the right ideas, the right interests, the right values, even the right spiritual concerns. Mental fashion is a "skilled master of enthusiasm," causing many to overlook how slavishly they in fact follow along. Even those who should be fostering quality, individuality, and the ability to reflect — writers, critics, artists, editors, and so forth — are apt to present ideas and facts as trendy commodities. They help society hand itself over to trend and style as worthy guides of the human project. Fraser warns that when fashion becomes the framework for perception, it warps not only individual perceptions but also any reasonable picture of the world.

19. Ibid., p. 76.
20. Kennedy Fraser, *The Fashionable Mind* (Boston: David R. Godine, 1985), pp. 145-46.

The greatest drawback of an overfashionable perception is that fashion is concerned, virtually by definition, with surfaces, images, appearances. . . . When the mind surrenders itself to fashion, the first casualty is objective judgment — which is, to all intents, the mind itself. Fashionable perception is incapable of discerning any fixed truth about an object or event.[21]

Intelligence, on the other hand, demands honest, disinterested distinctions "born of an isolated, dogged, unfashionable side of the mind — a sort of gawky mental provincialism." Ironically, the market for mental fashion is especially vital among the college-educated who, having tasted intellectual activity, are now nostalgic for the literary enthusiasms of studenthood. As a result, society — with serious political and cultural consequences — comes to pattern itself on fashion.

I chose to present Goldsmith's and Fraser's ideas — found in two relatively short essays — at this point because they reinforce Baudrillard's and Ewen's main positions. Together the ideas of these four represent a form of cultural critique, disclosing a current situation in enough detail to engage the concern of religious people of any major tradition. But what can be done about this marketing of and embracing of illusion and surfaces, about this preference of impression over reflection, about the promise of salvation from the right commodities? What does this situation mean for religious people — and their leaders — living in the same society and culture described by our commentators? In the face of the socially fostered preference for illusion, will religious people be able to hold onto their unique understandings and judgments about reality? My own view is that religious persons can deal with these matters, though not easily. One route for understanding what must be

---

21. Ibid., p. 148. Ewen, who uses similar terminology about surfaces, cites *The Fashionable Mind* in his bibliography. Note too the similarity of Fraser's ideas to the following comments of Baudrillard about fashion's relation to simulation models:

Just as the model is more real than the real . . . , acquiring thus a vertiginous impression of truth, the amazing aspect of fashion is that it is more beautiful than the beautiful: it is fascinating. Its seductive capacity is independent of all judgments. It exceeds the aesthetic form in the ecstatic form of unconditional metamorphosis.

Whereas the aesthetic form always implies a moral distinction between the beautiful and the ugly, the ecstatic form is immoral. If there is a secret to fashion, beyond the sheer pleasures of art and taste, it is this immorality, the sovereignty of ephemeral models. . . . (*Selected Writings*, p. 186)

done lies in examining the complex notion of culture. This is the route I propose to follow here, because it offers religious people a helpful way of grasping the problem posed for religiousness by the culture of surface.

A Description of Culture

Several years ago, aware of the faith religious educators have in their own use of intentional educational efforts, I found I had become a skeptic, if not an unbeliever. Led by my doubts, I sought to examine the influences on religious people from the widest possible angle. A year-long study of the concept of culture gave me a new perspective from which to examine these influences. The description of culture I came to find most useful is the one offered by the late British scholar Raymond Williams in his book *The Sociology of Culture*. Williams's approach stresses cultural production and offers us a concrete way of thinking about the processes by which a culture comes to be and works. It thus demystifies the obscure notion of culture held by many people. Williams describes culture as "a *signifying system* through which . . . a social order is communicated, reproduced, experienced, and explored."[22]

Every social order needs a signifying system to communicate its inner core in various modes: in conceptual categories, but also in nonlogical symbols such as images, heroes and heroines, rituals and narratives. The signifying system sets forth a particular social order's story of reality — that is, its imagination of what the human project is all about. A painful question I can silently ask myself about my own undergraduate students is: Who are your heroes or heroines? It is an important question because such models make the goals proposed by the culture concretely imaginable and pursuable. Besides giving rise to helpfully painful questions, Williams's description is about the church itself, a social order with its own symbols, rituals, heroes, and heroines, and with its own imagination of the purpose of the human project. As a goal, the church's social order is called the kingdom or God's holy commonwealth; as a current embodiment of efforts toward that goal, it is called the *ekklēsia*.

Those striving for a living discipleship thus dwell in two cultures: the wider social culture and economic system of our nation, and the

22. Raymond Williams, *The Sociology of Culture* (New York: Schocken Books, 1982).

narrower religious culture that exists within that wider "secular" culture. An important difference separates these two cultures. The narrower religious culture makes a bold and overt claim that *its* meanings are ultimate and salvific, and they hold a decisive place in directing the behavior of those who embrace these meanings. As we shall see, for those who live this claim rather than merely utter it, the claim establishes religious meaning as the standpoint from which the wider culture is approached and judged. Since the religious culture's meanings are prior, they relativize the claims of other social orders and signifying systems.

This rendition sounds compact and neat until we realize that the wider culture also claims that its meanings are ultimate, but it rarely does so explicitly. The wider culture's claim is implicit and thus quietly made as an assumption about reality. Ironically, the implicit claim can be more powerful than the explicit one. It is hard enough to counter a claim that is not clearly made; it is harder still to challenge a claim that is not admitted to exist. Even when unrecognized, the pull of these contrasting claims comes to reside in every religious person, including religious leaders. Perhaps this has always been the case, but today electronically depicted imaginations of reality bring the culture's implicit claims to people in ways both visceral and subtle.

The Church and the Wider Culture

As a signifying system by which a social order is communicated, the church does not stand against the wider culture.[23] Standing squarely within that wider culture, it welcomes and applauds every feature fostering the authentic humanization of persons. Because it embraces Jesus' imagination of human possibilities, the church rejoices in the ways in which social systems promote the human project. However, the church is clearly a zone of judgment, assessing both the social order and its signifying system by the criteria of its own meanings — that is, Jesus' vision of the dignity of persons and the need to live out his imagination of God's holy commonwealth. The way in which these assessments are made might be summarized in this brief formula: Quick to affirm what enriches the human project but unafraid to point out what diminishes it.

---

23. In using the term *church* I do not specify any particular denomination. For my purposes here, I prefer this general word to get at any embodiment of the Jesus tradition.

As a tradition, even in my idealized description, the church carries within it vestiges of the positive features of the many cultures within which it has existed. Its music, its rituals, its dogmatic formulations, its forms of communication, and its polities have been influenced by twenty centuries of embracing what was humanizing in the various cultures it met. This positive influence on the church still continues in varied ways, such as the application of management science to the coordination of ministries in dioceses. So the church does exist within the wider culture, but the wider culture also exists within the church — and not always in positive ways. Patriarchy, sexism, homophobia, polities that operate out of domination-subordination thinking — vestiges of these inhumanities can continue to infect the church. If Roman Catholics wince at the brutal intolerance of dissent and the hostility to reform in their own history, some Lutherans must likewise wince at Luther's connivance with the German princes of his day and his exhortations to unquestioning civil obedience.

Here, obviously, I have not gone far enough. There is another possibility. The church could become so enamored of the social order in which it lives and of that order's values and assumptions that its own tradition becomes distorted so as to fit comfortably within the wider system. The church then becomes the dominant culture in a religious mode or with religious trappings. I suspect that the *signifying system* does not change, at least not in dramatic ways. It seems to remain the same system of symbols, metaphors, and values it has always been. The deeper and more telling change is this: the *social order* that the religion communicates, reproduces, explores, and experiences has shifted from the one imagined and longed for by the tradition to that lived by the dominant culture. The religiously imagined social order continues to be spoken about, but not longed for. If we reread some of the studies of the Christian churches in Germany during the Nazi era, we would find telling examples of how this shift could take place. The Eucharist continued to be celebrated, the traditional hymns were sung; but the new times they represented had been replaced with an opposite. We could also study the Afrikaner Christian churches in South Africa. But then any of us might look to churches in our own hometowns to find more accessible examples.

This "tension of the social orders" and of their corresponding cultures is an ongoing, inescapable dilemma for the church, if only for the fact that its people *live* the wider culture, inhabiting its social,

251

economic, political, and communications structures the way we inhabit and are subtly shaped by a suit of clothes. These structures represent the material conditions of their lives in a way the church's structures do not — and probably cannot. As I have said, we can opt out of this tension, but then religious vision becomes diminished and even dies. If we embrace the tension, the result will be a liberating religious struggle. Even with the tension embraced, we would have to expect that different persons would stand at different points all along a continuum of struggle.

As a zone of meaning claiming ultimacy, the church is called to this struggle. To whatever degree it is faithful to the ultimacy of its religious vision, it becomes also a zone of judgment in two ways: it judges the wider culture, and at the same time it is itself judged by the gospel. The gospel, in its ideal of the holy commonwealth announced by Jesus, constantly brings the church in its local, regional, and international embodiments before the bar of its own criteria. Embedded in all the books of the New Testament one can find examples of this kind of inner judgment. Those who were branded and sometimes murdered as heretics were often those who were applying these same criteria to the church of their day. As historian Lester Little reminds us,

> All heretics are reformers . . . ; by definition they work within the system. Heresy occurs within the faith. . . . Heretics seek change by proposing or making alternative choices; they challenge the exclusive rights claimed and exercised by the prevailing, established authorities. They labor on behalf of aggiornamento; when they are in the prevailing party they are venerated as reformers and maybe even as saints; when they lose, they are cast out and trampled upon as troublesome heretics.[24]

The Church's People and the Religious Vision

With the prevalence of electronic communications, especially electronic storytelling, everyone — including those seeking to be disciples — has unlimited access to compelling, acted-out versions of reality. Particularly through television, everyone has access to vivid imaginations of what

24. Lester Little, "Evangelical Poverty, the New Money Economy and Violence," in *Poverty in the Middle Ages*, ed. David Flood (Werl/Westf: Dietrich-Coelde-Verlag, 1975), pp. 21-22.

life is all about. In consumerist capitalism, many of these imaginations are part of a strategy for orchestrating consumption. They are paid for by commercial interests. Shown in a context that stresses the centrality of having, the stories themselves often enough involve dramatizations of good and evil, with the good being the good of having and the evil being that of having one's goods snatched away. Here we have a world of signification that is packaged for people. It is not the culture of the people but the culture concocted for the consumption of the people. The main kind of agency envisaged for people is to watch someone else's story and then buy the products behind it. Under certain common circumstances, thus far not fully assessed, electronic communications tend to diminish cultural agency among many people, in the sense that they tend to be living in someone else's world of meaning and tend to be passive or mute when it comes to articulating their own world of meaning.[25]

How do religious meanings fare in such a cultural climate? In answering this question, one principle must be kept clear: *Religious meanings do not maintain themselves.* Their endurance is an achievement of intentionality. Because the meanings of a religion represent realities that are not easily evident, those meanings need to be worked at actively if they are to retain their hold on our imaginations. This would be true even if we did not live in a culture that actually imagines for us, via electronically communicated enactments, the meaning of the human project. Religious meanings cannot be maintained without cultural agency on the part of all those involved. This conviction is behind the idea that regular participation in worship is a potentially important part of religious living. If one does not regularly gather with a chorus of others who hold these meanings in common, the meanings themselves can come to seem illusory — to be replaced, ironically, by illusions.

Christianity has used many procedures to maintain its religious meanings. All of them are forms of cultural agency, calling people to work with and on the meanings that bind the community together. The goal of such work is the practice of discipleship. The basic procedure called for in a time of increasing cultural passivity is dialogue aimed at

25. Of course, as events in eastern Europe have made evident, electronic communications can under certain conditions enhance cultural agency among whole peoples. Televised police attacks on unarmed people in Romania inspired a popular insurrection and the establishment of an entirely new social system.

living out the meanings in specific forms of practice. Dialogue is an authentic and key form of any cultural agency, but it is *the* seminal form of religious cultural agency. As a grappling with the religious zone of signification and with the religious problematic, dialogue lays the groundwork for testing the truth-claims of a religion by the acid test of practice.

Intentional religious practice cannot operate in a vacuum. Practice needs a stance if it is to avoid being sucked into the vortex of commercially orchestrated culture and if it is to contest that culture. Someone could rightly say, "We already have a stance, the gospel." But that answer begs the question. Which gospel are we talking about, the Reverend Jerome Fallbadly's, or Ignacio Ellacuria and Oscar Romero's? The answer to this question is not always clear among Roman Catholics. The preaching I most often hear at the Eucharist is a version of religion Reaganomics: "Are you religiously better off — filled with more religious comfort — now than you were four years ago?" That message has its correlate in the genre of ads that exhort: "Move ahead; move up; have more." Or there are the religious correlates of the genre of self-enhancement ads: "You are the best; have the best." Their religious form is: "You are good, and God's love makes you a better you. There's nothing to worry about. Pray and put everything in God's hands." Or the genre of "pamper yourself" ads: "God wants you to be happy, to feel better about yourself." In other words, get more religious capital or get more of the religious goods, and you'll be more secure. These are the "Be-Happy Attitudes," and they emanate not only from the Crystal Cathedral, but from a variety of religious edifices. These are not stances that question the dominant culture; instead they embody it.

All cultures have their meanings distilled in such stances, which direct patterns of practice. Some stances express the culture's inner core more faithfully than others. For the religious culture of the church, there can be stances that express the gospel with a dramatic clarity that sets those who embrace those stances apart from the dominant culture and even from others within the church. What would some such stances be? One might be solidarity with victims. If a community struggled to live that seminal aspect of the gospel, if it studied the conditions of the victims and the causes of those conditions, the community would have a stance that would show up the false promises of a consumerist culture and the brutal economic policies of its society. Such a stance could lead a community to embrace for their study, not a single issue, but a whole range of matters threatening human dignity. That stance would increase the discomfort level of a community, casting a searching light into the shadows of its own corporate way of life and the ways of life of its individual members.

Another stance — one that has been critiqued back and forth for many years — might be the option for the poor. To disengage even the notion of "the poor" from elitist assumptions is difficult. To disengage activity on their behalf from assumptions of superiority and of dominative power is even more difficult. Whatever these difficulties, as an option proposed for a particular community this stance is as rare as an honest Pentagon budget. In a society where money promises salvation, solidarity with the poor is bound to be unpopular. In such a society, a more radical gospel stance would be the option *for poverty,* that is, for countering the forced poverty of so many with the voluntary poverty of those seeking to follow Jesus. In our economy, someone proposing this option might be accused of cultural blasphemy or even mental instability.

Yet Aloysius Pieris holds that any true Christian spirituality is a spirituality of poverty, adding that because of the Hydra-like quality of Mammon, it is also a spirituality of struggle. Pieris says,

> a Christian is a person who has made an irrevocable option *to follow* Jesus; this option necessarily coincides with the option *to be poor;* but the "option to be poor" becomes a true "following of Jesus" only to the extent that it is also an option *for the poor.* Christian discipleship or "spirituality," therefore, is a coincidence of all these three options.
>
> The (theo)logical force of this argument is derived from two biblical axioms: the irreconcilable antagonism between God and wealth, and the irrevocable covenant between God and the poor, Jesus himself being this covenant. These two principles imply that, in Jesus, God and the poor have formed an alliance against their common enemy: mammon. This is what justifies the conclusion that, for both Jesus and his followers, spirituality is not merely a *struggle to be poor* but equally *a struggle for the poor.* . . .
>
> The irreconcilable antinomy between God and money (Matt. 6:24), or more precisely between *Abba* and *Mamona* (to use two emotionally loaded and, to that extent, untranslatable Aramaic words that the synoptics place exclusively on the lips of Jesus), is the vital nucleus of the gospel message as expanded in the Sermon on the Mount. Growing intimacy with the one and constant repudiation of the other

characterize the whole mission of Jesus on earth. He is our covenant with God. Whoever has a pact with mammon is excluded from fellowship with his Father, "for no one can serve two masters." The rich young man is asked to become poor before becoming his disciple (Matt. 19:21).[26]

A third stance, which has every bit as much "edge" and is as "unthinkable" as the other two, would be the option for nonviolence. As is probably obvious by now, adopt any one of these three, and the other two become necessary correlates.

A stance engages judgment. Without a stance there is no judgment, because there are no norms. Norms configure a stance, and the stance engages judgment.[27] As Christians we claim that our norms are rooted in imitating Jesus' imagination of human possibilities. Religious persons have the potential to critique culture as an almost natural outcome of their religious commitment. Religions propose networks of meanings laden with transcendence and ultimacy. Such networks relativize — or at least have the potential to relativize — the positions of society and culture. Especially when religious conviction brings communities to embrace the concerns of the marginalized, religious conviction merges with social critique.

To put the matter another way, a religion bears within it "resources of hope," based on its religious vision.[28] The religious imagination comprises an alternative vision of life as a reality "hoped for" and worked for in the light of that hope. Such an imagination means that in spite of desperate and long-standing injustice and oppression, in the face of death itself, religious people can harbor an alternative understanding, deeply contesting inhuman social structures — including possible inhuman elements within the religious structures themselves. This alternative understanding of a reality beyond "reality" does not

26. Aloysius Pieris, *An Asian Theology of Liberation* (New York: Orbis, 1988), p. 15.

27. Here I do not deal with a complex question — namely, the judgment of judgment. If judgment is based on norms, must not norms themselves be held up to scrutiny? Francis Fiorenza's work on this question is helpful. He points out how praxis itself tends to push against its own criteria by being a source for the discovery of new truth and for a critique of ideology. See his "Foundational Theology and Theological Education," *Theological Education* (Spring 1984): 119-20, and the sections on criteria in *Foundational Theology: Jesus and the Church* (New York: Crossroad, 1984).

28. See Raymond Williams's posthumously collected essays, *Resources of Hope* (London and New York: Verso Books, 1989).

wait impassively for change but works actively at the most subversive of activities: keeping alive a memory of an alternative way of living. From this perspective there persists an alternative social possibility, meant by God to become an actuality. Its becoming an actuality is basically a work of God, a holy task in which persons carry forward God's will. From a religious point of view, one's religious vocation calls for one to protest and contest what is inhuman — even when one judges that little might be accomplished. No wonder those wanting to keep a social system unquestioned and unchanged find the religious imagination "dangerous." Indeed, one would have to admit that it represents a volatile social force that in certain circumstances could be a potent force for evil.[29]

Points for Further Study

By way of conclusion I wish to point out three matters needing more attention if a distinctive religious culture or zone of meaning is to function properly.

The first of these has to do with the possibility that a religion could opt for forms of domination and use its considerable power to justify that option. Religious history bristles with examples of religious groups seeking to dominate the social order in one way or another, especially through violence. Even barring violence, in a time when so many social forces are struggling not for dialogue and mutual understanding but for domination, it is possible for the church to view the end time as the day when it will be able to impose its vision. This is just another guise for Mammon.

The aping of dominative power in the interests of religion has subtle forms. Religious people could move beyond embracing their own religious vision to claiming it as the only religious vision possible. While a person may believe that his or her religious vision is "the truth," it is a dangerous step to then claim that it must be true for everyone. There could be ways, for example, of proposing Lindbeck's thesis on religion

29. A body of religious thought espouses nonviolence as a fundamental way of avoiding such evil. A thought-provoking analysis of the religious bases of violent social conflict *and* of its opposite, cohesive social pluralism, can be found in Aloysius Pieris, "Faith-Communities and Communalism," *East Asian Pastoral Review* 26, 3-4 (1989): 294-310.

as a specific culture so that the distinctive religious culture becomes the right stuff that makes us "the best." Religious leaders are told they should be enthusiastic because their product is truly the best.[30] They should not be afraid to market their goods. This is evangelization infected by Madison Avenue. Such an approach avoids the deeper question of the integrity of the religious vision. When local churches, for example, struggle to live the gospel from a radical stance, taking risks and bearing burdens to follow that vision, their way of life possesses an integrity that may be evident to some outside their fellowship. Again and again in the New Testament, danger, suffering, and oppression are taken as signs of authenticity.

In a pluralist situation, religious communities will have to find allies, religious or not, who are willing to challenge the society to become economically and politically a more human social order. Such allies can maintain their own distinctiveness while finding common ground for action together, even though disagreements over important matters will still occur. But visions of domination short-circuit such collaboration.

A second matter needing attention is that of the local church as a community of discourse. I have already stated my belief that religious meaning is maintained by dialogue, specifying that such a community is characterized by cultural agency. This is all the more true in a time of electronic communication of acted-out versions of the meaning of life. The sacredness of each person as a religious subject is crucial here. In some denominations one gets the impression that the individual is a good member only when she or he is a consumer of the religious meaning produced by elites. Cultural agency is achieved when each person becomes an original co-producer of religious insight. I am not saying that a person "invents" the religious language, but that a person learns to speak it by trying to speak it out of the self, thereby achieving some elements of originality.

The current pope is not coherent on this very point. Having written important treatises on both culture and the human person as a subjectivity, he does not apply his own principle to doctrinal matters. At many places in his encyclical on labor he emphasizes the person's

30. For an examination of a proposal for dealing with the "two cultures," the religious and the secular, see William L. Sachs, "Willimon's Project: Does It Make Sense?" *The Christian Century*, 19 April 1989, pp. 412-14. Sachs's questions suggest the complexity of the issues once a concrete proposal is made.

vocation as producer instead of consumer. However, in his exhortation on the role of the laity, some passages hint that a layperson's *doctrinal* vocation is to "swallow and follow." In doctrinal matters, hegemonic control will be maintained in the name of a special enspiriting given to the hierarchy. I am not denying special gifts within a community; I am denying that they are enhanced by suppressing dialogue.

When I read enthusiastic acclaim for the Catholic moment, I suspect that at some level it celebrates social controls that the acclaimers long for in their own denominations. In other words, they applaud Allan Bloom in religious drag. The complex truth about the Catholic moment must attend to the creative disaffiliation of Roman Catholic women resisting the sexism in their tradition, of gays, of those wanting an open dialogue on the giving and taking of life, on clerical celibacy, on the cultural captivity of the chaplaincy through military rank (and, let us not forget, military pay), and so forth. What the Catholic moment in fact represents may be intense disagreement about points of polity and doctrine by persons who refuse to be marginalized by those in power. The Catholic moment is dissent refusing to be intimidated by intolerance.[31]

Any local church opting for the sort of dialogue I am suggesting here will need to find ways of dealing with conflict. Sometimes when I read about ways of managing conflict in business or in the church I wonder if the basic idea is that of managing in a manipulative sense. We refuse to let conflict interrupt business as usual. Perhaps a more appropriate use of management techniques would be "managing" to live with disagreement when disagreement seems irresolvable, managing to love one another when we disagree. We do not need the churches to ape the use of dominative power used by governments. We need the churches to help societies imagine new forms of social collaboration in spite of conflicts or in the midst of conflict. Among the common tendencies some commentators find in postmodernism are moves toward smaller groupings, more local control, and greater openness to differences — all humanly creative tendencies.[32] There may be wisdom for our time in such tendencies.

31. In a creative essay Rubem Alves seems to say that such dissent from within the institution is a key character of the Roman Catholic ethos. My copy of Alves's essay, entitled "Protestant Ideology," is in typescript, translated by James and Margaret Goff from "A Ideologia do Protestantismo," *Cadernos do ISER,* no. 8 [Rio de Janeiro] (April 1979): 46-49.

The third matter involves greater attention to the life practices of each member and to the communal life practices of the local church. How much work needs to be done in this area can be seen in the fact that we hardly have a language by which to speak of it. By "life practice" I mean how people actually live, the very specific material conditions of their lives — both the conditions imposed on them by circumstance and the conditions they impose on themselves. These life practices are found in the size and locale of their dwelling, who their friends are and how they interact with them, the way they eat and drink, what and when they eat and drink, their work and the time needed to get to and from work, what they do with their leisure time, what they read and what they are paying attention to by means of their reading, what films they see, what they watch on television, the way they think about and use money. These activities become patterned in what I am calling practices, and these practices shape how people live, what their spirits are all about — what some of us would call their spirituality.

A brief example of the importance of life practices was suggested to me by a student. He explained why some Irish bishops are not very concerned about the high percentage of unemployed youth in his country. He said, "To understand why the problem doesn't engage them, find out where the various Irish bishops take their meals, who cooks those meals, who shops for and how payment is made for those meals. Find out who joins the bishop at those meals and how often. When they eat outside their residence, with whom do they eat and who pays the bill. You'll find out," he said, "that almost never do these men eat with unemployed youth. They eat with an entirely different, almost opposite, social class. And when they eat fancy, wealth pays the bill. That's why the bishops aren't so concerned with unemployed youth."

At the communal level, life practice embraces a similar range of patterned activities: the way the community comes together, the voices that are heard, the voices that are heeded, the personages that are celebrated in the community, the persons whose numbers are dialed by the staff or whose doors are approached, the way physical resources are used, the way monetary resources are used, the style of living of those

32. On this controvertible point, see Jane Caplan, "The Point Is to Change It," a review of Bryan D. Palmer's *Descent into Discourse*, in *The Nation*, 13/20 Aug. 1990, pp. 173-75; Frederic Jameson, "Postmodernism, or the Cultural Logic of Late Capitalism," *New Left Review* 146 (July-Aug. 1984): 53-92; and Kellner, "Postmodernism as Social Theory."

who serve the community, the kinds of issues that arise in the homilies, the ways (or lack of them) to respond to those issues. On what occasions or in what circumstances in a year has recourse to power outside the community been taken — say, to the law or to the police — and why? Does the church have investments, a portfolio? What is in it? I for one have never once heard the issue of investments raised by individual members of any congregation I have ever attended. And yet money is one of the most symbolic human creations, with sacramental power for good or for ill. The peace-activist slogan "Pray for peace; pay for war" (always intoned ironically) echoes this ambiguous symbolic value of money. C. Ellis Nelson reminded us years ago that the very arrangement of buildings on a church property is itself sacramental of its priorities. Such tangible arrangements can belie the stated commitments of the church. The perennial challenge of the church — this problem of being what we say we are — is the particular sticking point for disciples in a culture of illusion.

The problem culture poses for religious persons in this time of electronic communications will not disappear. The spirit of our age described by Stuart Ewen, Jean Baudrillard, Barbara Goldsmith, and Kennedy Fraser is likely to remain for some time. Only by going, like Moses, deeper into the mountain of God, by embracing their distinctive religious vision, can religious groups find the resources for contesting what they judge to be humanly unacceptable in the wider culture. Eventually this journey into the mystery of God is to be taken not just by Moses-like leaders but by the whole people of God, like the Israelites trudging into the desert. The people cannot survive religiously as passive receptors of religious meaning, but only as coproducers struggling to express religious insight for today. This struggle is the sign of religious vitality.

Fashioning Christians in Our Day

JOHN H. WESTERHOFF

Christianity is fundamentally a particular way of life corresponding to a peculiar perception of life and our lives; and "Christians," wrote Tertullian in a lapidary phrase, "are made, not born."[1] Baptism is the sacrament by which the church makes Christians — that is, by which persons are raised to new life in Christ, incorporated into Christ's body (the church), infused with Christ's mind and character, and empowered by the Holy Spirit to be Christ's continuing presence in the world. Through Christian initiation within a Christian community of faith, persons are formed and transformed into the persons that baptism establishes them to be. This process, historically known as *catechesis* — "to echo the Word" or "Christening" — is the means by which a community re-presents Christ (his life, teachings, death, and resurrection) in symbol, myth, rite, and common life and thereby fashions novices so that they might join the community in representing Christ to the world.

Catechesis is a complex process, difficult in any historical era, but especially difficult in the United States today. George Lindbeck, at the close of his book *The Nature of Doctrine*, states categorically "the impossibility of effective catechesis in the present situation."[2] While there is every reason to believe he is correct, I intend to make an attempt at describing a faithful catechetical program for our day. It is based upon

---

1. Tertullian *Apologetic* 18.
2. George Lindbeck, *The Nature of Doctrine* (Philadelphia: Westminster, 1984), p. 133.

the contention that any faithful catechetical endeavor necessitates an understanding of "church" as an ecology of intentional, interrelated, distinctively Christian institutions that provide an alternative to and are in creative tension with similar institutions within society — that is, families, congregations, and schools in which deliberate, systemic, and sustained efforts are made to fashion Christians.

Underlying this radical proposal is a particular interpretation of social life in the United States today. In his book *Education and Pluralism*, the educational philosopher Thomas Green writes, "The very idea of the *polis* [in the United States] contains implicit reference to the fact that though the community must be one, it must also be many; though it must have unity, it will inevitably contain diversity. A resulting tension is inevitable."[3]

Green explains that pluralism may be viewed either as social reality or as ideal; he then goes on to contend that within our American understanding of democracy, pluralism is an ideal — that is, it is valued and cherished. Our society, for example, does not just tolerate but encourages a variety of individual opinions to flourish and contend with each other. Further, it encourages individuals to unite together in voluntary associations for mutual benefit and social influence. The underlying assumption behind this commitment to the ideal of pluralism is that no particular culture, ethnic group, race, or religion has a monopoly on truth or is so rich in itself that it may not be further enriched by others. Further, it assumes that interaction between divergent groups is essential for a healthy society.

Pluralism as a reality — that is, as the presence of variety and diversity — is impossible to question. The enormous complexity of American society is readily apparent. While some groups strive to live in relative isolation, most are immersed in this country's cultural, racial, ethnic, and religious diversity through participation in its vast network of social institutions. However, turning that reality into an ideal is somewhat problematic. At least from one Christian perspective, while the ideal of cultural, racial, and ethnic pluralism may be desirable, the ideal of religious pluralism must be questioned, for such a proposition is founded on the assumption that differences between religions are not a matter of truth, conviction, or commitment but rather solely a matter of opinion and private individual concern.

3. Thomas Green, *Education and Pluralism: Ideal and Reality* (Syracuse: School of Education, Syracuse University, 1966), p. 7.

Such a proposition is simply not acceptable to many Christians. "The gospel," writes Lesslie Newbigin, "cannot be accommodated as one element in a society which has pluralism as its reigning ideology. The Church cannot accept as its role simply the winning of individuals to a kind of Christian discipleship which concerns only the private and domestic aspects of life."[4]

In a society in which religious pluralism is valued and cherished, any confident statement of ultimate belief, any claim to proclaim the truth about God, God's purpose for the world, or God's will for personal and social life is liable to be dismissed as ignorant, arrogant, or dogmatic. The natural result is the privatization, relativization, and subjectivization of Christian faith and life, a condition antithetical to the gospel. Religious pluralism may be a reality with which we Christians must cope, but I do not believe it can be an ideal we celebrate in principle.

To return to Green, our convictions concerning pluralism are extraordinarily important for education — and I would add especially for catechesis, the making of Christians. Our convictions concerning ethnic, racial, cultural, and religious diversity will influence the flexibility we are willing to allow schools in accommodating such diversity. More important, it will influence our conclusions concerning the place and role of public and parochial schools for Christians.

Green identifies three possible understandings of pluralism and how a society might function in each case. One extreme understanding he names "structural assimilation." This understanding encourages interaction and friendships across ethnic, racial, cultural, and religious groups in every aspect of social life, including marriage. As such, this understanding results in an open society rather than a pluralistic society. Insofar as this has occurred in the United States, some ethnic, racial, cultural, and religious minorities are troubled, for they are aware that this understanding discourages any sense of distinct identity and makes it extremely difficult to transmit distinct understandings and ways of life from generation to generation.

At the other extreme is what Green calls "insular pluralism." In this case all social relations are exclusively confined to one's own ethnic, racial, cultural, or religious group. As such, this understanding does not result in a pluralistic society either; it merely provides a means for

---

4. Lesslie Newbigin, *The Gospel in a Pluralist Society* (Grand Rapids: Eerdmans, 1989), p. 222. See also his *Foolishness to the Greeks* (Grand Rapids: Eerdmans, 1986).

maintaining the coexistence of different societies living alongside each other. While only a few groups have adopted this understanding, it remains extremely difficult to accomplish. Such an understanding, however, has the distinct advantage of preserving identity-conscious groups, and it does make possible the transmission of particular understandings and ways of life from generation to generation.

Green favors his third option, which he calls "half-way pluralism," because as he contends it alone makes possible true pluralism. This understanding is founded upon a differentiation between primary and secondary associations. Significantly for Green, there is only one primary association: the family. All other associations are secondary. Therefore, "half-way pluralism" would discourage intermarriage between different ethnic, racial, cultural, and religious groups, but it would encourage interaction and association of these diverse groups in schools, hospitals, restaurants, stores, mass media, neighborhoods, and workplaces. Accordingly, pluralism is defined as "a social order founded upon the principle of harmonious interactions for common ends, among distinct familial units, each of which possesses both positive self identity and openness to others."[5]

Serious problems result, however, when understandings and ways of life practiced by primary and secondary groups conflict, a situation most likely to occur in schools. As a consequence, nothing that any particular ethnic, racial, cultural, or religious group cares strongly about will be introduced into a school curriculum unless there is consensus, or the others do not object, or it can be introduced in an "objective-comparative" manner. This has been particularly devastating for religion in that it has kept both the study of religion and more importantly the practice of religion out of most public schools. Nevertheless, even our most enlightened understanding of what is appropriate to a public school curriculum limits the school to the teaching of religion and denies the teaching of persons to be religious.

Now while this "half-way" understanding of pluralism and education may be reasonable for ethnic, racial, and cultural diversity, it is not reasonable for those who wish to transmit Christian faith, character, and consciousness to the next generation. Further, it becomes particu-

5. See John Westerhoff, "In Search of a Future: The Church-Related College," in *The Church's Ministry in Higher Education,* ed. John Westerhoff (New York: UMHE Communication Offices, 1978), p. 197.

larly problematic when we examine the assumption that schools are secondary associations. In point of fact schools may have become the most significant primary association in contemporary society. By the time children are twelve years of age, they have spent more hours in school than they have spent with their families and religious community combined. Indeed, it would take seventy-five years of attending church and church school regularly to equal the school's influence in the first twelve formative years of a person's life.

Further, schools are not solely instructional institutions in which reading, writing, and arithmetic are taught. Schools are fundamentally agents of enculturation. As Philip Jackson notes, more than ninety percent of the time a child spends in school is spent on enculturation, while only ten percent is spent on instruction. The hidden curriculum of the school is, it appears, more influential than the stated curriculum.[6]

In the light of this situation, it appears obvious to me that Christians need to question seriously their support of public schools, or better, they need to consider seriously the formation and reformation of parochial schools. The rest of this essay will explore how Christians are formed and what sort of parochial schools are needed in conjunction with family and congregation if authentic Christian faith and life are to be maintained and transmitted from generation to generation in a pluralistic society.

The Catechetical Process

Earlier we named the process by which Christians are made as *catechesis*. Catechesis necessitates three deliberate or intentional, systemic or interrelated, sustained or lifelong processes essential to Christian faith and life: formation, education, and instruction.

Instruction aids persons to acquire that knowledge and those abilities useful for responsible personal and communal Christian life in church and society. For example, through instructional processes persons acquire a knowledge of the content of Scripture as well as the ability to comprehend its meaning and interpret its implications for daily life and work. Instruction alone, however, can produce a person who knows

6. See Philip Jackson, "The Daily Grind," in *The Hidden Curriculum and Moral Education,* ed. Henry Giroux and David Purple (Berkeley: McCutchan, 1983).

all about Christianity but who does not intend to be Christian. Nevertheless, without the benefit of instruction, persons may not know what faithfulness is, what it implies, or how to decide what is faithful.

Education aids persons to reflect critically on their behavior and experiences in the light of the gospel so that they might discern if they are being faithful and when they might need to change their behavior. For example, through critical reflection on the ways in which we live together as families, congregations, or schools, we can reform them to be more faithful. Christians, therefore, need to make education a natural way of life and not just a program, as they engage in critical reflection on every aspect of their lives.

Formation aids persons to acquire Christian faith (understood as a particular perception of life and our lives), Christian character (understood as identity and appropriate behavioral dispositions), and Christian consciousness (understood as that interior subjective awareness or temperament that predisposes persons to particular experiences). For example, Christian formation is the participation in and the practice of the Christian life of faith. We do that by identifying with a community, observing how persons in it live, and imitating them.

Instruction informs us in terms of knowledge and skills believed by the community to be important for communal life. Education reforms us by aiding us to discover dissonance between how we are living and how we are called to live. And formation both conforms (nurtures) and transforms (converts) us through a process best understood as apprenticeship.

Formation is related to a natural process called *enculturation; when enculturation becomes intentional it is called formation.* Education is necessary for faithful formation, and instruction is important for faithful education, but formation is foundational because it is the primary means by which Christians are made. Still, formation as a process has not been given the attention it deserves. The reasons for this are varied, but among the most significant is that in recent years catechists have been more concerned with teaching doctrine and rational convictions about truth than they have been with faith understood as a community's perception of life and our lives, to which loyalty, trust, and devotion are to be given. Further, a primary concern of catechists has been the teaching of moral decision making and problem solving, which has led them to a neglect of the persons who make the decision and the character of those persons — that is, their identity and disposition to behave in particular ways. And finally, catechists have tended to focus on individual subjective experience to the neglect of consciousness or temperament, the interior awareness that makes any particular experience possible or probable.[7]

While instruction is a useful means for transmitting beliefs and teaching decision making, and education is useful for making sense of and interpreting experience, only through formation do persons acquire Christian faith, character, and consciousness. George Lindbeck, in his seminal work *The Nature of Doctrine*, mentioned earlier, provides an analysis for understanding why this is so.

In this book, Lindbeck explores four "theories of doctrine." His first theory emphasizes the cognitive aspects of religion and stresses the ways in which church doctrine functions as intellectual propositions or truth claims about objective reality. His second theory emphasizes the experiential aspects of religion and stresses the ways in which church doctrine is derived from reflection on subjective feelings and existential experiences. His third theory combines the first two.

Lindbeck's fourth theory of doctrine, which I contend can be correlated with the other two, he names "cultural-linguistic." This theory emphasizes the cultural aspects of religion and stresses the ways in which church doctrine functions as a comprehensive, informing, interpretive scheme embodied in communal symbols, myths (sacred narratives), and rites. Like a culture, doctrine is a communal phenomenon that structures and shapes human thought and experience, rather than a description of subjective experience or objective or propositional statements, accepted on the basis of some authority, about objective reality.

Of course, the term *culture* has such a multiplicity of referents, along with an acquired vagueness, that it makes many suspicious of its usefulness. Still, I believe it is a particularly helpful category in explaining how Christians are formed, especially how Christian faith, character, and consciousness are formed. Culture, as I use the word, refers to socially established structures of meaning or significance, their related

7. See Peter L. Berger and Thomas Luckmann, *The Social Construction of Reality* (New York: Doubleday, 1966); Clifford Geertz, *The Interpretation of Cultures* (New York: Basic Books, 1973); Alasdair MacIntyre, *After Virtue* (Notre Dame: University of Notre Dame Press, 1984); Stanley Hauerwas, *Character and Christian Life* (San Antonio: Trinity University Press, 1975); James Wm. McClendon, Jr., *Ethics* (Nashville: Abingdon, 1988); and Philip Greven, *The Protestant Temperament* (New York: Random House, 1977).

symbolic actions or patterns of behavior, and their resulting artifacts.[8] Culture describes a people's learned, shared understandings and ways of life, the framework within which they perceive the world about them, interpret events and experiences, and act/react to this perceived reality. From a cultural-linguistic perspective, religion is the idiom for dealing with whatever is most important and foundational. At the heart of culture is religion, and at the heart of religion are the perceptions that define its social construction of reality or its worldview and ethos. Because a cultural-linguistic understanding of doctrine stresses the means by which human thought and experiences are shaped, molded, and constituted by cultural and linguistic forms — participating in a community's rites and internalizing its sacred narrative, for example — its emphasis is on intentional enculturation or formation. It is therefore useful to understand how culture is sustained and transmitted from generation to generation.

Enculturation is a natural process of formal and informal, intentional and unintentional means by which children are inducted into a community and acquire its culture. In pluralistic cultures the process of enculturation is complex and difficult, even for those ethnic groups that attempt to isolate themselves from the general culture and its numerous subcultures.

Acculturation is the process by which persons learn to adapt to the general culture while still maintaining their own particular subculture. This process is similar to learning a second language without either becoming completely bilingual (in terms of thinking as well as communicating in both languages) or making the new language one's primary language. Acculturation is easiest when applied to technique and taste — such as eating with knife and fork rather than with one's hands, eating raw rather than cooked seafood, or driving a car rather than riding a bicycle — and it is more difficult when it enters the realm of symbols.

In any case, it is possible to be enculturated in one culture and acculturated to function in a second culture without losing the fundamentals of one's primary culture. Nevertheless, only if this is done intentionally, forcefully, and consistently will an ethnic group be able to continue over time as an identity-conscious cultural community in a pluralistic society.

8. See Geertz, *The Interpretation of Culture*, chap. 1.

This implies that for Italian-Americans to maintain Italian culture, for example, a number of conditions will be required: close-knit families; an Italian-speaking congregation; a stable, boundary-conscious neighborhood of Italians; a parochial school with Italian teachers; and the presence of mass media resources representative of Italian culture. Where these conditions do not exist, each succeeding generation of adults will provide a less than adequate form of enculturation for their children. The result will be that in three generations the adults will no longer be *Italian*-Americans, except in name. Intermarriage, mobility, diversified peer groups, mixed neighborhoods, public schools, and mass media make enculturation into a particular subculture difficult, if not impossible.

Assimilation is similar to enculturation; it is the process by which adults are inducted into a new culture through conversion, thereby leaving behind the first culture into which they had been enculturated. For example, there are adult immigrants who discard their ethnic heritage when they arrive in the United States and immerse themselves so fully in American culture that they no longer think of themselves as, for example, Scotch-Americans, but as Americans who left Scotland. Their children are then enculturated into U.S. culture, never knowing themselves as anything but "Americans."

Assimilation is a process related to believers' baptism or adult baptism, while enculturation is a process related to infant baptism for the making of Christians. As processes they are similar. The problem is that while we attempt to shape our children to be Christians, they are also being influenced by the dominant culture. If we can discover how to enculturate them as Christians and acculturate them to be U.S. citizens, we will have been faithful. But in doing so, we run the risk of their being enculturated to be U.S. citizens and acculturated to be loyal members of an institutional church.

Formation is the primary means by which Jesus taught. Vernon Robbins, in his book *Jesus the Teacher,* claims that Jesus was a unique teacher. Instead of waiting for potential students to seek him out, sit at his feet, and take notes, as in the schooling tradition, Jesus sought and summoned students to follow him, to become companion-apprentices, as in the itinerant tradition. Jesus then sent them forth to seek, summon, and commission others through a similar process of identification, observation, and imitation.[9]

9. Vernon Robbins, *Jesus the Teacher* (Philadelphia: Fortress, 1984).

Aaron Milavec, in his book *To Empower as Jesus Did,* makes the interesting observation that typically we translate the Greek word *didaskalos* as "teacher" and *didaskein* as "to teach." He points out that as a result of this translation, Pasolini in his film of St. Matthew's Gospel represents Jesus as a teacher without a classroom, traveling about delivering lectures in the form of homilies to convey beliefs and ethical principles. Milavec goes on to point out that these same Greek words can also be translated as "master" and "to apprentice" — that is, "to live with" or "to accompany," to have one's own life guided and shaped by life shared with a master.[10]

So it is that James — perhaps the first bishop of the church in Jerusalem, in what according to tradition was a homily delivered to the elect before their baptism — lays stress on the moral life expected of those who follow the way of Jesus; he therefore warns that not many of them should be catechists, for more will be expected of them (James 3:1). Why? Because catechizing implies apprenticing and the catechist is called to be a master to apprentices, which further implies that the catechist will focus her or his attention on an ever-deepening and loving relationship to Christ.

Similarly, the catechumenate in the early church was founded on the principles of an apprenticeship — that is, a formation process in which persons (catechumens) apprenticed themselves to the community and participated in its life and practiced its way of life accompanied by a sponsor, a master (catechist) who represented the community.

Thus the making of Christians involves the practice of living a particular way of life. The process is similar to that used in learning a craft such as stonemasonry, a sport such as basketball, or an art form such as dance. The learner apprentices himself or herself to a master. Through observation, imitation, and practice the apprentice learns a multitude of skills. The apprentice also learns a language and is initiated into a history.

Christian apprenticeship is discipleship. If a person desires to become a Christian, he or she needs to practice praying the Lord's Prayer, ministering to the poor and needy, and performing other acts basic to being Christian. He or she also needs to learn a story so that words and actions merge together, shaping the heart, mind, and soul of the apprentice. Formation then is fundamentally the practice and experience of Christian faith and life.

10. Aaron Milavec, *To Empower as Jesus Did* (Toronto: Mellon Press, 1982).

271

Aspects of Communal Life

Formation, understood from the perspective of intentional assimilation or enculturation, involves eight aspects of communal life, each of which contributes to and influences the practices and experiences that are foundational and necessary for the making of Christians. We will examine each in turn.

1. Communal Rites

In 1925, Willard Sperry, then dean of the Harvard Divinity School, wrote *Reality in Worship*.[11] In a chapter entitled "The Occasion and Intention of Public Worship," he contended that the church shares with many other institutions common tasks that are religious in nature, and that many of these activities are done better by institutions other than the church. The one unique contribution of the church, he continued, is its cultic life. While the work of the church is real and intelligible through the life and actions of its members in daily life, the church is clearly defined whenever and wherever people meet together to address themselves to the act of liturgy. Liturgy is the original and distinctive task, the primary responsibility of the church. Everything else may be conceded, compromised, shared, and even relinquished, but so long as the church invites people to worship God and provides a credible vehicle for liturgy, it need not question its place, mission, and influence in the world. But if it loses faith in its liturgy, if it is thoughtless in the ordering of its liturgy or careless in the conduct of its liturgy, it need not look elsewhere to find vitality: it is dead at heart.

Cultic life refers to a community's rites — repetitive, symbolic, and social acts which express and manifest the community's sacred narrative, along with its implied faith and life. (Ceremonial acts are prescribed behaviors; ritual acts are prescribed words.) These liturgies include several kinds of rites: (1) rites of intensification that follow the calendar (once a week, month, or year) and shape, sustain, and enhance the community's faith, character, and consciousness, as well as increasing group solidarity; (2) rites of transition that follow the life cycle and promote meaningful passage for persons and the community from one stage of life to another; and (3) rites of initiation that induct persons

11. Willard Sperry, *Reality in Worship* (New York: Macmillan, 1932).

into the community. Through these symbolic actions, persons practice the Christian life and make the Christian community's narrative their own. (Importantly, all the other aspects of formation that will be considered later are encompassed in a community's rites.)

Within secular culture there are numerous rites that are intended to shape the community's worldview and value system. They too are repetitive, symbolic actions expressive of the community's understandings and ways. The dominant secular rites called "spectator sports" are intended, for example, to support individualism (even in team-oriented sports we award a most valuable player), aggression (the most popular sports are often violent), competition (a tie is considered unsatisfactory; someone needs to win), and cooperation — but the kind that supports nationalism (raising the flag and singing the national anthem as well as cooperating with your team in order to beat the other team). Advertising is another form of cultural rite; it supports an economic system based on self-interest and consumption. These rites and others constantly attempt to enculturate us into the society's understandings and ways; this explains why, when persons in the early church entered the catechumenate to be formed as Christians, they were no longer permitted to attend public spectator sports. If we are to be formed as Christians, we must take our Christian rites seriously. This implies making participation in the church's liturgy the heart of formation.

2. Environment

Our church environment includes architectural space and artifacts, along with sights, sounds, smells, and tastes. We shape our environment and it in turn shapes us. The history of architecture and art is the history of culture. For example, a culture in which specialization and differentiation dominate is more likely to construct space for particular activities: bedrooms for sleeping, dining rooms for eating, and so forth. One's environment encourages or discourages, facilitates or hinders particular behaviors. Our understandings of the purpose and the proper use of space influence our perceptions, dispositions, and consciousness.

In some churches there is a space for a vested choir and clergy that is separated from the space for the congregation; this arrangement could be seen to imply that the sacred and the secular are appropriately and necessarily separated. Further, by not permitting many normal activities (eating, drinking, talking, and the like) within worship space, we make

273

JOHN H. WESTERHOFF

that separation more severe, thereby lessening the church's influence on daily life and work. Churches that use small silver bowls for baptism make it difficult to understand baptism in terms of drowning and being brought back to life or as being fully washed. Churches that display pictures of a white Anglo-Saxon Jesus without any other images of Jesus distort the nature and character of Jesus as the Christ. In that regard, it is fortunate that we do not know what Jesus looked like, and it is therefore appropriate to use a great variety of images.

3. Time

Our orientation toward past, present, and future, the structure of time in terms of particular activities, and the ordering of time in terms of the calendar — all provide structure for understanding the meaning and purpose of our behaviors. There is the Hallmark card calendar that orders time with occasions such as Mother's Day, Halloween, St. Patrick's Day, the Fourth of July (Independence Day), Memorial Day, birthdays, and so forth. Many churches celebrate such days and thereby encourage a secularization of the church. For Christians the celebration of baptism days and the church's year — Advent, Christmas, Epiphany, Lent, Easter, Pentecost, and so forth — are more important. The stories we celebrate shape our faith and life. One year when Mother's Day and Pentecost corresponded, many churches celebrated Mother's Day and then wondered why the Holy Spirit was not alive in their lives, or the church infused by its presence. Just as serious a time warp is the ecclesial calendar that celebrates days such as Stewardship Sunday, Theological Education Sunday, Mission Sunday, Rally Day, etc., all of which are more likely to make loyal members of the institutional church than to form Christians.

4. Communal Life

Communal life encompasses the governance or polity, the programs and events, the economics and budgets of a community, all of which support behaviors and suggest that some are more valuable than others. Communal life also encourages particular behaviors and makes others possible, for it establishes the ways in which people are to spend their time, energy, and money and therefore how the church understands its mission and ministry.

How many churches have a sign when you enter that says, "If you spend too much time, energy, and money in this building, you are neglecting your ministry"? Most churches teach that service to the institutional church and its members is ministry. Further, many congregations create a budget and then have a stewardship drive to get pledges to support it, using the methods of modern fund-raising — and then wonder why their people do not live a life of Christian stewardship. Other churches make church growth a goal, using secular means to attract and integrate members — and then wonder why their church is seen as a social club with which people make a contract rather than a covenant, so that if the church says and does what they believe, they stay and support it, but if not, they leave and begin another church.

5. Discipline

Discipline refers to behaviors that are taught, practiced, and celebrated within a community. We live in a society where people lack and indeed do not like discipline. They think they can be virtuous without practicing the virtues. They want instant health and weight loss without the discipline of exercise and dieting over the long haul. They want to become Christians overnight without effort. But to be Christian and maintain a relationship with God takes years of hard work and discipline.

Simplicity, for example, is an aspect of the spiritual life. But if we are to learn to live simply we need to practice buying things only for their usefulness and not for their status, to reject anything that is addictive, to develop the habit of giving things away, to avoid buying now and paying later, to learn to enjoy things without owning them, and to develop a deeper appreciation of creation. Especially important is the practice of critical reflection and resistance to non-Christian influences.

6. Social Interaction

Social interaction refers to who does what, with whom, for what purposes: the natural, normal, unconscious ways in which people relate to and treat each other. The following poem by Alice Walker illustrates this dimension of formation:

Sunday School: Circa 1950
"Who made you?" was always
the question.

275

The answer was always
"God."
Well. There we stood,
three feet high,
heads bowed,
leaning into
bosoms.

Now
I no longer recall
The Catechism
or brood on the genesis
of life.
No.

I ponder the exchange
Itself
And salvage mostly
the leanings.[12]

If persons grow up in an environment that is highly competitive, individualistic, and aggressive — that is, an environment in which conflict
is resolved by acts of violence — they will as adults behave in these ways,
perceiving them to be the way life is intended to be.

7. Role Models

Role models are persons past and present who are acknowledged and
celebrated as exemplars of the Christian life; they are "masters" to whom
children and initiates are apprenticed — teachers, for example. Who are
the people we memorialize, install, congratulate, and celebrate within
the church? Many churches have plaques on the walls of rooms to
remember wealthy men who have funded them, establishing these men
as models for the next generation's understanding of being Christian.
Churches install all sorts of people — church school teachers, choirs,
etc. — but mostly those who work within the church, thereby establishing that ministry is serving the institutional church. Churches cele-

12. Alice Walker, *Living By the Word: Selected Writings 1977-1987* (San Diego:
Harcourt, Brace, Jovanovich, 1988), p. 27.

brate and congratulate people all the time (sometimes even church teams who win football games), but neglect the saints among us that we want the next generation to imitate. Some churches do celebrate certain saints, but mostly men and clergy. When other churches eliminated the celebration of saint's days, they began to celebrate the lives of other "saintly" persons, thereby teaching how the church believed Christians should live their lives.

8. Language

Language refers to the naming of and the descriptions of behavior. It includes both verbal and nonverbal means of communication, our vocabulary and our grammar. Our language reflects our understandings of life. For example, how many times do we say "I have" something. We have friends, cars, degrees, jobs, mates, etc. We possess and own things and people — but avarice is a sin. Some come to church because they "*have* no friends." For the Christian the question is not "Do I have a friend?" but "Am I a friend?" To be a friend is Christian. We claim Jesus is our Savior, which means that we are not victims to heredity or environment but free from their influence and able to make moral decisions. But people sometimes say "I *can't* do that for you this week," which establishes them as a victim to a previous decision. It would be more appropriate for a Christian to say "I will not to do that for you this week," which establishes us as moral persons who make free decisions as believers in Jesus Christ and members of his church.

In his defense of a cultural-linguistic understanding of religion, George Lindbeck explains that to become religious involves becoming skilled in the language or the symbol system of that religion. And the grammar of religion, like that of any language, cannot be explicated or learned except by practice. One of the functions of the theologian is to teach Christians how to talk so that they might live as Christians.[13]

In his essay entitled "The Church as God's New Language," Stanley Hauerwas cites Hans Frei's observation that Barth took the classical themes of "communal Christian language molded by the Bible, tradition and constant usage in worship, practice, instruction and controversy, and he restated or redescribed them . . . [so as to] recreate a universe

13. Lindbeck, p. 131.

277

of discourse, . . . instructing [the reader] in the use of that language by showing him how. . . ."[14]

The English philosopher John Austin, in *How To Do Things With Words,* explains that the primary function of language is not so much to say something as to do something. We humans perform actions through our words: we promise, pledge, apologize, forgive, judge, rebuke. As a consequence, the words we speak have effects on us and on others; they alter relationships. Austin goes on to suggest that the most important word-acts we perform are those that ritualize, for they not only express us but also shape us. Liturgical speech is performative; it is deemed effective in that it does what it says: "I baptize you," "I absolve you," and so forth. Further, he points out, we participate in these word-acts, these rites, primarily to submit ourselves to their discipline so that we might become disciples.[15]

Parochial Schools

Having examined various contexts for formation, it should become clear that they are all interrelated and that together they all provide the basis for being intentionally Christian in our contexts of primary association — that is, in our homes, congregations, and schools.

Previously we suggested that the making of Christians in our day may necessitate that the church maintain parochial schools related to congregations, to which Christian parents will send their children. I will now turn to examine the nature and character of such a Christian school. But first a few comments.

When I speak of a "parochial school" I do not mean simply a church-related or church-sponsored school, nor do I have in mind a quality public school in which religion is taught and the day begun with prayer and Bible reading. I am talking about a *Christian* school, a school that is intentional about every aspect of its life and the formation of Christians.

14. Stanley Hauerwas, "The Church as God's New Language," in *Christian Existence Today* (Durham, NC: Labyrinth Press, 1988), p. 57; citing Hans Frei, "An Afterword," in *Karl Barth in Re-View,* ed. H.-Martin Rumscheidt (Pittsburgh: Pickwick Press, 1981), pp. 110-11.

15. J. L. Austin, *How To Do Things With Words* (Cambridge: Harvard University Press, 1975).

When I talk about the importance of a parochial school, I do not want to give the impression that I believe that having such schools will provide the solution to all our problems. Only if the home, the congregation, and the school unite and are intentional and consistent in their efforts will the church (understood as a combination of all three of these) have the possibility — and only the possibility — of forming Christians. I also want to make clear that without the school, the home and congregation may have little chance of succeeding. Of course, we still have the tremendous influence of the mass media with which to contend, but we do have some control over its influence.

Now while I believe that a parochial school's mission must be the same as the church's — namely, to make Christians — it is a *school* and therefore appropriately will have to live with some paradoxes if Christians are to be in but not of the world. For example, while it has a religious purpose (habits of the heart), it will also need to have an educational purpose (habits of the mind); while it must aid students to acquire a positive self-identity as Christians, it will also need to help students learn to be open to the world; while it must prepare students for life in God's reign, it will also need to prepare them for life in society; while it must model itself after a community of Christian faith, it will also need to model itself as an instructional institution that teaches science, math, history, English, and so forth.

If I were to begin to imagine a Christian school intentionally engaged in the making of Christians, it would look something like this: worship would be at the heart of its life, with each day set in the context of prayer and the celebration of the Eucharist. In the place of singing the national anthem and saluting the flag, the community would pray for the nation and its leaders. While supporting athletics, there would be no spectator sports, and non-competitive, non-aggressive games would be encouraged. Students would be rewarded for cooperation and other Christian values. Communal projects would dominate over individual ones as life in the classroom would be understood as ritual performance.[16]

The school would order its life and its activities according to the church year and would avoid celebrating secular holidays. Advent would be a contemplative season, Epiphany a season of witness, Lent a season of self-examination, and so forth. All of this would influence the cur-

---

16. See Peter McLaren, *Schooling as a Ritual Performance* (London: Routledge & Kegan Paul, 1986).

riculum of the school so that the church's holidays would shape the school calendar and its activities. The school would provide an environment conducive to Christian faith and life. The architectural space would unite the sacred and the secular. The importance of prayer would be highlighted by the presence of a meditation chapel. Quality Christian art and artifacts would communicate the Christian story.

Every aspect of school life would encourage the practice of behaviors consistent with Christian character. Faculty would be expected to set an example in terms of simplicity of life, compassion and service to those in need, prayer and meditation, and the stewardship of life and resources. The school would provide role models through its faculty and administration, and by celebrating those in the past whose lives were exemplary. Life in the school would be focused on the behavior of persons — past and present — who model faithfulness.

The school would develop its curriculum around work, service, study, and play. The arts would play a significant role in the life of the school so that the intuitive way of knowing would be given as much attention as the intellectual. The school would be concerned about how people treat each other and would encourage relationships between blacks and whites, rich and poor, young and old, wise and simple, and males and females that make friendship possible. Groupings based on age and ability would be avoided.

And finally, verbal and nonverbal communications — the way people talk, their vocabulary and grammar, and their use of stories — would be taken seriously. All of this is to say that the school would be radically different from any public school in that its aim would be to make Christians as well as to "educate" persons as human beings.

Recall that the early church chose not to avail itself of the protection it could have had under the Roman law as a *cultus privatus* dedicated to the pursuit of a purely personal and otherworldly salvation for its members. Instead it chose to confront society with a social and this-worldly alternative. In doing so it necessarily embodied aspects of the culture, but also remained separate and distinct.

When that society began to disintegrate, the young church was called upon to provide a foundation for a new society. The church accepted that role and sought to construct a society in which all of public and private life was controlled by Christian revelation — a *corpus Christianum*. As it did so, the church became less separate and distinct. And we are its products.

But the *corpus Christianum* is no more, and we cannot go back to it; nor for that matter can we return to the first era of the church's life. The synthesis of church and society has ended. A post-Constantinian era has emerged, an era in which the making of Christians is increasingly problematic.

For too long the church has worked at being respectable and desirable by making few demands. For too long the church has attempted to make Christian faith and life credible and acceptable to the rest of the world. It has lost its status as a community of "resident aliens."[17]

The church must become a more intentional faith community, must stop worrying about church growth, and must begin to shape its people to be Christian in an alien world. To do that it will need to take seriously the creation of Christian schools for the making of Christians. The question that remains is this: Do we who claim to be believers in Jesus Christ, and who by our baptism are members of his church, have the imagination and commitment to do so?

Is the church, at least in its mainline Protestant expression, serious about making Christians? Is it willing to give up its commitment to public schools? Are congregations willing and able to create and support Christian schools? Are parents willing to send their children to such schools and to support them? Are there enough faithful, knowledgeable, and able teachers willing to accept a call to teach in them?

Of course, to liberal Protestants all these questions may seem inappropriate. They may consider advocating Christian schools to be a sectarian move. But if they do, the burden is on them to offer a faithful and viable alternative for the fashioning of Christians in our day.

17. An image taken from St. Paul's letter to the Philippians. See also Stanley Hauerwas and William H. Willimon, *Resident Aliens* (Nashville: Abingdon, 1990).